Digital Suffragists

Digital Suffragists

Women, the Web, and the Future of Democracy

Marie Tessier

The MIT Press

Cambridge, Massachusetts | London, England

The MIT Press would like to thank the anonymous peer reviewers who provided comments on drafts of this book. The generous work of academic experts is essential for establishing the authority and quality of our publications. We acknowledge with gratitude the contributions of these otherwise uncredited readers.

This book was set in Stone Serif and Stone Sans by Westchester Publishing Services. Printed and bound in the United States of America.

Library of Congress Cataloging-in-Publication Data

Names: Tessier, Marie, author.
Title: Digital suffragists : women, the web, and the future of democracy / Marie Tessier.
Description: Cambridge, Massachusetts : The MIT Press, 2021. |
Includes bibliographical references and index.
Identifiers: LCCN 2021000496 | ISBN 9780262046015 (hardcover)
Subjects: LCSH: Women--Political activity--United States. | Political
    participation--Social aspects--United States. | Internet--Political aspects--
    United States. | Communication in politics--Technological innovations--
    United States. | Democracy--Social aspects--United States.
Classification: LCC HQ1236.5.U6 T44 2021 | DDC 320.082/0973--dc23
LC record available at https://lccn.loc.gov/2021000496

10 9 8 7 6 5 4 3 2 1

Contents

Introduction

U.S. Representative Alexandria Ocasio-Cortez was walking up the steps of the U.S. Capitol building on a summer day in 2020 when she was confronted by a Republican colleague. The world was in the middle of a pandemic, her district in New York City was the epicenter of coronavirus epidemic in the United States, and her constituents were economically devastated by layoffs, illness, and business closures.[1] The intensifying poverty in an already economically distressed area was leading to an increase in crime, the New York City Democrat had recently said.

Ocasio-Cortez's perspective on rising crime had not gone over well with some of her Republican colleagues, who tended to blame the Black Lives Matter movement for criticizing police violence and impinging on law enforcement. On the steps on the Capitol, in the middle of the day, with a reporter looking on, U.S. Representative Ted Yoho, a Florida Republican, angrily told Ocasio-Cortez that she was "disgusting" for suggesting a link between poverty, unemployment, and crime, according to witnesses.

Later that day, after Ocasio-Cortez cast a vote and went back outside, Yoho said, "fucking bitch," according to a report in *The Hill* newspaper by the reporter who witnessed the exchange.[2]

After news of the encounters broke in the media, Ocasio-Cortez spoke on the floor of the House of Representatives about the exchange. She underscored the particular vulnerability of lower-income women to this kind of hostility from men in the United States.

"Representative Yoho put his finger in my face, he called me disgusting, he called me crazy, he called me out of my mind. And he called me dangerous," Ocasio-Cortez said. "Representative Yoho's comments were not deeply hurtful or piercing to me. Because I have worked a working-class job. I have waited tables in restaurants. I have ridden the subway. I have walked the streets in New York City. And this kind of language is not new. I have encountered words uttered by Mr. Yoho and men uttering the same words as Mr. Yoho while I was being harassed in restaurants. I have tossed men out of bars that have used language like Mr. Yoho's, and I have encountered this type of harassment riding the subway in New York City. This is not new. And that is the problem."[3]

What erupted in the media and in a solemn hour of condemnation on the floor of the House of Representatives was a catalog of women's experiences with misogynistic hatred that routinely rises up when women do their jobs or violate someone's expectations about how women are supposed to behave.

New York Times readers were quick to add their opinions to several stories about the incident. Nearly everyone spoke of the issue as specific condemnation of a particular man and other men like him. Yoho's words had a familiar ring, many said.

"There are too many men like Rep. Yoho in both business and politics who feel that they can say anything to women and get away with it because they are part of the good ole boys club. I have two daughters that are professionals and I would be extremely angry if anyone said to them what Rep. Yoho said to Congresswoman Ocasio-Cortez. I can also see my youngest daughter reacting the same way as Rep. Ocasio-Cortez," VMG of New Jersey wrote. "I wish her a long and successful career in politics. We need more people like her in Congress."[4]

Others raised similar points, sometimes using the popular abbreviation AOC for the youngest woman ever elected to Congress. Characteristically, few women commenters used their full names and locations in comments related to sexism. "For women everywhere, AOC's remarks perfectly encapsulate all that they continue to endure due to careless and entitled men," Cousy in New England wrote.[5] "As a 54[-year-old] woman who has mostly been resigned to this behavior, I cannot thank AOC enough. I am trying not [to] be ashamed that my generation didn't take care of this. I am going to focus instead on my gratitude to her for giving the most articulate summary of sexism that I have ever heard."

After a year and a half in Congress, Ocasio-Cortez was used to being a lightning rod. She also showed her mastery at turning opponents' words back on themselves.

"I never spoke to Rep. Yoho before he decided to accost me on the steps of the nation's Capitol," Ocasio-Cortez wrote on Twitter, where she has more than three million followers. "Believe it or not, I usually get along fine w/ my GOP colleagues. We know how to check our legislative sparring at the committee door. But hey, 'b*tches' get stuff done."[6]

The fact that this was not Ocasio-Cortez's first widely reported experience with vulgar public criticism is also sadly reflective of a broader truth about women in public life globally. When women speak up, they are attacked, often in vulgar and threatening terms. When they offer ideas in the office, they are ignored and interrupted.

For many people, that kind of overt attack in public is rare. Misogyny is not always a palpable, experience of daily life. Yet the subtext remains a part of people's lived experience. Unfortunately, all of these experiences have their effects. These attacks on women—and myriad forms of criticism, interruptions, and false assumptions about how to measure equality—have a purpose. They exist to deny and diminish women's voices. And to a great extent, it works.

The fact is that women are routinely criticized, demeaned, threatened, interrupted, and characterized as wrong, unruly, disgusting, and out of place when they exercise their rights as citizens or do their jobs as elected officials or try to ascend to leadership positions throughout society. Indeed, using the language of "disgust," as Yoho did, is a moral judgment used to shun people who violate gendered expectations, scholars point out. In recent years, it has been used repeatedly against women in the United States who challenged Donald Trump for the presidency, against a journalist who asked Donald Trump difficult questions, and also in the wide open public in an angry man's contempt for an elected member of Congress. In Australia, the opposition leader to Prime Minister Julia Guillard routinely questioned women's fitness for office, echoing ancient messages about who should be in charge.

In the twenty-first century, when most parents in industrialized nations support their daughters' right to work and control their own lives, it is common for many people to believe that women have achieved equality.

Despite the good will of many people and laws that support women's rights in much of the world, women's voices remain markedly muted in public life, even when they have seats in government and around the tables of power throughout society.

That is the topic of this book—how women's voices are derailed and disrupted online and how that antagonism continues to influence women's confidence in sharing their views on public affairs in the digital public square. It is not so much about the many victims of misogyny online, though that is part of the picture. Rather, it is about the loss to democracy when women's voices are limited.

The promise of women's equality in democracy is failing when women's voices remain quieted and marginalized. That is the central argument of this book about discussions of public affairs online.

Women's voices remain sharply underrepresented in public life and in electronic media. The representation of women in news is beginning to change online. Much remains to be done.

Clearly, women's engagement in news comments is one mirror of a broader cultural trend of women being underengaged and underrepresented. It's not a stand-alone problem for news sites or any single platform for conversation about public affairs.

In fact, women's voices are missing and underrepresented in debates about public issues in every forum where public affairs are discussed. Even when women have seats at the table, their voices are outnumbered and underrepresented in proportion to their representation. This problem extends to the most powerful women in the world, including women on the Supreme Court of the United States. Women's voices are to a great degree censored out of public debate by interruptions, lack of support, discrimination, and self-censoring.

A little more than a century after white women in the United States won the federal right to vote, women remain stalled in many broad measures of equality, even as women's qualifications and legal rights have grown by leaps and bounds. The impact on women of color is worse. Gender-nonconforming people are just beginning to be accepted in public life.

Change is slow, and bridging the gender inequality gap has taken time. White women earned the right to vote in the United States with the Nineteenth Amendment in 1920. But it was not until the first year that I cast a ballot, 1980, that women voted in the same proportion as men in a presidential election.

Sixty years passed between white women's suffrage and women's equal participation in voting.

How long will it take before women's voices are included as half of public affairs conversations?

This book is about how the twenty-first-century voices of women speaking online reflect the horrible burdens borne by our grandmothers, great-grandmothers, and great-great-grandmothers. They were not even permitted inside the buildings and the rooms where public affairs were discussed. They were jailed for trying to vote just a century ago in the United States. Women's voices online reflect their experiences in real life and the online harassment they see in their daily lives. This book is about how real life and antagonistic digital realities reinforce ancient laws and reinforce ubiquitous implicit expectations of gender segregation.

A new wave of scholarship and commentary sheds light on the various ways that woman-hating behavior—much of it subtle and widely accepted—shapes public life today.[7] The philosopher Kate Manne frames all of this behavior brilliantly as a matter of logic: it is "down, girl" behavior.

The barriers women face to full citizenship are a matter of culture, in real life and online. We live in a culture that persistently limits women's full citizenship through "social environments in which women are liable to encounter hostility due to the enforcement and policing of patriarchal norms and expectations." This is the definition of misogyny that Manne describes in her 2018 book *Down Girl: The Logic of Misogyny.*[8]

It is vital to understand this environment as a result of a pervasive culture, then, and not the specific act of a hostile man (though Representative Yoho's behavior was certainly misogynistic). If misogyny and sexist behavior were simply the artifacts of individual behavior, sexism could be cleaned up by calling out a few bad actors. Many people believe that's the answer. But it's not a realistic solution to a problem that is rooted in millennia of cultural norms.

Misogyny and the marginalized public voices of women are much bigger than a few bad actors or even political parties full of bad actors. Misogyny is a fact of life, and its ongoing consequences for the citizenship of women are evident in every forum where public affairs are discussed, as the evidence throughout this book shows. Democracy will continue to fall short until public affairs discussions justly represent all the people.

It's no wonder that twenty-first-century women remain, as scholars have written and proven empirically, the Silent Sex.[9] (More on that in chapter 2.)

As I illustrate throughout the book, Ocasio-Cortez's experience on the steps of the Capitol reflects so much more about the historical burden that women bear. It also illustrates the intersection of gender and race where women of color find themselves particular targets for misogynist and racist attacks.

Curiously, that intersection of race and gender has not been in the spotlight in much of the public conversation about Ocasio-Cortez's remarkably successful public voice. Rather, the attacks on her have been characterized as either racist or sexist, depending on the language used and the topic of the conversation. But the fact that Ocasio-Cortez is a New York–born woman of Puerto Rican heritage stands out as a clear example of the extraordinary burden of prejudice and marginalization that women of color face, as the leading scholars of critical race theory and intersectional feminism have been pointing out for three decades.

A year before the scene on the steps of the Capitol, Ocasio-Cortez and three other new members of Congress had already become the focus of racist and misogynistic backlash, sometimes within their own party. But the double burden was not always acknowledged. Curiously, the attack was in racist terms, and most mainstream commentators missed the intersectional message that targeted the congresswomen as women. No similar comment has been directed at the president's male detractors. One in particular, U.S. Representative Justin Amash, left the Republican Party under pressure after he broke from the GOP and announced that he would support the first impeachment of President Donald Trump. Like Congresswoman Rashida Tlaib, who is also from Michigan, Amash's parents are immigrants from the Middle East. They share the same citizenship profile, but he was never asked to leave the country.

Ocasio-Cortez had defeated a Democratic incumbent to win her place on the ballot in 2018 and vowed to challenge and upset establishment Democrats in Washington, D.C. When she arrived in Washington early in 2019, she formed an alliance with three other new women of color in Congress: Tlaib of Michigan, Ayanna S. Pressley of Massachusetts, and Ilhan Omar of Minnesota. The four women challenged the expected ascension of the powerful Democratic leader Nancy Pelosi to be Speaker of the House. Their challenge did not succeed, but their reputations as a united team willing to raise their voices earned them public contempt in some quarters (and respect in others).

President Trump encouraged the derision in starkly racist terms that had been uncommon in public life in the forty years before his presidency. Even though three of the four women were born in the United States, Trump asked, "Why don't they go back" to the countries "from which they came"? Though the attack was transmitted online, its effect was very much the same as the confrontation on the steps of the Capitol.

As I describe throughout this book, the language Trump used embodied historic themes that have been used to silence and disempower women and racial minorities for centuries. That he directed this anger and vilification at four women of color as if they were not in fact democratically elected public servants underscores the way that women of color bear extra burdens. Only Omar is an immigrant. She was born in Somalia and immigrated to the United States as a child. Of course, Puerto Ricans are U.S. citizens whether they are born in New York or in Puerto Rico, a U.S. territory.

Trump characterized the elected officials' voices as rude and out of place. He said they were using their elected positions "loudly and viciously telling the people of the United States, the greatest and most powerful Nation on earth, how our government is to be run."[10]

Here's the thing. These women were telling the United States how the government is to be run. The four women *had earned their places in* the government by winning democratic elections, by definition. Under law, that's called *democratic sovereignty*—voters electing their representatives to government.

The Fossils of White Male Supremacy

Trump's attack was remarkable because he openly invoked the fossils of male white supremacy, using themes that go back at least as far as *The Iliad* about the silence and exclusion that are expected of women.

It was in *The Iliad* that Telemachus, the son of Odysseus and Penelope, told his mother to shut up and pay attention to domestic tasks while he handled the "matters of men." The British classics scholar Mary Beard says this was the first example in Western history of a man telling a woman to shut up, and it was directed at his own mother.[11] (According to Homer, this method worked, though I have my doubts.)

The important thing is that when Donald Trump said these women's voices did not belong in Washington—or even in their own country—his tweets were more than a social media distraction and a rallying cry to racists. His attack was one more link in a long chain of powerful men working to silence women by saying that their voices were not appropriate in the Forum.

Notably, outrage in Congress, in the media, and from the public focused mostly on the president's overtly racist language. What many people missed was the misogyny at the heart of the attack. And that, in fact, was the dog whistle encoded in the heart of the overtly racist message: Women do not belong. Women of color, especially, don't belong.

*   *   *

I have been moderating comments at the *New York Times* since 2007, the year the first iPhone went on the market. Little did I realize the discoveries that awaited.

Comments on the news are a primary form of political communication in the twenty-first century. More than half of people in a 2015 survey said they have left comments on news sites and on social media. Three-quarters reported reading comments. The preferred place to comment was on social media, people reported, but politics and public affairs were a primary motivation for posting, according to the Center for Media Engagement at the University of Texas at Austin.[12] News sites were also a popular destination for commenting and reading comments.

It is my conviction as a journalist that news sites have an obligation to host conversations for intelligent discussion of public affairs. News media have splintered in recent years, weakening their place as the primary destination for public conversation. Still, promoting public engagement in civic affairs is a fundamental mission of ethical journalism, and it is in that vein that I offer my thoughts for fulfilling that purpose. Social media are an alternative site, but preliminary results from a controlled study of news sites in 2020 showed that eliminating comments on news sites did not give rise to additional comments on social media.[13]

From my earliest days online, I noticed a significant gap between men's and women's participation. A lot has changed as the *New York Times* made the change from primarily a print-oriented product, as it was when I started, to a digital-first publication. The company has succeeded in getting a larger proportion of women to subscribe.

My work moderating comments, it turns out, has been a kind of archaeological excavation. Down at the bottom of my work site, as I pondered women's lagging engagement, what I have uncovered are the fossils of gender segregation in public life. I unearthed the bones of women's silence in a culture where women's voices still are routinely and publicly derided. The silence of disadvantaged minorities is down there, too. I ultimately found the bones of gender segregation as reflected in classical Greek literature through the millennia, about who could speak in the Forum.

As long as men have created ruling councils and legislatures, societies were defined by the rights and the voices of men alone.

Sadly, the fossils of historic gender segregation and the official exclusion of women from the public square have functioned as the new bones of digital technology and the public conversations they support. Most women do not suffer the harangues targeted at Ocasio-Cortez, but the fossils are still there, providing the foundation of our public conversations.

It's as if the semi-silent voices of women throughout the world remain mired in the same tar pits that claimed La Brea Woman, the ten-thousand-year-old hominid found among other fossils in the California's La Brea tar pits. It's the twenty-first century, but many hurdles remain. The forces silencing women are the forces of millennia. It's not a simple task to keep the past in the past, and now it has been digitally reframed and cast out into the world as if it were something new. But it is very, very old.

Sometimes, the digital public square is good for women's voices. It has had some powerful organizing effects, as evidenced by the Global Women's March in January 2017 and by some of the successes of the #MeToo movement and the Black Lives Matter movement, both launched by Black women on social media. Sometimes, women find their collective voices, often when they feel they have reached a tipping point of solidarity with like-minded comrades. It helps when they feel they are part of a give-and-take conversation with each other and not subject to outsider criticism.

Hillary Clinton's campaign for president in 2016 was one time when feminist women found common cause and when they found forums to discuss their differences. This is the power of social organizing that scholars have heralded for women, minorities, people with disabilities, and other disadvantaged groups, such as gender-nonconforming people. These areas of solidarity also can form blind spots. That was certainly the case for white female supporters of Hillary Clinton, many of whom did not recognize that most white women, historically, vote Republican. They were stunned when Trump won a plurality of white women's votes in 2016. Sadly, electronic media are also a powerful organizing force for hate, as global hate movements have coalesced with the rise of social media.

News sites played a role in moderating conversations among women in the deep winter days of the U.S. presidential primary season in February 2016. Former Secretary of State Madeleine Albright spoke on behalf of Hillary Clinton's campaign at a Saturday rally in New Hampshire. At the time, the Clinton campaign for the Democratic nomination for president was confronting a remarkable division between older women and younger women. Women over age forty-five supported Clinton by wide margins, polls showed. Women under age forty-five supported U.S. Senator Bernie Sanders of Vermont by an overwhelming margin of two to one.[14]

In her remarks, Albright appealed to young women to understand how much all women had to gain from a woman in the White House.

"We can tell our stories about climbing the ladder. A lot of younger women think it's done. It's NOT done. You have to help. Hillary Clinton will always be there for you. Just remember," Albright continued, using a phrase that she had used through decades in public life, "there's a special place in hell for women who don't help each other."

Just days before the New Hampshire primary, Albright's remark touched off a round of criticism. Many people heard her remark—and a similar, dismissive aside from feminist leader Gloria Steinem—as tone-deaf critiques of younger women, as if they failed to understand the issues and historic significance of Clinton's candidacy. The *New York Times* headline: "Gloria Steinem and Madeleine Albright Rebuke Young Women Backing Bernie Sanders."[15]

Shortly after, Sanders won the New Hampshire primary with 60.8 percent of the vote.[16] The only segments of New Hampshire voters that Clinton carried were Democrats over age sixty-five and those with annual incomes $200,000 and above.[17]

As it turns out, liberal women's responses to the controversy were a prototypical example of public conversations about women in progressive politics.

"I have a college age daughter, who understands why I prefer Hillary Clinton's pragmatism to Bernie Sanders's much more appealing call to arms. But she admires Sanders and his message, and her friends are all 'feeling the Bern,'" Cathy from Hopewell Junction, New York, wrote in response to an Albright op-ed a few days after the primary.[18] "Hillary Clinton needs to make her case to my daughter's generation who have been convinced she is a dishonest shill for corporate greedsters, that she is indeed progressive, that she is indeed working for their future. She doesn't need to try to get young votes by playing the feminist card. They don't buy it."

Albright spelled out her convictions in an op-ed *mea culpa*: "My Undiplomatic Moment."[19] She apologized for giving offense but reiterated her conviction that women who want to see progress for women do need to support women's progress by voting for women candidates. "We cannot be complacent, and we cannot forget the hard work it took us to get to where we are," Albright wrote. "I would argue that because of what is at stake, this is exactly the time to have a conversation about how to preserve what women have gained, including the right to make our own choices, and how to move forward together."

Women explained their points of view, responding in droves.

"When I was an employment lawyer I regularly saw women abused and pushed out at work simply because they raised their hands and had a good idea," Mara Dolan wrote in a comment from Cambridge, Massachusetts.[20] "Women must work together to change the culture and get in the habit of helping each other out. It takes an experienced woman to fully understand the depth of sex discrimination in this culture. Vote for whoever you choose, but do so knowing that having a woman at the top is the most powerful method for change."

Others said that supporting a single woman candidate does not respond to their policy concerns for women. "The Democrats should thank Senator Sanders for energizing young people and the middle class. The Democrats have not adequately addressed the challenge of income inequality, rising college costs, and the crushing burden of student and parent debt for college expenses," Lisa wrote from New York City.[21] "It is not sufficient for one woman to become president if it means that the status quo of income inequality continues. That's not how we help other women."

In many ways, the outpouring of women's responses to the stories about Albright and Steinem's remarks were emblematic of women's response to civic debate online and also the way they use news comments to build a sense of belonging and community.

- Women reacted strongly and publicly to an issue that is central to defining women's place in public life.
- Women spoke in personal terms about symbolic issues that go to the heart of their identity.
- Women made clear where they saw common ground with Albright's perspective, and they made clear when their perspectives were different.

As these examples show, many women also avoided giving their full identity in public comments, just as many avoided revealing their identities in comments about attacks on Alexandria Ocasio-Cortez and her colleagues.

If we looked at these comments on their own, we might see them as the ordinary conversation of women interested in politics. But it was not ordinary. Women's overwhelming reaction to the story about what women voters owe or do not owe a woman candidate was revealing in several ways.

First, women strongly asserted their views. That is unusual as a general rule but common in areas where women are assumed to have authority. In fact, it is unusual in many contexts both on and off the internet. Second, women spoke about their political views in deeply personal terms, explaining their views and their particular qualification to comment in the context of their lived experiences. And third, women emphasized areas of agreement as well as disagreement.

The themes in response to these stories reflect the themes from more comprehensive, empirical work done to analyze comments on another issue of intense interest to women—domestic violence. In a study spanning several forums on news sites and on social media, scholars analyzed the civility and sense of purpose many women commenters expressed when the topic was a video of a U.S. football player punching his fiancée to unconsciousness in a hotel elevator.

Throughout the communities where women were encouraged to speak, they outlined their personal experiences, they affirmed each other's experiences, they worked to raise awareness of the dangers faced by women in abusive relationships, and they offered solutions.[22]

In a similar vein, women activists around the world, including India, have used online communities to bolster the movement against street harassment.[23]

My View from the Heart of Public Discussion

As I've moderated thousands of comments to the Opinion pages of the *New York Times* online from the outset of article comments at the *Times*, the dearth of women's voices has been obvious. From the earliest comments in late 2007, through President Barack Obama's first inauguration day and his presidency, through the Trump presidency, women are consistently outnumbered in comments about public affairs. These numbers swell when women feel personally affected, when the topic is within the bounds of gender-normed topics such as education or health, and when women's rights are directly at issue.

As I outline in chapter 1, women's voices are lagging in news comments at the *New York Times* and at leading news sites worldwide, as research at the *Times* in 2015 and elsewhere has shown in the years following. Women were outnumbered three to one in news comments then, just as women are underrepresented in Congress, on political discussion programs on television, in prime minister's offices, and in leadership positions throughout the work world.

To me as a feminist, a journalist, and a lifelong proponent of participatory democracy, the lagging voice of women has also been painful. Here I was, moderating a premier global forum on public affairs, day in and day out, and women weren't participating to the same degree as men. Could the *New York Times* really call it "the best conversation on the web" if women are not equal voices?

And what was going on? There is literally no barrier to participation, other than registering at NYTimes.com. While some privacy advocates may find that onerous, setting up that minor bar is one way for the *Times* to know that a real person is connected to a user profile and the comments that stem from it. It helps deter antagonists who thrive on disrupting constructive conversations.

Women's low participation was also a head scratcher because the company's high standards for civil conversation fit with women's preference for a nonadversarial forum. *New York Times* moderators reject personal attacks and various kinds of hateful language, except to the extent that they are directly relevant to a news story. So when columnist David Brooks in 2011 called Donald Trump a "blowhard,"[24] *New York Times* commenters rejoiced in the freedom to call Trump a blowhard, and we approved those comments—for that one day. The next day, the name calling was again off the table. Similarly, when contributor Christopher Buskirk said critics of the U.S.

president had a monotonous message of "Orange Man Bad," playing off a popular meme, moderators published comments with that unflattering description of the president's remarkable skin tone.[25]

Across the internet, comments are generally recognized as "the bottom of the web," as Northeastern University's Joseph M. Reagle has memorialized in a book title.[26] But the *New York Times* set out to be different.

From the very beginning, the *New York Times* established one of the most protected spaces on the internet for open, civil discussion of public affairs. When the company first introduced its internal comment moderation technology for articles other than blog posts, one of the biggest concerns was whether hosting an open forum might tarnish the company's claim to be the most "authoritative newspaper in the world." What could go wrong for the company's reputation for seriousness and thought-provoking conversation?

The *Times*, after all, is a news organization whose style manual bans references to "the familiar barnyard epithet, and the farm animal to which it refers."[27] The company has high standards—so high that generations of journalists have laughed about the persistence of a sometimes Victorian approach. For example, the late Molly Ivins sometimes spoke of a story draft she submitted, referring to a pol with "a gut the size of Rhode Island." Her editor changed the language to say the man had "a protuberant abdomen."[28]

So day by day, as I sorted people's comments, I pondered: What was going on?

I've looked at comments from many sides now, up and down, and still somehow, it's comments' illusions I recall. But I do know comments. After more than a decade moderating national and international conversations at one of the smartest publications in the world, I really, really know comments.

My argument is that democracy is failing when half the population is not fully represented in civic debate, and technology companies and public affairs forums have an obligation to fix it.

Public forums have to redesign their conversations to reflect a fair representation of women, minorities, and other marginalized groups. Women's low status in public conversations both undermines democratic influence and reinforces existing inequalities.

Bringing women's voices to equality is a multifaceted, systemic issue of the public affairs ecosystem. It's not enough to simply call on women to speak up. We do need to change public conversations, but it is fundamentally a design problem. It's a function of comprehensive social design, web design, workplace design, and conversation design.

If we are to solve the deficit in participatory democracy, a core piece of the puzzle is solving the problem of the gender gap online, where young people in particular live and talk. It's a crucial foundation of democracy in the digital age.

News organizations are part of the solution. And yet news organizations themselves have been thrust into the uncomfortable position of no longer controlling the distribution of their content. The primacy of social media and online searches now accounts for much of what people see, read, and respond to. A Reuters Institute study of news consumers in the United Kingdom in 2018 showed that people with lower social status relied far more heavily on social media and other news-sharing methods than people with high social status, who tended to get news from news sites directly.[29] And technology companies' purpose and priorities are different than the public service impulse that historically has rested in news.

The social media, search, and advertising distribution systems that dominate digital commerce are fundamentally different from the public affairs news organizations of the print era, Columbia University professor Emily Bell argued in her seminal 2014 speech, "Clash of Cultures." "The 'two cultures' of engineering and journalism are very different. They do not share the same motivations, they have not shared the same skills, they do not seek the same outcomes and they certainly do not share the same growth and revenue models. Yet now they occupy the same space in terms of conveying news and discussion to a broad public," Bell said[30]

Becoming a Curator of Voices at the *New York Times*

As a feminist who came of age during the height of second-wave feminism, I have long understood women's low levels of representation in government and business. I have experienced firsthand the ways that I was questioned and seen as overly aggressive when I used the same hard-nosed investigative reporting techniques as my male colleagues. I always felt most at home in a room full of women committed to improving women's lives and making progress for women's rights around the world.

Somehow, though, I was unprepared for the dearth of women responding to opinion pieces at the *New York Times*.

The first day I got broadband internet in 2007, I was sitting in my home office in Bangor, Maine, looking at a lot of websites that had become too cumbersome for my landline phone connection to load. At the time, Facebook was in its public infancy. Apple CEO Steve Jobs had just announced the release of the first iPhone, ushering in the era of touch screens and a minicomputer for every hand.

As I clicked around the news, I scoured the website of the *New York Times*. There, at the bottom of the home page, was a little button: Work for Us.

I looked over the job openings, and one caught my eye—community moderator. The *Times* was embarking on an effort to create the smartest conversation on the web, and it was hiring a few journalists to build a thoughtful online forum.

I wondered whether the paper would let me do that job from my home office in Maine. As a journalist and a lifelong proponent of civic participation, it seemed like my résumé was an exact fit for the job, even though I had twenty years of journalism experience and the job description was for an entry-level worker.

I wrote an ambitious letter of application, outlining my qualifications to build a vision for a global community of thoughtful discussion at a time of epic change in the world and in the digital revolution in journalism. So much was at stake for journalism at that time. News organizations were folding entirely. Thousands of journalists were losing their jobs every year. The remaking of the advertising ecosystem proceeded as digital advertising drained readers and advertising revenue from newspapers.

By 2020, 55 to 70 percent of digital advertising revenue would be going to Google and Facebook, and print advertising was plummeting.

A few weeks after I sent my letter of application, I got a call from Heather Moore, the community editor for the *Times*, and I told her it had long been my wish to be editor of letters to the editor. Curating democratic conversation was my idea of an ideal job. "Really!" she said. "Really," I replied.

Some weeks passed.

In September 2007, Heather Moore phoned to offer me the *New York Times* job. She said I could work from home, since the Community team was being built as a remote workforce. My youngest child was in kindergarten, I was part of a small team building a new forum for civic conversation at the *New York Times* online, and I could do it from my home office in Maine.

The internet is a wonderful thing.

My Road Less Traveled to NYTimes.com

My path to my job moderating and curating comments to the Opinion pages of NYTimes.com was a circuitous one, but it also unfolded in the most natural way.

I have spent a career working in both women's organizations and newsrooms. At the heart of all that work was a devotion to women's voices, a devotion to fulfilling the promise of democracy itself— government by the people.

I remember the moment that my academic interest in government hit me like a lightning bolt. I was a student in a 100-level political science class at the University of Michigan, sitting in a large lecture as the professor described the work of government as something that transcends the arguments of political parties. Professor George Grassmuck—a one-time aide to President Gerald Ford, a University of Michigan graduate—explained that the unspoken agreement in Washington, D.C., at that time was that the work of the people must get done, even when politicians disagree.

This, I thought to myself, is what politics should be—fulfilling the will of the people, come what may.

By the time I entered my junior year of college, I knew that I wanted to work at the heart of the democratic experience. By my senior year, I was planning to move to Washington after my graduation.

When I did move to Washington in May 1983, I had secured an unpaid internship with U.S. Sen. Donald W. Riegle, a Democrat from my home state. Day after day, working in his offices on Capitol Hill, staffers listened to a live feed of "debate" that was taking place on the Senate floor. The closed-circuit audio system was known as "the squawk box." Across the airwaves all day every day, long lines of senators read speeches about this or that vital pork-barrel project in their home states. After a few weeks of this, I asked a colleague if the subject ever changed. "Not really," said a legislative correspondent, a recent graduate of Yale University who answered constituent mail from Michigan week in and week out. "Senators just talk about these projects all the time so they can tell the voters that they're really, really working hard to get their projects funded."

I learned a lot during that internship. It was not, however, the thrill of political theory as I envisioned it.

In August, I got my big break, thanks in no small measure to my dubious post–Title IX softball batting skills (thank you, Title IX). I batted in three runners in the bottom of the final inning of a recreation league softball game. I was safe at third, the game was tied, our best batter was coming up, and I had just become a minor sensation in the Capitol Hill softball league. From that moment, my Washington reputation as the intern who hit the three-RBI triple preceded me. And the conversations that followed proved to be a link to my future.

Three different people called me the next day at Senator Riegle's office, trying to recruit me to play on their District of Columbia football league teams. One was a congressional staffer married to a woman at the League of Women Voters, which had some openings he said I might find of interest.

The next day, I stopped in at the League of Women Voters office and received a copy of the job description. I wrote a heartfelt letter of application about the history of women's voting and my passion for women's issues and for an all-inclusive democracy. The inspiring Mary Stone, who led the League's efforts on government and voter services for many years, gave me the job. And she proved to be a supportive boss.

A year later, I took a League position working on the 1984 presidential debates. This, I felt at the time, was an apex of democratic ideals—creating a forum for major party candidates to exchange views publicly in a forum where their strengths and weaknesses would be on display.

And it was this experience with the debates, largely, that led me to journalism. I loved working for the League of Women Voters and have always admired the group's devotion to good government and voter education. The white suffrage movement's racism has since chronicled by numerous historians, and summarized succinctly by the *New York Times*'s Brent Staples.[31] At the time, the suffrage movement's white supremacy had been scrubbed from its recorded history.

At the same time, I was growing frustrated with the way that my work was going into the world with someone else's name on it. This is the nature of nonprofits. Staff members work for the organization, and the organization's leaders bring the ideas into the world.

During the debates, however, I saw something else. Dozens of journalists and television producers worked to carry the broadcast and write stories about the debates. And when they were over, those producers, reporters, and photographers moved on to the next story.

I had found my calling. After interviewing for a number of television jobs, I went to graduate school at the Missouri School of Journalism at the University of Missouri. I studied print, radio, and television news reporting and producing—the original multimedia approach. And I retained my commitments to ensuring equality for women and to informing and engaging citizens in the acts of participatory democracy.

My first job in journalism was at the *St. Petersburg Times*, now the *Tampa Bay Times*, as a metropolitan reporter and copy editor for two years. Then I moved to Washington, D.C. Before long, I was caught in the nascent gig economy, juggling part-time jobs at National Public Radio and the *Washington Post*. My new husband and I were tired. And then my husband's old job came open at the University of Maine, and I decided to embrace the gig economy and make a go of independent reporting from Maine.

Soon, I discovered the Journalism & Women Symposium, then based at the University of Missouri. When feminist news sites began to spring up, I found my passion. I wrote for the late Rita Henley Jensen, founding editor of Women's eNews, and for the late Mary Thom, the news editor at Women's Media Center who was a longtime editor and one-time managing editor of *Ms.* magazine. I developed an expertise in writing about domestic violence and served for four years on Maine's Domestic Homicide Review Panel.

And then I got the job at the *New York Times*.

Defining Terms

Here it is important to define some terms, especially *gender, gender identity, misogyny, sexism, race,* and *intersectional feminism.*

Gender and Gender Identity   Gender is a multifaceted cultural system of classifying people by sex. In the past and in most media research, people are largely identified as women and men. Scholars and activists call this the gender binary. Gender is now understood to be a matter of cultural expectations and experiences and not strictly about a biological sex at birth.

In addition to men and women, scholars and scientists now recognize transgender men, transgender women, and nonbinary and other gender identities as scientifically valid. These identities have always been with us, but they have not been honored or represented in science and the media. The overwhelming body of scientific evidence and cultural practice around gender is opposed to thinking of gender as a two-sided binary of women and men.[32]

And so one of the feminist's dilemmas is how to talk about the burden of misogyny on women of all races and on transgender and other gender-nonconforming people without reinforcing outdated and damaging binary stereotypes. This book is about the continuing burden of silence and discrimination that misogyny creates in digital society. This creates particular burdens on women of color in societies still dominated by white men. I have worked to acknowledge the limitations of this approach but ask my readers to understand that reporting on trends and binary-based research is not intended to erase underrepresented people. It is writing about the data we have.

I will be using the language of women and men throughout the book, adding more inclusive data where it is available and acknowledging the deficits without excessively reiterating the same issue.[33]

Sex   Scientists understand sex as referring to biological characteristics. It is one factor influencing gender identity. Sex and gender have interactions that are relevant for technology, but the two terms need to be understood separately.[34]

Misogyny and Sexism   The term *misogyny* refers to the cultural reality that women and gender-nonconforming people are punished, marginalized, and silenced for violating gender norms. The term "sexism" is the justification for misogynistic behavior—that is, "it is not women's purpose" to behave in such and such a way. These definitions follow the deep philosophical analysis from Kate Manne in *Down Girl: The Logic of Misogyny.*[35] Individual acts can be sexist or misogynistic, but they stem from the culture of misogyny. Manne expanded her theories in *Entitled: How Male Privilege Hurts Women.*[36]

The existence of misogyny or sexism is not a matter of debate, and I will not expand on that.

Race   Scientists recognize that race is an artificial system of categorizing human beings that has very little to do with biology.[37] Race is, however, a relevant social category for talking about how power is unevenly distributed in society. As critical race theorist Kimberlé Williams Crenshaw describes, race is a method for imposing power systems in society.[38] I use the language of race with this understanding.

Intersectionality   Scholars have developed a body of work to discuss the double bind of racism and sexism that is experienced by women of color and gender-nonconforming people, a field pioneered by Crenshaw and followed by many others. Crenshaw's body of work shows that traditional categories of social activism around race (which center on Black men) and traditional white feminist movements (which center on white women) have had the harmful effect of marginalizing women of color. The burden on Black women is so great that it has its own name—*misogynoir*, coined by Moya Bailey.

"The interpersonal domain of power refers to how individuals experience the convergence of structural, cultural and disciplinary power," Patricia Hill Collins and Sirma Bilge write in the second edition of *Intersectionality*. "Such power shapes intersecting identities of race, class, gender, sexuality, nation, and age that in turn organize social interactions. Intersectionality recognizes that perceived group membership can make people vulnerable to various forms of bias, yet because we are simultaneously members of many groups, our complex identities can shape the specific ways that we experience bias."[39]

Throughout this book, I recognize the unique combined effects of race and gender that affect women and nonbinary people of color. Systems of power have different effects on different kinds of individuals in complex ways in a variety of contexts. The theory and practice of intersectional feminism have reframed the inadequate way that social justice movements have talked about race and gender.

I acknowledge that as a white middle-class woman with a certain set of life experiences, I can only do my best to understand my limitations and consult intersectional sources where appropriate.

An Online Mosaic of Misogyny

In this book, I present the political, institutional, historical, communication, and web design challenges that function to suppress women's voices in civic affairs online. Equality is an uphill task. And yet we will not truly have a democracy until we climb this hill.

Chapter 1 outlines the way that women's voices are limited in public comments on news websites around the world. In democratic societies where women have an equal vote, they do not have an equal say in the forums where public officials and pundits assess public opinion.

Chapter 2 addresses the way that women's voices are systematically underrepresented in all kinds of democratic forums. This includes news websites, letters to the editor, school board meetings, town meetings, and public bodies up to the U.S. Supreme Court. Interruptions and selective enforcement of rules work against women, often in settings where gender identity does not appear to be relevant on its face. I review the way women's voices reflect other markers of inequality where positions of power and influence are concerned.

Chapter 3 addresses the way that communication throughout society embodies gendered patterns. It discusses how those gendered patterns behave in real life and how they have been reframed, reshaped, and transferred to online communities of all kinds.

Chapter 4 looks at cyberharassment, misogyny online, and the work that is being done to assess new conduits for hate in the internet age. If the first ten- to fifteen-year span of broad public use of the internet worked as an open season for misogynists online, what effect has it had on deliberation? Cyberharrassment has a particular effect on young women, who have come of age online and been targeted in ways that were unimaginable a few years ago. Women of color also bear special burdens and are disproportionately targeted for abuse.

Chapter 5 makes the business case for engaging women in public affairs conversations on news websites and in other online discussion forums. Engaging women not only fulfills the civic goal of a supporting a democratic society, but it also serves the business purposes of commercial news and social media. New tools and committed leaders are making huge strides to elevate women's voices and views to equality across news media.

Chapter 6 explores the way that historical patterns of gender and race discrimination have become baked into new technologies such as comment forums. In fact, the leading business methods of technology development often compound discriminatory assumptions rather than open products to the widest markets. New waves of technology designers are reimagining how developers approach product design, and it bodes well for the inclusion of women and other underrepresented groups in comment forums.

Chapter 7 introduces emerging methods for gender-informed technology and business development.

Chapter 8 outlines recommendations for reenvisioning democratic debate in the digital age. The populist wave of politics that ushered in the Brexit vote in the United Kingdom, the presidency of Donald Trump in the United States, and a host of nationalist movements around the world are clearly a backlash to changing demographics. But the way that nationalist movements have coalesced has also clearly been driven by the organizing potential of the digital age.

For women to claim our speaking time in the democracies of the future and to move to equal power in government and society, we have to be speaking online in the most popular forums. We have to have leaders and a grassroots willing to bring women's policy and political priorities more clearly into the open. And we have to create online forums that truly represent a democratic world.

1
Women and News Comments

Smoke blotted out the sun and gave a hellish orange glow to skies over San Francisco and much of the West Coast of the United States in the summer of 2020. Forest fires burned millions of acres in California, Oregon, and Washington state. Red, gray, and black skies dominated major cities as people struggled to breathe, and roads closed because of low visibility. Thousands of homes and businesses were incinerated.

Fires burned for weeks. Scientists had a strong consensus: regular, raging wild fires were part of the future in the U.S. West because of climate change. "Climate change, in the words of one scientist, is smacking California in the face," Thomas Fuller and Christopher Flavelle wrote in the *New York Times*.[1] A year earlier, fires were so intense in Australia that the season was known as "Black Summer."

In response to the California fires, readers from around the world underscored how predictable it was that many in the United States would suddenly take the fires as a sign that climate change required public action, though the science had long been known.

"Every now and again climate change reaches a new peak of undeniability, and the agenda-setting class decides it's important enough to focus on. But they always talk about it like it's just recently that it's been clear," Tim Moerman wrote from Ottawa, Ontario.[2] "I was working for an environmental nonprofit in 1996 and we were talking about the actual melting ice caps and collapsing ice shelves then. Can we please stop retroactively giving ourselves a pass by rewriting history?"

Phillipe wrote from Paris, urging people in the United States to overcome their complacence.[3] "One would think that the vivid images coming out of California would spawn a new awakening and a unified reaction to climate change, but that's not happening in America," he wrote. "America's inability to accept the urgency of climate change and reject those politicians who choose to ignore it, your failures have become everyone's problem. Any sane leader would view the pictures of San Francisco's smoke riddled skyline and immediately react with all resources available, but that's not happening."

Throughout the discussion online, one characteristic prevailed. It looked as if the people concerned about climate change were mostly men. Offline, Gallup poll results over a period of eight years showed that women have a higher level of scientific understanding about climate change and that women are slightly more concerned about it than men.[4]

Just three of the eleven comments highlighted as NYT Picks, which moderators choose to represent a variety of views, were from commenters with names likely to be female. Elizabeth from Roslyn, New York, wrote about a lack of response from the Trump administration.[5] "The real question for Trump is how do the fires and resulting damage to life and property affect his reelection?" Sarah Turner of Ojai, California, wrote about poor forest management over a long period of years as an underlying cause of the massive fires. "The main reason for today's mega-fires has less to do with global warming, and more to do with our fire suppression policies for the last

100 or so years," she wrote.[6] "Before white settlers, they now believe that the entire range of the Sierra Nevada completely burned every five to thirty years."

Shelby, from Out West, wrote about the danger of breathing in Marin County, California, and 113 degree Fahrenheit heat and said family on the East Coast did not accept the science of climate change.[7] ("Shelby," a British place name that traditionally was a boy's name, is now ten times more likely to be given to a girl.[8] This comment displays the way gender identification of commenters can only be approximate, not certain.) "This morning, the air outside our front door is considered too dangerous to breathe," she said, citing the specific measure of particulates in the air. "Yet, when I chat with my conservative relatives back East, all people whom I love, they do not accept that this situation is being caused by human activity. What is a person supposed to do in the face of this?"

Two of the NYT Picks had display names that were not gender identified. They were from online handles "Pucifer" (a character name from the online game *World of Warcraft*) and "Young Jedi" (a Star Wars reference, but Jedis are men three-to-one, according to fan sites). Across the 628 comments that were published on the story, male names predominated in those comments with an identifiable gender. Nongendered display names were less common, and names that are typically women's were even less common. Changes in European privacy laws and corporate policy at the *New York Times* mean that registration data for commenters is now obscured for staff working on the back end.

The climate and wildfires story reflected broad patterns of conversation at the *New York Times* that I have been studying and trying to understand since my first days moderating comments. Similar patterns prevail across the site. And it turns out the same pattern prevails on other news sites throughout the world.

One big shortcoming of all these analyses is that they do not account for race as a measure of inclusive community or for the diversity of perspectives that a more carefully constructed sample of readers would provide. It does not account for gender beyond the outdated binary. This is one example of the way that critical race theory looks at mainstream news media as not accounting for race and thereby as "erasing" the presence of people of color throughout society.

The reasons for a paucity of identifiable comments from people of color is not difficult to understand. Indeed, news industry research has shown that a decisive majority of Black and Hispanic communities distrust mainstream media and doubt their accuracy.[9] This, research shows, affects the willingness of people to contribute to public conversations. All of the literature about women's voices on the internet reflect a deep distrust of the safety of online spaces, as I discuss in later chapters.

Meredith D. Clark, a scholar and former journalist, investigated for the Coral Project why some people's voices, especially those of Black women and gender-nonconforming people, are especially marginalized in news comments. The perspectives she gathered should give any thoughtful journalist pause about how to expand the voices heard in comment sections of any website:

> When it comes to commenting online, the women of color and nonbinary people of color in our sample and complementary in-depth interviews indicated they're more comfortable doing so under conditions where they feel they have more control, such as on their own social media pages. But when they do comment on online news websites, it's often in service to the profession and the public, stepping in to submit missing details or context in a story, or to advocate for their communities.
>
> "I try to weigh the cost-benefit analysis," explained Maia, a participant in the interviews. "What will I get out of posting this? Is anyone going to interact and say, 'oh, I learned something

about this from you?' Is it smart, engaging discourse? Or is it going to turn into an online version of what happens to me in real life: people dismissing what I have to say for a number of reasons."[10]

In an interview, Clark spoke about the structural reasons that Black voices and others are limited in an open forum in a mainstream news site. "Low participation in comments might be a revelation to people who were shielded from backlash for speaking up. But it's not a revelation to a woman of color who has spoken up in spaces that are thought to be a traditional white space, or it's thought to be a place where people with credentials speak," Clark said. "This is how race is structured in social and political conversations. It's how power works, and it's how conditions of power work together."[11]

It's Not Just about Government and Politics

The overrepresentation of men in comments also shows up in other areas of news, such as entertainment. The day that the pop star Prince died in the spring of 2016, my friend Dawn Fallik sent me a private message. She wanted to know about the comments that *Times* moderators had chosen as highlights of the reader conversation about his legacy.

"I'm looking at the Times Picks for the Prince story and all the picks are written by men," Dawn wrote at about 5 p.m., a few hours after the story opened to comment. "Seriously? Of all the comments, only the men have something real to say about Prince?" The absence of women's voices upset her, she wrote, "almost as much as Vice saying that Prince's great song 'Strawberry Beret' hit the charts."[12]

While the death of a musical genius is a cultural event and not an issue of public policy, Dawn's observation is nevertheless an important one. Women's voices are missing across broad areas of public interest and conversation.

Whose voices are being heard in all kinds of conversations taking place in open digital spaces? Are online discussion forums offering only variations of A Guy Nation? Or are open discussion platforms created to engage and reflect a broad range of public thought and expression?

As I looked at the highlighted comments on the Prince story at that time, about 5 p.m., I saw that one NYT Pick was from "Kimberley from San Francisco," a more commonly female name. Others had men's names, and two had genderless display names, such as lgt525 from Ann Arbor, Michigan.[13] While not a flawless method of identification, matching display names to lists of gendered names is one that researchers use.[14]

In 2016, working in the back end of the *Times*'s first comment-moderation system, I could look at other clues to gender that are not available on the live website. I looked for gender clues in registration information for comments from EP in Morristown, New Jersey, or The-JadedCynic, with the display location listed as "Work."[15] Two other highlighted comments with gender-ambiguous display names (how appropriate for a story about a gender-fluid icon like Prince) had email addresses that indicated the account was linked to a woman reader. As an example, if I were to leave a comment with the display name MTT, moderators at that time would have been able to see my email address on the back end. Email addresses often give clues about gender if the email address is something like marie.tessier@randomdomain.

I replied to Dawn and told her that gender can often be hidden, and it appears women more often make the choice to appear anonymously. I explained that in addition to providing a range of views, the *Times*'s policy was to reflect a variety of locations, genders, and possibly races, if indicated. It's a guideline, not a hard-and-fast rule, and not all moderators take notice on every story. It's complicated on a popular breaking story like Prince's death, when numerous moderators are all approving, rejecting, and highlighting comments as they plow through hundreds or thousands of comments that come in during a short span of time. While gender has not always been embraced as a consideration across all *New York Times* comments throughout our daily rush, I had one clear answer.

"I'm working on it," I wrote.

By the time the story was closed to comment the next day, four of the twenty-seven highlighted comments (just 15 percent) were clearly from women. This is not far off from trends documented in news sites around the world, as I explain below. Three were from readers named Katherine, Lady Scorpio, and Carolyn. Another with the display name Easy E wrote in the text of her comment, "Oh, this Minnesota girl is sad." Because of an apparent technical glitch, Kimberley's comment no longer appeared on the live page.

Empirical Data

The wild fire and Prince stories turn out to be good representations of gender dynamics in online news comment sections. In recent years, studies of the *New York Times* and more than forty other major news websites around the world show that women are outnumbered in news comments about three to one.

In 2015, just 28 percent of comments from people with identifiable gender on the *New York Times* website were from women, according to study of nearly a million *Times* comments by Emma Pierson. Pierson was then a statistics blogger, a writer, and a Stanford University graduate student. Beginning in 2021, she will be an assistant professor at Cornell Tech, the New York City technology campus of Cornell University.[16] Pierson studied comments by gender and uncovered broad themes.

In essence, Pierson's work showed that news comments at the *New York Times* online reflect the same gender roles and lack of women's voices that are reflected in many other aspects of public life.[17] Women are underrepresented in parliaments, in business leadership, in political leadership, in front-page bylines on major news sites, on Sunday morning political talk shows, and in nearly every other measure of leadership. Only men have been presidents of the United States and so on. More data are presented later in the chapter about women's representation in office and in other areas that reflect more movement toward equal representation in public life.

In addition to women's voices being outnumbered three to one, women's comments were concentrated in areas that are traditionally seen as women's domains, such as parenting, health, fashion, and education. The Op-Ed Project, a nonprofit organization that began as an effort to increase the number of op-ed essays submitted to newspapers by women, describes these stereotypically "pink" topics as the four Fs—family, food, fashion, and furniture.[18]

A year after Pierson's study, the sociologist Andrew J. Perrin explored a similar phenomenon in letters to the editor, where women's voices are also vastly outnumbered.[19] Perrin also found that African Americans submitted fewer letters than white readers, an issue that the OpEd Project has subsequently taken up. In 2018, Caroline Kitchener wrote in *The Atlantic* magazine about the same phenomenon in a magazine where the readership is about evenly split between women and men. She received similar tallies when she asked editors in the *Kansas City Star*, *Chicago Tribune*, *Tampa Bay Times*, and *Toronto Star*.

Women and Comments around the World

As I stood at my computer station every day, vexed that the most common contributors to the *New York Times* Opinion conversations really were Tom, Dick, and Hari, writ large, it was also clear to me that the *Times* could not be alone. The *Times* leads news sites for its attention to civility and is one of just a few news organizations devoting substantial resources to comment moderation.[20]

For one thing, I knew that women's voices were being heard at the *Times* at levels that aligned with so many other markers of women's place in public life, where women remain terribly underrepresented in leadership. Could it really be the case that the number of women citizens speaking up on public affairs would naturally reflect women's representation in Congress or front-page bylines?

When I took a wider-angle lens and looked at news comments around the world, it became clear that the same dynamics inhibiting women's full-throated participation in *New York Times* comments were affecting news organizations the world over. As I surveyed the web, it seemed that other long-lived news organizations were doing no better at engaging women readers in their comments.

It turned out others shared my concerns. In 2015, a comprehensive global survey of leading English-language and Danish news sites verified my sense that women's voices are missing online, throughout the world. University of Sydney professor Fiona Martin undertook a three-year study financed by the Australian Research Council to make a comprehensive assessment of whose voices were being heard online.[21] She looked at age, race, gender, geography, income groups, immigration status, and aboriginal voices. Martin wanted to assess the scope of interactive media and to support the prospect that media should become true platforms of civic engagement and interactive relationships, not merely reproductions of past power structures.

Among her most significant findings was that women's voices are being left out of civic conversations across the web. Her research goals were not gender-focused. But gender is where she found the sharpest divide and the greatest shortcoming in democratic representation.

"The conversations at news sites are becoming the historical evidence of the *vox populi*," Martin said.[22] "There's a problem for journalists if their news sites are reflecting just one aspect of a society. You can't really call it a reflection of people's voices unless everyone's voices are included."

Martin catalogued, coded, and analyzed nine million comments from news sites around the world, including the United States, the United Kingdom, Australia, and Denmark. Results showed that women are consistently and overwhelmingly outnumbered in comments on news sites. Results from country to country were similar. A few sites had a preponderance of display names rather than real names.

At the world's largest and most prestigious publications, the arbiters of public issue debates in major countries, male-named participants dominate across all international and metropolitan populations.

At the *Daily Mail*, 63 percent of comments had identifiable men's names, 17 percent were identifiably female, and 20 percent were ambiguous. And this occurred at a publication with a reported total audience that is 55 percent female, much higher than other major metropolitan daily news organizations, where men typically make up a majority of the audience.

At the *Huffington Post*, men's comments were 79 percent of the total, and women's comments 20 percent. The comments in their system are tied to Facebook profiles, so gender-ambiguous names and pseudonyms are minimized. (Facebook's policy is to require real names, but pseudonyms are not uncommon.)

At the *New York Times*, in the Australian study, identifiable men's names comprised 72 percent of comments, women's names 10 percent, with 18 percent ambiguous. This is within range of the comments on the Prince story discussed at the beginning of the chapter.

At the *Sydney Morning Herald*, identifiable men's names made up 70 percent of the comments, women's names made up 9 percent, and 21 percent were ambiguous.

The *Guardian* and the *Washington Post* had curious results. In both of those publications, screen names or pseudonyms predominate, and they are largely gender ambiguous. The *Guardian* had 76 percent of comments with gender-ambiguous names, 21 percent men's names, and 3 percent women. The *Washington Post* had 72 percent gender ambiguous names, 12 percent men, and 6 percent women, with 10 percent unaccounted for.

Remarkably, even on the sites where pseudonyms predominate, the *Guardian* and the *Washington Post*, women's representation with full names is even lower than where more people are using their full names (see figure 1.1).

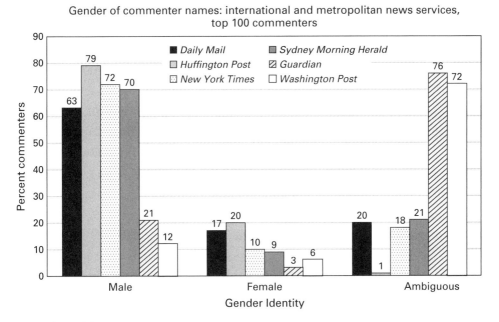

Figure 1.1

Gender bias in commenters' names in six international and metropolitan news sources. *Source:* Fiona Martin, "Getting My Two Cents Worth In," *#ISOJ*, April 15, 2015, https://isojjournal.wordpress.com/2015/04/15/getting-my-two-cents-worth-in -access-interaction-participation-and-social-inclusion-in-online-news-commenting.

On the websites for the British Broadcasting Corporation, Australian Broadcast Corporation, and U.S. Public Broadcasting Service, comments with men's names were 40 percent to 54 percent of the total comments. Comments from women were 5 percent to 12 percent of the total. And 41 percent to 49 percent were from people giving ambiguous or ungendered display names.

One program stood out. "The Conversation," a digital native web-based international site, hosted a comment section where full names were encouraged. Even there, women were outnumbered by more than three to one. Men contributed 77 percent of the comments; women contributed 22 percent of the comments. Eliminating display names did not alter the familiar ratio.

In systems where full names are ensured via Facebook, the *Huffington Post*, and the *Orange County Register*, a major news site near Los Angeles, women's comments were 20 percent and 21 percent of the total. So women were outnumbered four to one on sites where full names are used.

One site did considerably better than others, with 35 percent of comments from women. The *Texas Tribune* is a nonprofit, nonpartisan site dedicated to civic news and engagement in a state that is home to about 10 percent of the United States population, the second biggest state by population after California. One important difference between the *Texas Tribune* and other major news sites with a regional focus is that the *Tribune*'s purpose is to augment existing news coverage in the state. Among its purposes is to engage people with journalism and public affairs through more than fifty live events each year. That means its mission can rise to a different level of interaction, which is a hallmark of its approach.[23]

The trend of women's underrepresentation also bore out in metropolitan or regional news sites in the global study. The *Liverpool Echo* had 80 percent of comments from men, 6 percent from women, and 14 percent from people using pseudonyms or gender-ambiguous names. Two Australian news sites with large numbers of pseudonyms had fewer than 10 percent of comments coming from women using full names. The *Illawarra Mercury* had 56 percent of comments from men, 9 percent from women, and 34 percent from gender-ambiguous display names. The state service *North Territory News* had 49 percent of comments from men, 7 percent from women using full names, and 39 percent from people using pseudonyms.

Pierson published her results in 2015, at about the same time that civic discussions flashed open on questions of sexual abuse, fame, and the abuse of power by celebrities. Stories about sexual abuse are a perfect example of the profound differences between men's and women's views and reactions have clear relevance for public policy. What people say in the public sphere influences public perceptions, and it also can mean the difference between convictions and acquittals in court. The degree of empathy for someone who alleges sexual assault has huge implications for public policy, Pierson argued.

In the years since Pierson's study of comments on at *New York Times*, much has changed with the advent of the #MeToo movement and the subsequent convictions of such entertainment powerhouses as the former movie producer Harvey Weinstein and comedian Bill Cosby. News talk show host Charlie Rose, host of a PBS talk show and co-anchor of *CBS This Morning*, has lost his career, as has NBC's former *Today* show anchor Matt Lauer. Congressional hearings probed the high school behavior of a man who was subsequently confirmed to sit on the U.S. Supreme Court. In those cases, some of the men were finally held accountable in public when multiple people came forward to document patterns of abuse that spanned many years and multiple victims.

An ordinary woman accusing a man of sexual assault or sexual misconduct is in a far different power dynamic. Women accusing ordinary men who are not stars or power brokers face an entirely different set of power dynamics. The *New York Times* reporters Susan Chira and Catrin Einhorn detailed the limits of #MeToo trends in

2017. They ran an extensive story about pervasive sexual harassment and assault against women who were Ford autoworkers, many of whom are Black.[24] Social class, race, and public focus all have a direct effect on what justice can be achieved.

Because #MeToo took on a life of its own in 2017 and 2018, I want to rewind to an earlier conversation before sexual assault and harassment became everyday topics of conversations. An earlier conversation about an acclaimed movie director allows more subtlety about the facts in evidence, underlying attitudes about justice and men's reputations, and the extent to which women who make stand-alone allegations are believed.

In 2014, Dylan Farrow published an open letter on Nicholas Kristof's *On the Ground* blog at the *New York Times*.[25] She resurfaced her allegation that Woody Allen, her adoptive father, had sexually abused her. The blog post came as Allen was nominated for another Oscar.

"The message that Hollywood sends matters" for sexual abuse survivors, Farrow wrote. "Woody Allen is a living testament to the way our society fails the survivors of sexual assault and abuse."

In a pattern that is typical of women's communication generally, comments from women routinely affirmed the value of Dylan Farrow's account and expressed sympathy. Many of them said they were incest survivors, too.

"Not being believed is a testing of one's strength to which a young child should not be subjected. I believe you because I know how these secretive betrayals of a child's innocence can take place. They happened to me too," Vivienne Woodhead wrote from Gloucester, Massachusetts.[26] "I did not speak out because I was too young and too traumatized. There are more predators like our fathers out there than people will believe. For all the discussion of the issue over the last twenty years, acceptance of the survivor's word is still difficult for those not involved. Speaking out is an unimaginably brave act and I salute you."

Some women shared details of their own experiences. "Who feels it, knows it! The smell of Old Spice makes me sick to my stomach and words spoken a tad too softly by any man make my deception radar go up . . . even after almost 60 years," Joyce Marie Wright wrote from Brooklyn, New York.[27] "The physical scars of my father's abuse have long since healed but the emotional trauma remains. My abuse came during the 50s when there were no words for me to articulate, and no listeners who had the mindset open enough to hear me even if I had the words. I see nothing much has changed since then. Those who pretend otherwise should be ashamed of themselves!"

Other women said Dylan Farrow's detailed account showed why so many in Hollywood were wrong to stand by Allen in the face of serious allegations. "This is very well done and she seems imminently credible," Katie in North Carolina wrote in response to Farrow's letter.[28] "Artistic talent does not excuse child abuse—nothing does. I'm sickened by all of these prestigious actors who are so eager to work with Woody Allen."

In contrast, many men expressed skepticism about Farrow's allegations, and criticized Nicholas Kristof for featuring the letter on his blog. Men also expressed much more concern for Allen's reputation, given the fact that no criminal charges ever were filed.

"There is nothing in Dylan's letter or apparently in the investigation to convince anyone that the abuse really happened. It seems important to find if it actually happened, not for the benefit of Dylan, who clearly believes that it did, but for the many who withhold judgment, horrified by the story of the abuse, but concerned that it may be a manufactured memory," wrote WHM of Rochester, whose email address, visible to moderators on the back end of NYTimes.com, indicates a man's name: "It is inappropriate for Nicholas to again air this horrific and oft-repeated allegation, when even he does not know if it is true."[29]

Many others stressed the use of criminal courts as appropriate avenues for the issues to be raised and cast aspersions on the accuser's motives. "Public accusation. Now, press charges or else forget about it," Paul wrote from Virginia Beach, Virginia.[30] "If there is basis to the accusation, try to prove it in court. But salacious slander via the press hardly seems fair and cannot be taken seriously."

Many men also sympathized with Farrow. "There are no words to describe the horror visited upon Dylan Farrow. Her bravery in the past and with this letter are astounding," Bill Palmer wrote from Oakland, California.[31] "Should we pay attention to the artistic works of a moral monster and predator? For me, an ethical dilemma for which I have no glib answer."

Some men said that before the open letter, they had withheld judgment about the allegations, which had been covered off and on over the years. They changed their minds, they wrote, after reading the deeply personal appeal from Farrow.

"I've been a fan of Woody's work for a long, long time. I've obviously been aware of the accusations regarding his daughter," Jeff Holcomb wrote from Evanston, Illinois.[32] "But never have I allowed them to strike home. Until now."

The different ways that women and men responded to Farrow's open letter serve as a perfect illustration of why the lack of women's voices online is a problem in a democracy. Women's and men's views on policy issues—and the criminal and civil court results of sexual abuse are clearly public policy issues—differ sharply.

As in these examples, Emma Pierson's analysis of *Times* comments showed a profound gender divide in support for Dylan Farrow in the comments—a divide that tracks public opinion surveys about sexual assault allegations in general. Women overwhelmingly supported Farrow. Men were evenly split, she wrote.[33]

Knowing that women are more likely than men to believe reports of sexual abuse, the difference has enormous implications for public life, Pierson wrote:

> Regardless of whether you believe Dylan Farrow's story, the gender gap in sympathy (which several other studies have found as well) should trouble you. It implies that in Congress, the police, or the

military, where women are underrepresented, opinions will be skewed against survivors of sexual assault. (The importance of equal representation applies to men as well, of course: we would not want sexual assault trials to have entirely female jurors.) And because men and women's opinions differ in many other ways as well, the undemocratic implication is simple: when one gender is underrepresented, the views that are heard will not fairly represent the views that are held.

The outpouring of women's support on the Dylan Farrow blog post also reflects other ways that women express themselves online. Those will be addressed in depth in the chapter on gender and communication. But it's noteworthy that women weighed in on a topic that is deeply felt among women—sexual assault. It's a topic where women have a feeling of investment and efficacy, an issue where their views are expected. Because sexual assault is considered a women's issue—though abuse occurs to boys and girls, men and women—women know their voices will be heard by others in an open forum, even if a child is not believed by investigators or even family members.

To show just how much an impact that men's and women's different perspectives are for the public record, consider this example. A few years after the open letter, *New York Times* columnist Bret Stephens displayed the difference in understanding between the more victim-centered perspective that women generally express and the more skeptical perspective that men generally displayed in 2014. In 2018, Stephens wrote that Woody Allen had been "smeared" by unproven allegations. "Since the State of Connecticut declined to press charges against Allen, it is what we have to go on," Stephens wrote. "Shouldn't the weight of available evidence, to say nothing of the presumption of innocence, extend to the court of public opinion, too?" Ultimately, he had to make a profound correction to the column that undercut the validity of his point about Woody Allen and so-called "cancel culture."[34]

Stephens's 2018 column first went to press saying that only one investigation had been conducted of Dylan Farrow when she was a child and that it had concluded she had not been abused. As myriad previous stories in the media had outlined, however, four different court cases had decided against Allen, supporting the mother's wish to control Allen's access to her children. The judge in the custody case rejected the conclusion of the study Stephens cited. Maureen Orth covered the story for the magazine *Vanity Fair*. In 2014, she outlined a judge's finding that "Allen's behavior toward Dylan was 'grossly inappropriate and that measures must be taken to protect her.'"[35]

Even with facts displayed in depth over a long period of years, even well into the #MeToo era, a prominent man's skepticism persisted and cast the alleged victim in skeptical terms, even when a judge had ruled against the alleged abuser. The differences between men's perspectives and women's perspectives matter a great deal. The historic dominance of men's voices in the media matters a great deal, too. And #MeToo has fallen well short of persuading influential voices to take a broad view of a complicated topic.

Women's voices and other underrepresented voices matter.

On other topics that are not considered explicitly a female domain, as rape and sexual abuse are, women are far less likely to participate in discussion. Examples as varied as the stories about wild fires, climate change and Prince outlined at the beginning of the chapter illustrate the empirical reality.

The shortfall in women's comments is also reflected in letters to the editor at the *New York Times* and at other media. As *Times* editors set out to boost women's voices in other parts of its news and opinion reporting, a history graduate student, Kimberly Probolus, sent a letter in 2019 expressing her disappointment that the letters section always featured a predominance of men. She wrote with a historian's flair:

> In 1855, Nathaniel Hawthorne wrote to his publisher, "America is now wholly given over to a damned mob of scribbling women." Although he was referring specifically to sentimental novelists, his letter expressed the larger belief that women's writing was not worth

reading or publishing, that their words and ideas didn't matter, and that their work was, to use the language of Hawthorne, "trash."

As a historian, I see this playing out not only in the antebellum period, but also in the postwar era when I read letters to the editor. As I scan through various national newspapers, day after day, year after year, I find myself hoping that someday, *eventually*, women will be represented proportionally. I am always disappointed; they always skew male.[36]

The *New York Times* editor of letters to the editor, Thomas Feyer, and staff editor Susan Mermelstein responded with a commitment to invite, support, and keep track of the section's performance on gender representation. Up to that time, they wrote, only about a quarter to a third of letters submitted came from women. Again, women wrote most regularly on topics that are typically a female domain. This gender disparity problem is not unique to the letters page. Online comments on articles and the unsolicited op-ed submissions news organizations receive skew heavily male. Nor is this issue unique to the *Times*, they wrote: "As for our letters page, we make our selections regardless of gender. But we are sensitive to gender imbalance, and as editors of a space dedicated to readers' voices, we are determined to have it reflect more closely society as a whole. Going forward, we're committing ourselves to work toward a goal of parity on a weekly basis."[37]

A year later, the editors reported back. The proportion of letters to the editor from women had improved to 42 percent of the total. Submissions from women still hovered at 25 to 30 percent, according to Feyer and Mermelstein. "There were consistent patterns: Politics, the economy and foreign affairs? The majority of submissions come from men. (Women represented just over a third of the published letters about politics.) Parenting, health, education and relationships? A larger percentage from women," they wrote. "Some of the results surprised us: Homages to stick-shift cars? We published letters from five women, and none from men.[38] And we published a plea from 33 writers, all of them women, to stop using the term 'quid pro quo' in the impeachment inquiry, in favor of the more explicit 'bribery' or 'extortion.'[39] Overall, though, we're not satisfied yet. While there was a small uptick in letters from women right after we announced the project, we still sometimes find ourselves struggling to ensure that women's voices are heard on a wide variety of topics."[40]

I posted a similar appeal to women to write comments at about the same time.[41]

Having a goal is terrific, but the struggle to hear from women is real. As Andrew J. Perrin wrote in 2016, submissions to letters to the editor reflect the same aspects of social inequality as other forms of political participation.[42]

As frustrating as it is to watch, we do know why women do not contribute more often. Many measures of gender inequality remain fixed at women contributing 25 percent, and there are real-world consequences when women assert their authority online, at work, and in public life. A lifetime hearing "down girl" has its effects.

The Voice Gap and the Puzzle of Missing Voices

The enormous shortfall in women's voices in news comments or in letters to the editor is no surprise to anyone who has observed women's representation in other parts of public life. Women remain vastly underrepresented in Congress,[43] in front-page bylines,[44] on op-ed pages, and on Sunday talk shows in the United States. Similar patterns pertain in most other countries, though some countries are doing far better with women's representation in government.

As Facebook's Sheryl Sandberg notes in her book coauthored with Nell Scovell, *Lean In: Women, Work, and the Will to Lead*,[45] women volunteer their voices less in the workplace, too. Girls participate less in classroom discussions when they see themselves as less efficacious, research shows, especially in science, technology, engineering, and math. Unless a school takes innovative approaches to inclusion, girls speak up in subjects like English but do not fully participate in subjects that traditionally have been seen as domains of men and boys.

These themes of gendered communication are explored more fully in chapter 3.

When I first started investigating the absence of women's voices in news comments across the media, internet use and digital media were not the primary ways that most news consumers received news. The mobile web was a distant dream.

I soon figured out, however, that when it comes to women's voice in public life, the women's movement and civic organizations have an odd set of invisible barriers to overcome. As with the examples of the comments I shared in the introduction about abuse directed at a congresswoman, misogynistic behaviors are usually blamed on individual bad actors like Congressman Ted Yoho or antagonists like Donald Trump.

Throughout the years that I puzzled over women's reluctance to comment at NYTimes.com, scholars and policy makers in the United States, Europe, the United Kingdom, Australia, and other countries had questions of their own. What kind of citizen interaction in media would indicate full participation in an information society?

Martin describes the hallmarks that scholars look for when they assess how well or poorly media are engaging communities in civic problem solving:[46]

- Are media engaging with the public and creating content to solve civic problems?
- Are media hosting and facilitating public commenting and debate?
- Are scholars in Europe looking for media opportunities for people to produce content and express themselves in online political communication?

When some people use media a lot and others hold back or don't have access, the gap is often described as "the digital divide." During the coronavirus pandemic in 2020, the term was used most often to describe gaps between families with excellent access to the internet and computer technology and families with no internet connection and a lack of computers for children to use to attend school remotely or complete their studies.

The digital divide between women's and men's voices online is much more about public voice. It most definitely includes socioeconomic disparities in access to the technology. And scholars argue that the media need to close these gaps. "Recent media studies also suggest inclusive digital media strategies need to recognize potential participants, attend to how discussions could be better hosted and consider user obligations to listen and respond to others in a conversation," Martin writes. Others ask "how online journalists can better facilitate and respond to comments."[47]

While a huge gender gap prevails in online comments, public perceptions of online forums differ sharply from the data about who is actually submitting comments. A 2014 Pew Research study of internet users found that the vast majority of people believe that comment sections and other online communities outside of gaming are equally welcoming to women and men (see figure 1.2).[48]

To achieve something like democratic engagement in the digital age, news sites need to find ways to create a legitimate democratic forum that broadly represents people's voices. When sites first went online in the 1980s and 1990s, editors felt they were opening the gates and a raucous new form of democracy would prevail. As I describe in later chapters, this was soon shown to be an unrealistic fantasy, though it retains mythic power. Rather, a wide-open internet gave rise to new vectors for the aggregation of hate and imposed steep costs on women who spoke up at all, regardless of whether they were violating any known gender norms.

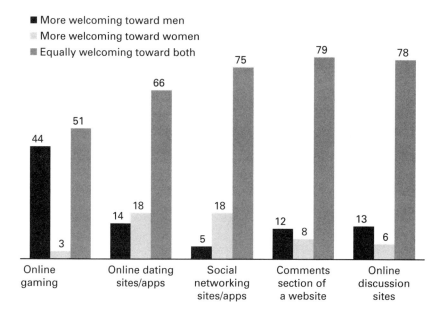

Figure 1.2

How welcoming are online "neighborhoods" to men and women?

Note: n = 2,489.

Source: Pew Research Center, American Trends Panel (wave 4), survey conducted May 30 to June 30, 2014, https://www.pewresearch.org/internet/2014/10/22/part-2-the -online-environment.

The dream of a one-person, one-voice kind of democratic forum remains just that—a dream. Historians always knew that that type of utopian vision was never in the cards for online conversations about public affairs. Media leaders, however, did not.

By and large, the online world naturally reflects and recreates culture and social power dynamics that exist in real life. Worse, online media recreate historic social and power dynamics. Online media, particularly social media, have created some advantages for social networking that have breathed new life into political organizations. But those same advantages have also allowed antagonists to coalesce as well.

What editors did not fully appreciate is the way that freewheeling, unattended open forums, *as they were conceived*, naturally evolved to be platforms where antagonists were allowed to dominate and where thoughtful readers feared to tread. The forums naturally reframed existing power dynamics in society, and in some ways reinforced barriers to public conversation.

These antagonistic, often hateful experiences can be a form of social risk that technology companies have taken too little responsibility for, the writers Catherine Buni and Soraya Chemaly say.[49] Similarly, the ways that social media algorithms draw together like-minded people created the risk of genocidal forces coming together in Myanmar, they write.

One foreseeable risk of creating an "open" internet where individual voices have more power than a more centralized mass media setting was the way that traditional systems of power would arise to police gender norms. As the Australian political scientist Jessica Megarry describes it, social media have given men the opportunity to conduct surveillance of feminist activities.[50]

All over the world, women experience complex social barriers to sharing their views online, as I describe in the next chapters. Some of the barriers are from present-day antagonism like trolls. Some may stem from direct experience with hostility online. Much more of it is the silence that has followed women and people of color through millennia—followed them right onto the internet—from a historic foundation in legal exclusions from power. Like many issues of culture and social power, there's no one single fix. The first step is understanding how women's voices fit into the larger society.

2
Women as the Silent Sex

Like many women in politics, Toni Carter was elected to office in Ramsey County, Minnesota, with an agenda focused on education, juvenile justice reform, and other human needs such as providing light rail to more neighborhoods in St. Paul.

Also like many women, Carter says she could tell her proposals and comments did not always carry the same authority as others' comments, even when she was the expert in the room. "Sometimes, my voice would just sit there, almost like nothing was said," says Carter, who went on to win reforms and better rail service in low-income neighborhoods. "I believe trying to have one's voice heard is a common experience for women, and especially for women of color."[1]

Women's experience of being unheard in public affairs is so ubiquitous that a landmark study from Princeton University and Brigham Young University has described women as "the silent sex."[2]

Women's voices and influence lag in public affairs settings, far below their already low level of representation in government—despite years of other kinds of progress for women in education, in the workplace, and in leadership positions in business and government.

Women speak less at public meetings, they make fewer motions, and they're more frequently subject to negative interruptions. Such interruptions are a key mechanism that suppresses women's participation, data show.

"We hear from women, 'we need to be better,' 'we can't make mistakes, because the consequences are just brutal,'" says Kelly Dittmar, a professor with the Center for American Women and Politics at Rutgers University in New Jersey. "Women know the reception is going to be skeptical, so they wait to speak up until they have overwhelming evidence and support."[3]

An obvious question arises if women's voices are outnumbered three to one or four to one in online conversations about news and public affairs, as outlined in the previous chapter. Are women's voices heard any more clearly or equally in other kinds of conversations on public affairs? The emphatic answer is no.

Women's voices are outnumbered three to one in many aspects of public life, most notably in Congress, where the proportion of women is about one of every four members. Measuring women's power in the real world requires a multidimensional view of political power.

In civics classes and in politics, people often talk about "one man, one vote," as the late Supreme Court Justice Earl Warren once summarized a theory of political representation. Empower people to vote, the theory goes, and political power will follow. When the suffragists marched to win power at the ballot box, many people characterized women's right to vote as the epitome of political equality.

"How long will women need to wait for liberty?" one suffragist's sign said.

It's notable here that divisions between white women's power and the political power of Black people took a big turn in the United States after the Civil War. Though people advocating for the abolition of slavery and people advocating for women's right to vote had worked together for years, the end of the Civil War marked a disastrous division. The leading power brokers of the day determined that only one group would be getting the vote—either Black men or white women, as historian Lori D. Ginzberg describes in her spell-binding biography, *Elizabeth Cady Stanton: An American Life*. A lot of things happened, but the bottom line was that Stanton and Susan B. Anthony, the great women's suffrage leaders, aligned themselves with prominent white supremacists in order to put women's votes ahead of those of newly emancipated Black men.[4]

This, too, is part of the story of women's voices. Not only were Black men and white women pitted against one another for a chance at an equal voice, but Black women were left out of the picture entirely. Even at the beginning of the twentieth century, white suffrage leaders tried to segregate public events like a march on Washington in 1913. Black women such as journalist Ida B. Wells refused to accept the scheme and solved the problem herself. Rather than walk at the back of the parade, as white leaders insisted, she and some allies waited along the parade route and jumped in front of their state delegations in the middle of the parade.[5]

But Black citizens were to be denied the vote in effect, despite their alleged protection under the Constitution. Winning white women's right to vote, however, was barely the beginning for women's representation in democracy.

For years, advocates for women's political participation have appealed to women to vote in the democratic process. "It's a man's world," according to one slogan from the League of Women Voters, "unless women vote." In fact, for decades after the Nineteenth Amendment to the U.S. Constitution was ratified, empowering women to vote throughout the country, women's voting participation lagged far behind men's.

The first time I cast a national ballot was in 1980, sixty years after women won the right to vote. As it happened, the first time I voted in a presidential election was also the first time women voted in the same proportion as men. That was the year Ronald Reagan defeated incumbent President Jimmy Carter. Women have been voting in greater proportions than men ever since.

It took generations for women's voting participation to reach equality.

As the United States approaches a century of white women's voting, many measures of women's political power fall far short of equality.

The social traditions and attitudes that suppressed women's voting turnout for sixty years continue to suppress other aspects of democratic power and influence. Such factors also influence daily life and political participation of all kinds. Indeed, similar patterns are found in workplaces, colleges, and public schools.

To gauge the way individuals and disempowered groups exercise political power, scholars identify several measures of action, authority, and influence. These measures give a detailed view of who has power in a democracy, how power is exercised, how power is inhibited, and how it is influenced by social and cultural practices.

Here are some metrics that political scientists use to describe political power. I've given them commonsense names.

- *Seats at the table*. Representation at the tables of power. In the context of women's political power, advocates have traditionally emphasized winning more seats for women at the tables of power. Political scientists call this *descriptive representation*.

- *Speaking turns*. The number of turns each member of a democratic forum speaks. This is one part of what the political science literature refers to as *discursive equality*.

- *Speaking time*. The number of minutes each member of a democratic body speaks. Speaking time can be measured for each speaking turn or for the total speaking time over several turns. This is another aspect of discursive equality.

- *Policy power*. The degree to which women's distinct policy preferences are adopted and implemented. Political scientists call this *substantive representation*—literally, do my views have equal power in the end?

- *Power expectation and authority*. The expectation that any particular individual is entitled to have power in a democracy. People's power expectations are influenced by social and demographic factors such as race, gender, income, and geography. Political scientists call this *symbolic representation*.

In real life, women and men talk face to face, over the phone, in letters, in town halls, on city councils, on juries, and in public forums. They talk in committees, in legislatures, and in political movements.

Or, more accurately, women often are silent much more than men in public policy conversations. Even when women attend public forums, they do not participate as much as men—just as fewer women submit comments online. And when women do speak, a growing body of research shows that they are heard less often, wield less influence, and have a diminished power to influence legislative agendas.

In other words, political officials like Toni Carter in St. Paul, Minnesota, and scholars who study women in politics, like Kelly Dittmar, are perfectly accurate when they say women face uphill battles. We do.

Women's muted voices online, in other words, mirror our muted voices in the real world. The low rate of women's participation in online forums is a mere reflection of women's underengagement and invisibility in public affairs of all kinds. Worse, the reflection of women's underengagement in political affairs has an incredible shrinking effect. Women's speaking turns in elective office don't even rise to our minimal number of seats at the table, except in uncommon situations.

Common Wisdom

The conventional wisdom about online comments is that an open forum is an egalitarian forum where everyone has equal access and equal opportunity. No one stands in the way, and no gatekeeper is deciding, in most cases, whose comments should be posted. Many people assume that the veil of anonymity available in most online forums means women can participate freely, without gender barriers.

Assuming equality in an unequal world, however, is a fundamental error. It's an especially big problem for women in politics and public affairs. Rules and institutions that appear, at face value, to be gender-neutral often have terribly unequal effects in the real world.

The Silent Sex

A variety of data support the longtime concerns of women in office, like Toni Carter, that their voices go unheard, even after they win seats on elected bodies. Comprehensive data from school boards, Vermont town meetings, and community meetings in rural Indian villages and Israeli kibbutzim all show that women's voices are underrepresented in mixed-gender groups throughout political life.[6]

Women rarely take up more than a quarter to a third of discussion turns and time where public policy is discussed across a range of institutions and settings, except when women are in a majority, women are chairing a committee, or institutional rules and culture are deliberately inclusive and affirming.

"Society signals that the domains of power are still reserved for men," says Tali Mendelberg, a Princeton University professor who with Christopher F. Karpowitz coauthored *The Silent Sex: Gender, Deliberation, & Institutions*, published by Princeton University Press in 2014: "Women still have confidence in their views, even when they see that their status is low. But they're not confident that what they have to say is valued, and that in turn shapes how willing they are to speak and what is discussed."[7]

Conventional wisdom about women in politics often looks to the number of women in a legislature or in elected office to gauge women's political power. Decades of research about women's influence, however, have shown that there are many more gaps between voting power, elective office, and the power to enact policies than many people may consider.

Scholars have measured women's influence in policy outcomes in a variety of countries. In parliaments and councils from London to Rwanda to New Zealand, an increase in the number of women in a legislature has not resulted in policy outcomes that reflect women's policy values.

"Larger numbers of women in the legislature do not consistently increase women's influence, or the substantive representation of women's distinctive priorities and perspectives," Karpowitz and Mendelberg write in *The Silent Sex*: "The reasons include the overriding influence of party membership and the allocation of power according to the party's position in the legislature, women's lack of seniority, the imperative to represent constituency interests rather than women's distinctive concerns, women's heavy dependence on male elites and patrons who are the gatekeepers to elected positions or resources, and male legislators' backlash against women's legislative gains."

In short, Karpowitz and Mendelberg write, "Increasing numbers help, and sometimes backfire."[8]

One of the most comprehensive data sets about women's participation in open forums comes from Vermont town meetings. Starting in 1970, University of Vermont professor emeritus Frank M. Bryan tracked participation at town meetings. Throughout the state, many municipalities make binding legislative decisions at open meetings where all registered voters may vote. It's in the tradition of Athenian democracy, which Bryan praises as "real democracy."[9]

Among Bryan's findings is that women's attendance and participation have gone up steadily over time, though men still dominate (see figure 2.1).

At Vermont town meetings, women's attendance is now close to equal. However, women still take just 38 percent of the speaking turns, the data show. When Bryan started tracking meetings in 1970, women took 20 percent of the speaking turns.

Starting in 1970, a researcher tracked how many women spoke at town hall meetings in Vermont, and how often. Both have risen over the decades, but men still dominate.

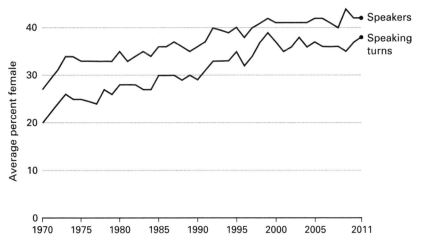

Figure 2.1

Having their say: Women speaking at Vermont town hall meetings, 1970 to 2011.
Source: Frank M. Bryan, *Real Democracy: The New England Town Meeting and How It Works* (University of Chicago Press, 2004).

"The women's movement did result in a huge increase in women's participation," Bryan said. "It still takes a lot of moxie to get up and speak."

Over five decades, Bryan developed an extraordinary data set about participation in open forums. At the time that his book was published in 2004, Bryan and his students had recorded 238,603 acts of participation by 63,140 citizens in 210 different towns.

Among the insights in the data are some measurements about which conditions tend to boost women's participation and which have the effect of discouraging it.[10] Some of those characteristics echo other findings in communication research about women's willingness and interest in sharing their views. In Vermont town meetings, women are more likely to speak in smaller towns, and they're more likely to speak in smaller gatherings. "So much of what you find looking back in the data is common sense," Bryan says. "When conversations take place on a more human scale, person to person, the behavior is more humane. It isn't rocket science."[11]

Oddly, though, the proportion of women attending tended to lower the overall number of women participating.

One woman, MTL, who said she had been on a town select board in Vermont—the New England equivalent of a city councilor—wrote on NYTimes.com that men's and women's interests vary with the topics of town meetings:

> I have attended a lot of Vermont town meetings, and been on a town select board. I think what the research does not show is that a good part of the discussions in Vermont small town meetings has to do with roads, road equipment, and trucks. The men can argue forever on the merits of these things, but the women aren't really all that interested. It's not intimidation. Women speak plenty when they want to.[12]

"Speaking in public is one of the great fears around the world, along with spiders," Bryan says. "The smaller the group, the easier it gets, and equality naturally follows."[13]

Another Vermont resident, Liz Weinmann, wrote on NYTimes.com that all the Vermont women she knows are "bold" and often face discouraging behavior from men in meetings:

> None of the bold women I have met here are driven by the implicit adage of "go along to get along." And, sometimes that makes us stand out in ways that less vocal women (not to mention, some pompous, loud "mansplainers") don't appreciate. Some of the most effective leaders of nonprofits in Vermont—especially in the town of Rutland (about 4 hours from NYC and Boston)—are strong women who contribute to our communities in the way of education, quality of life, social justice and, especially, legal issues affecting women. Yet there are countless times I've seen (and been) a lead participant in important meetings about strategy, budget and social issues and some man begins a serious discussion with a superfluous comment about a woman's outfit—despite the fact

that the woman in question clearly demonstrates she's the most prepared person in the room. As the beloved Vermont poem goes, ". . . miles to go before we sleep."[14]

As Weinmann's experience reflects, women's participation still falls short of equality. Women take fewer than four out of every ten turns speaking, according to the Vermont data.

"Civilization has evolved dramatically since the days of early Athens when women were not even considered citizens," Bryan wrote in his 2004 book. "Now we have an accurate measure of how far we've come. Not far enough. Not yet."[15]

Even more striking results emerged when Karpowitz and Mendelberg set out to measure women's participation and influence on one of the most pervasive and powerful small public bodies that affects every community in the United States—school boards. School boards are especially important for a study of women's voices because a seat on the board generally is an elective office with a high proportion of women elected officials.

The results were striking (see figure 2.2). Nearly nine times out of ten, 88 percent of the time, women spoke less than their level of representation on the board.[16] In fact, women did not achieve equal talking time to their male colleagues until they had at least two-thirds of the seats on a school board.[17]

Notice how women move up the chart of equal turns as more women are included on the school board. (Boards that are all men or all women are excluded.) In the upper right quadrant, the dots represent school boards where women are in the majority and the level of equality for speaking turns. In the lower right quadrant are school boards where women are in the majority but still do not reach the line of equality.

In the lower left quadrant are school boards where women are in a minority and where men are taking far more speaking turns than their representation on the board would reflect. In the upper left quadrant are a few school boards where women are in the minority but also have equal speaking turns or better.

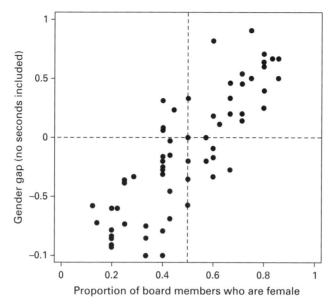

Figure 2.2
Balance in speaking turns, by proportion of women's seats on a school board.
Source: Christopher Karpowitz and Tali Mendelberg, *The Silent Sex: Gender, Deliberation, and Institutions* (Princeton University Press, 2014), 299.

To fully understand the pivotal importance of the school board study, it's helpful to understand why Karpowitz and Mendelberg chose that particular public institution. Focusing on the small-group discussion in democratic life is one of the more important insights of Karpowitz and Mendelberg's work on women's voices. While many national conversations about women's representation look to Congress, state legislatures, or television news shows like *Face the Nation* and *Meet the Press* to gauge the reach of women's political power, Karpowitz and Mendelberg focused instead on the most basic political institutions that are diffused throughout the country—the small group.

Across all of politics, many of the most important public decisions derive from small-group deliberations like city councils, planning boards, and legislative committees. These panels and councils make binding decisions about taxes, education, public salaries, roads, public transportation, and many other aspects of standards of living. Juries are another small-group example where profound public power is exercised daily, making binding decisions about such constitutional values as life, liberty, and property.

Moreover, research shows that small-group conversations are where political persuasion takes place.[18] So a study of women's voices in small groups targets a place where women have broad access and profound impact.

School boards are an important bellwether for women's voices for a variety of reasons, Karpowitz and Mendelberg write. First, education is a subject area that has long been in women's domain, where women's role as teachers and leaders is longstanding and where women hold substantial numbers in elective office. Boards have tremendous power in raising revenue, setting spending priorities, setting agendas for schools, adopting curricula, negotiating labor contracts, and contracting with corporations—all in a setting that broadly affects the futures of every community.

School boards represent a best-case scenario for women's voices, in a pattern that affects every community in the United States. Since education is a traditional female domain, it is also an important point of entry for many women starting a political career.

To study school boards in a way that reflects real-world conditions, Karpowitz and Mendelberg built a data set that looked at a full range of real-life situations. Women hold a little under half of all school board seats, about 44 percent, according to survey data from the National School Boards Association.

To allow for robust interpretation of data across a variety of settings, Karpowitz and Mendelberg designed their study to include a full range of scenarios. They included school boards from small communities. Nationwide, men are about two-thirds of the members of school boards in small districts. They included midsized school districts and large urban school districts. Women hold about half the seats in districts with more than 7,500 students, or 51 percent of the seats.[19]

Karpowitz and Mendelberg studied transcripts of boards where women had the majority. They sampled boards that had men in the majority. They sampled boards where women were the chair and where men were the chair.

In the end, research for *The Silent Sex* had two basic findings about public bodies where women enjoy some of the highest representation of any government office. First, women school board members do not achieve an equal voice until they are in a supermajority. Second, the inequality in women's voices can more or less be cured when a woman is chair of the board.

As Karpowitz and Mendelberg analyzed transcripts of school board meetings, the effect of women's numbers was remarkable. Adding more women to a school board had a dramatic effect on women's participation in governance (see figure 2.3).

This graph represents how close or far away is equality under different conditions. Perfect equality occurs when each member of a five-person school board takes one-fifth of the turns speaking and each person makes one-fifth of the motions. If any one person takes more than 20 percent of the turns or makes more than 20 percent of the motions, at least some other members will receive less than equal representation.

In fact, the presence of more women in the conversation had what in a medical setting would be called a dose-response relationship. As the numbers of women go up, so does the participation of women in making motions and speaking.

This is not merely a data set about volume or length of speech. This data set weighs the turn taking of women and the turn taking of men as individual members of elective office. In most scenarios, men are taking turns far out of proportion to their representation, while women are functionally rendered to the back bench.

Even though the effect of having more women is remarkable, the chart also illustrates the limits of representation.

Having seats at the table is not enough. Not even having a majority of women on a school board is enough to ensure that women

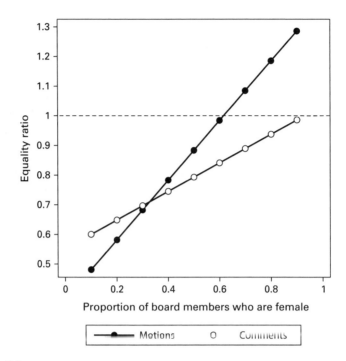

Figure 2.3
Speaking turns and motions by proportion of women on a school board.
Source: Christopher Karpowitz and Tali Mendelberg, *The Silent Sex: Gender, Delibera-tion, and Institutions* (Princeton University Press, 2014), 287.

have an equal voice. In fact, women had to hold two-thirds of school board seats before they could reliably achieve equality in making motions and even bigger majority to achieve an equal voice.

Another "wow" metric emerged from the school board study—the corrective power of having a woman chair a public body. On school boards where women were in the minority, having a woman chair effectively brought women's comments from half that of men to just over the line of equality (see figure 2.4).

When a woman chairs a school board meeting, women's voices are much more likely to be heard. Their voices are heard more than equally. When a man chairs a board where women are in the minority, women's voices get about half as much time as their

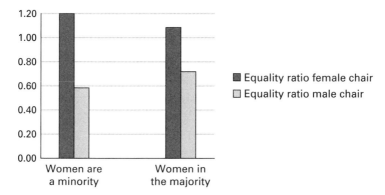

Figure 2.4
Source: Christopher Karpowitz and Tali Mendelberg, *The Silent Sex: Gender, Deliberation and Institutions* (Princeton University Press, 2014), 406, table A10.1.

representation on the board. When women have a majority and a woman is chair, women get slightly more than equal time. If a man is chairing a board that has a majority of women, women get about two-thirds as much time to speak as their representation level would suggest. The effect was even larger than having a majority of women.

"Regardless of the gender composition of the board, women are much more likely to reach our standard of equality, and even exceed it, if the board chair is a woman," Karpowitz and Mendelberg write. "We interpret this evidence that formal authority in the form of a leadership position in the meeting can be a critical factor for women's equality of voice."[20]

The Small Group and the Bigger Picture

The results of the Karpowitz and Mendelberg study need to be considered as one focal point in a bigger picture of women's vast underrepresentation in the halls of power. Much of the work for women's progress involves revisiting the persistent barriers that hold women back in many fields.

Leaders in a broad range of civic and other organizations have long called for women to rise to leadership positions. Women's ascendance to power has always been seen as a stepping stone to fulfill broader progress for women, as Madeleine Albright argued in 2016. The National Women's Political Caucus was founded in 1971 to promote women as leaders in the mainstream Democratic and Republican parties. And yet women remain remarkably underrepresented in elective office.

Women began receiving an equal number of college degrees around 1980 when I was an undergraduate at the University of Michigan. As Facebook's chief operating officer, Sheryl Sandberg, outlined in her seminal book *Lean In*, women's progress has stalled in achieving leadership roles—decades after women achieved an equal number of college degrees and surpassed men's participation in many fields. Men still hold the vast majority of leadership positions in government and business.

The lack of women's voices holds true online, the same way that women's voices are missing and underrepresented in debates about public issues in other forums.

By the turn of the twenty-first century, women around the world and institutions of all kinds were well aware of the way women were missing from many aspects of public life. In 2016, 101 women were members of the U.S. House of Representatives, or 23.2 percent. Forty-four women of color were included in that number. Twenty-six of the hundred seats in the U.S. Senate were held by women, including four women of color.[21] Around the world, eighteen countries have women heads of state, out of 142 counted in a World Economic Forum report.[22] While Nordic countries have parliaments that are about 40 percent women, most other countries top out with women's representation in parliaments at 25 percent.

In 2021, just 29 women serve as chief executive officer of Fortune 500 companies, or 5.8 percent.[23] This is true even as women lead the majority of small businesses that create the majority of jobs in the U.S. economy.

Like the comments sections of news websites and other public forums, women's representation in public bodies in turn defines the highly marginalized role that women's voices continue to play in democratic institutions, even a century after white women achieved the right to cast votes.

As public deliberations extend ever more into online spaces—a trend accelerated by the coronavirus pandemic in 2020—core issues of equality, access, and the public voice take on ever more urgency. Fifty years ago, the women's movement was pushing for seats at the table, but contemporary research into in-person deliberation proves beyond doubt that seats at the table fall far short of achieving equality.

In the 1970s, it looked like the hard part was going to be electing more women to public office. That's a start, but it's not nearly enough. Women need to speak up and be heard more. Institutions must be reimagined and restructured so that all people are willing to hear.

3

Women, Authority, and the Public Sphere

Communication Is Gendered

To understand women and public affairs conversations, we have to go back to beginnings. Women's opportunities to speak, women's willingness to speak, and expectations about women's entitlement to speak are all influenced by gender dynamics that go back to the beginnings of each woman's life. The gender dynamics go back to the beginnings of Western culture.

In part, gender dynamics begin developing at birth, as girls and boys are valued and encouraged or discouraged in different ways and as they express different ways of collaborating or competing with each other.

In the grand scheme, gender dynamics and women's speaking in public are embedded in cultures that are millennia in the making. With few exceptions, women have been legally and functionally excluded from discussions and decisions about public affairs until recent decades. In the United States, women have had the legal rights to vote and to own property for only about a hundred years. In many parts of the world, prepubescent girls are "given" to middle-aged men in marriage. With no self-determination, women are hardly empowered to change the terms of public affairs. Millions of women in the world are prohibited from even appearing in public alone, much less empowered to speak on matters of public concern.

Women are far from achieving political equality in the West, even as women have made enormous gains over the centuries. It's little wonder that one profound element of inequality is a diminished voice in public affairs.

In law and in culture, women have been silenced for millennia. Mary Beard, the University of Cambridge classics professor who is a prominent public intellectual in the United Kingdom, traces the Western tradition of silencing women to *The Odyssey*. She describes it as the first recorded example in Western literature of "a man telling a woman to 'shut up.'"

The Odyssey's narrative is as much a coming of age story about Telemachus, son of Odysseus and Penelope, as it is about Odysseus, Beard writes in the seminal essay "The Public Voice of Women" in the *London Review of Books* in 2014. Telemachus comes of age as he instructs his mother about when she should speak. In the crucial scene, Penelope, wife of the absent Odysseus, beseeches a man to sing a happier song than one about the difficulties that Greek heroes encounter returning home. As Beard writes,

> Telemachus intervenes: "Mother," he says, "go back up to your quarters, and take up your own work, the loom and the distaff . . . speech will be the business of men, all men, and of me most of all; for mine is the power in this household." And off she goes, back upstairs. . . . It's a nice demonstration that right where written evidence for Western culture starts, women's voices are not being heard in the public sphere; more than that, as Homer has it, an integral part of growing up, as a man, is learning to take control of public utterance and to silence the female of the species.[1]

Other women are silenced in Greek and Roman classics. Io, a lover of Zeus, is turned into a heifer. Philomela, in Ovid's *Metamorphoses*, has her tongue cut out to prevent her from reporting a rape. Tongues of other women also are cut out in other stories.

Fast forward twenty-five hundred years to colonial North America. As property-owning white men worked to create an independent nation independent of England in the eighteenth century, women were purposely excluded from democratic power, just as they were in Athens. This was merely a continuation of white male rule and the continued exclusion of women and all non-white people from matters of national or personal governance.

Abigail Adams famously beseeched her husband in 1776 to "remember the ladies" with legal protections and self-determination. She argued that women were often ill-used by husbands who had unchecked authority over property and had sole access to courts and administrative relief. John Adams's reply was dismissive:

> Depend upon it, we know better than to repeal our masculine systems. Although they are in full force, you know they are little more than theory. We are obliged to go fair and softly, and, in practice, you know we are the subjects. We have only the name of masters, and rather than give up this, which would completely subject us to the despotism of the petticoat, I hope General Washington and all our brave heroes would fight.[2]

Clearly, a historical arc bends from the ancient Greeks and Romans through eighteenth-century democratic revolutions and nineteenth-century efforts in the West to win votes for women up to the current day.

The point of recounting this history in the context of public debate on the internet is that the gender segregation imposed on Penelope is the same gender segregation that was imposed on white women in North America in the eighteenth century.

Throughout history, this primordial impulse to segregate women and define women's allowable spheres of influence remains very much alive and pulsing in online conversations. And that is only speaking of the history for white women, who still remained highly privileged by race.

This gender-normed culture of allowable and punishable speech continues to affect the willingness of women to speak online. It is the very definition of misogyny I offer in the introduction of this book. We continue to live in a culture that persistently limits women's full citizenship through "social environments in which women are liable to encounter hostility due to the enforcement and policing of patriarchal norms and expectations."

It's what Congressman Ted Yoho was doing to his colleague Alexandria Ocasio-Cortez on the steps of the U.S. Capitol. It's what Donald Trump was doing when he said four women of color who are members of Congress should "go back to" the countries "from which they came"—even though three of them are in the same country they came from.

It's this same misogynistic frame that women are reenacting daily when they hesitate to offer their opinions in meetings at work. It's a misogynistic frame that inhibits women from speaking up even when they have expertise and authority in the area.

The history of women's silence can be explained from every area of academic study. I portray the sum of those fields throughout this book. Some of the specific impulses and methods of gender segregation are described later in this chapter.

One thing, though, is certain and undeniable: women's silence is not just history. It's our current reality.

Legal Roots and the Long, Long Bridge to Equality

At the time the United States became a nation, women, enslaved people, and indigenous people were not full citizens. They did not have the right to vote, own property, or move about the country. Enslaved people and indigenous people did not have a right to life.

Once women did have the right to vote throughout the United States, in 1920, women rarely held office, were not taken seriously, and still encountered families and communities that did not value their participation. Just four years earlier, Margaret Sanger had been imprisoned for speaking publicly about birth control and for opening a clinic to help women control the size of their families. Susan B. Anthony was arrested for trying to vote. Suffragettes were jailed and often shouted down.

Another powerful act of citizenship was denied women at that time—jury duty. Those official slights consequently made a material difference in women's experience of criminal justice and civil legal relief. At the time that Sanger and Anthony were arrested, jailed, and tried, women rarely sat on juries, even though some Western states had always allowed women to vote and women were thus legally eligible to be part of a jury pool.

Five decades passed after women got the vote in the United States before women could serve on juries throughout the country. In the early 1940s, women could serve on juries in only twenty-eight states. The Civil Rights Act of 1957 gave women the power to serve on federal juries. And it was not until 1973—the same year as the *Roe v. Wade* abortion rights decision—that women were able to serve on juries in all fifty states.[3]

Because it took sixty years—or fifteen presidential election cycles—for women to vote in the same proportion as men, it is important to understand what was holding women back. Women no longer faced arrest, as Susan B. Anthony did in the late nineteenth and early twentieth centuries. But women and other disadvantaged groups face a cultural force field that creates a lag time between legal rights and enacting egalitarian ideals.

The lag time in women's speaking participation online is another real-life delay in women fulfilling the destiny of equality. Women's reticence—and some antifeminist backlash—in online forums parallels the long lag time between legal proscriptions and full equality in other aspects of women's role in the public sphere.

Stanford sociologist Cecilia Ridgeway describes the way these old methods of sex segregation and gender divisions work to recreate old "gender regimes" in the modern world. In her landmark book *Framed by Gender: How Gender Inequality Persists in the Modern World,* she demonstrates that the unconscious expectations about gender are acted out in how we perceive each other and behave in daily life. Those expectations in turn shape the culture of workplaces, public forums, and every place in person and online that women and men work and play together.[4]

"Our unconscious gendered biases prime gender stereotypes in our minds, working in the background, ready to be applied in the way we interact with other people," Ridgeway said in a talk at Stanford University's Clayman Institute for Gender Research. "The effect of these biases can be negligible or substantial, depending on our motives and the context."[5]

The remarkable thing about Ridgeway's research is that she tested this abstract sociological description of human behavior and social psychology in real-life settings. Her hypothesis was that the "gender frame" could be used to predict behavior in different settings. And the evidence she found fit her sociological theory, just as Karpowitz and Mendelberg's *Silent Sex* assessments of school board deliberations mirrored a controlled experiment with randomly assigned gender configurations. Essentially, we "rewrite" gender inequality into new institutions and issues as they are created and develop.

Ridgeway studied women with doctoral degrees in two different Silicon Valley startup settings—biotechnology and information technology. In biotechnology, women are now half of the students in biological sciences and represent more than half of all doctoral degrees in biological sciences, or 52.8 percent in 2017. In information technology, women engineers and computer scientists are steeply underrepresented in undergraduate majors and in doctoral degrees. Only about one in five computer science doctoral degrees are granted to women, or 22 percent in 2017.[6]

The gender frame prediction that unconscious biases would play out much more powerfully in the male-dominated field did recreate outdated gender regimes in the new institutional structure.[7] In Ridgeway's gender frame theory, then, male-dominated environments would consequently recreate gender inequality in similar proportions to women's representation. It's a bleak outlook for women's voices in the public sphere.

Thus the gender frame theory compounds *The Silent Sex*'s empirical showing that women's voices get a smaller platform until women control a supermajority of seats, Women's voices will never reach equality without broad political, institutional, and cultural changes.

Stepping Up to Political Power Takes Decades

Nonvoting women in the early years after women won the right to vote are a good example of the slow process of cultural change toward equality in women's political participation. The path from winning the right to vote in 1920 to women's equal participation in voting took sixty years.

In fact, some of the earliest systematic social scientific studies of nonvoters came from shortly after the Nineteenth Amendment took effect. The data provide a window into some of the cultural factors that held women back.

In 1920 and 1923, scholars at the University of Chicago collected door-to-door survey records of nonvoters in Chicago. They looked at federal Census records as well. They provide some evidence explaining the lag time between when white women won the right to vote and when women began to vote in equal or greater proportion than men in 1980.

Just under half of women in Chicago in 1920 cast a vote for president, or 46 percent. In contrast, 75 percent of men voted that year. When the mayoral race came around in 1923, about a third of women voted, 35 percent. For men, the turnout rate was 63 percent.[8]

The University of Chicago political scientists cited several reasons that women said they did not vote. The reasons included eleven women who did not want to disclose their ages to register to vote. Two other factors: "Disbelief in woman's voting," and "objections of husband."

Immigrant women from Germany, Ireland, and Italy were among those most reluctant to vote, according to the Pew Research Center's summary of the study. Older women were more likely than young women to be dubious about the wisdom of allowing women to express their political preferences. In the view of one elderly Irish woman, 'Women have no business voting. They would be better off staying at home and minding their own affairs.'"[9] It's almost as if Penelope herself were transported from the eighth century BCE to an Irish American neighborhood in 1920, so precise is the language.

The scholars concluded: "It was obvious that there were thousands of women in the city who still believed that woman's place was in the home . . . that woman is a flower for man to worship and that she should not spoil her beauty by mingling in his affairs."[10]

The underrepresentation of women in politics and various acts of political participation, then, has many bricks in its foundation, both explicit and implicit. Explicit gatekeepers with enforcement mechanisms are one part, such as Telemachus having the power to tell his mother to "shut up," as Mary Beard writes. Or founders such as John Adams might write women out of the Constitution, for example. Or husbands might disapprove of their wives' voting participation.

The second part is the implicit expectations and tactics that have been internalized and framed by women, men, and institutions across generations and across millennia. When women's votes were a new power, many women themselves described politics as a man's realm. Such implicit biases give rise to tactics and expectations that are real and substantial, and the consequences for violating those expectations can be brutal.

While a mythic figure like Io might have been turned into a calf, a woman who even writes about sexual assault in the current day might be subject to rape threats. In some cultures, a victim might be murdered in an "honor killing." In Western cultures, rape victims are frequently blamed with "slut shaming" on social media. These vectors of misogynistic attack are outlined in the next chapter. But the persistent framework is misogyny itself, which finds its expression in every era by punishing women for speaking.

Women's Voices Online

In the internet age, all kinds of conversations have taken on new forms. The generally inflammatory nature of internet conversations itself has gendered effects. In the same way that a prism in a sunny window refracts sunlight into separate rays of colored light, adversarial culture online refracts the wider pool of public conversation into gendered segments of political conversation. Men will have one kind of conversation, and the noisiest, most bombastic voices will tend to dominate. Women will largely avoid those conversations and have a different kind of conversation among themselves.

Cultural feedback mechanisms about who is entitled to speak on a subject take on new vectors in the online age. Backlash comes out in new public forms. Even if backlash is directed to a woman's email rather than the wide open public, the opportunities for anonymous mob attacks on particular targets have reached terrifying new speed and intensity. Such attacks give women example after example of reasons not to speak up. The efficiency and speed with which antagonists can congregate online, aggregate their forces, and then deploy hateful and intimidating messages at chosen targets have changed the nature of public life for women, as the next chapter about cybersexism makes clear.

"We have these huge cultural norms that are being uncovered and amplified in ways that we've never had to deal with before," said Soraya Chemaly, a writer and activist who is director of the Women's Media Center Speech Project. "There's a huge difference between someone calling you an asshole, and someone hammering you with gendered racial violence day after day after day."[11]

Gender Dynamics 101

I had my own steep learning curve about internalized forms of women's silence the first time I taught a college class, in 1991.

I was teaching a 100-level class in political science as an adjunct instructor. When I walked into class the first day, I noticed that about forty of the sixty students were men. It turned out that campus fraternities had a large collection of past exams for the course, and the course had a reputation of being an easy A.

I mixed up the seventy-five-minute class periods with a combination of shorter lectures and discussion periods. When I posed questions to the class, no women would speak. None.

I tried calling on women. They responded with trepidation, at best. Many demurred. Still, I could see in women's faces they had thoughts on the topics, and I could also see they clearly understood that I believed they had valuable perspectives. It was almost as if they were nonverbally telling me, "Sorry, I'm not going there."

Frustrated, I sought advice from the director of the University of Maine's Women in the Curriculum program, which had been formed years earlier to promote gender equality in curricula and classrooms. It was my first meeting with Ann Schonberger, whose door was always open to faculty wanting to improve classroom climate for women.

I described the dynamics and expressed my frustration.

"So," Ann said, "did you think that a lifetime of experience was going to go out the window because you were the one standing in front of the classroom?"

There was a long uncomfortable silence. "Yes," I thought to myself. "That's exactly what I thought." Surely, my body language at that moment communicated as much to Ann. Saying it out loud would have sounded incredibly stupid, but there it was.

In one sentence, a single scholar with a PhD in mathematics had said in twenty-seven words just about everything anyone needs to know about women's underengagement in public affairs discussions online.

Women's experiences in the public sphere are often punishing. Among the many things that Ann Schonberger knew in 1991 that I did not is that the field of gender dynamics was growing in every academic discipline. Since about that time, research has shown that girls and women speak less in classrooms, their views are less likely to be affirmed or encouraged, and they are interrupted sooner, as I describe in earlier chapters. Real-life examples about acceptable gender roles and behavior are present everywhere, just about every day of the week.

The academic field of communication studies has a subspecialty in gender and the way gender is expressed and communicated within societies and across culture. Since the 1970s, scholars have tracked the way women's contributions to conversations are received, the amount of positive and negative feedback women and men receive when they talk, and the way women and men influence the final results of political debate.

The literature on gender and communication is extensive. Indeed, no communication studies faculty would be considered complete without a gender specialist on board.

It's about Inequality and Authority

Karpowitz and Mendelberg, the scholars who carried out research for *The Silent Sex*, conclude—through rigorous, controlled experiments that are validated in real-world settings—that, in essence, the reason for women's underrepresentation in mixed-gender conversations of all kinds boils down to gender inequality in society. As a result, women are perceived as having less authority and have less influence and power. One way that power is expressed is through time in conversations and frequent interruptions (women are interrupted far more often than men):

> One of the pitfalls most advocates of deliberation neglect is gender inequality. Women are highly disadvantaged in many deliberative settings, and this disadvantage affects everything from how long they speak, to the respect they are shown, to the content of what they say, to the influence they carry, to their sense of their own capacity, and to their power over group decisions. All the more troubling, these problems can emerge even when the terms of discussion do not, at first glance, appear to disadvantage women. The problem is not that women are disliked or formally discriminated against; rather, the problem is that while women are liked, they are not given equal authority.[12]

And there is the heart of the problem, embedded as it is in decades of communication research. Women's underrepresentation on online forums and other public acts of political participation functions in part as a consequence of lifelong experience and millennia of experience that has explicitly denied women political power and equal status. Chapter 5 continues this discussion about the way women's voices are silenced and marginalized, perpetuating the cycle of inequality.

Women and Men Online

In the early days of the internet, most users were men, since the internet originated in the heavily male Department of Defense. As digital technology expanded to universities and their computing services in the late twentieth century, men still were the predominant users.

Computer use and internet access remained decidedly heavily male domains into the 1990s, according to numerous scholarly accounts of the period.[13] By 2000, those gender divisions had completely changed. At the turn of the millennium, half of all internet users were women. By 2005, more young women than young men were using the internet. At the same time, 60 percent of Black women were using the internet, compared to 50 percent of Black men.[14]

As computers and internet use came to be extensions of daily life for a majority of people in the West, some utopian assumptions came to be received as common wisdom. The first false assumption was that traditional gender dynamics would be transformed in computer-mediated communication by the absence of physical and auditory cues. Some scholars claimed that computer-mediated communication "makes the gender of online communicators irrelevant or invisible. This allows women and men to participate (and be recognized for their contributions) equally, in contrast with patterns of male dominance traditionally observed in face-to-face communication."[15]

Contrary to that common wisdom, however, studies of online conversations of all kinds have shown for twenty-five years that technology-facilitated communication reproduces the existing gender status quo.[16] These findings, coming from communication and computer science disciplines, were harbingers of Cecelia Ridgeway's research in sociology.

In the early days of contemporary chat rooms, communication scholars documented communication patterns and found a long list of gendered characteristics. The use of pseudonyms did not change gendered linguistic styles.

In fact, 89 percent of linguistically gendered behavior in early internet chat-based conversations on six different chat channels "indexed maleness and femaleness in traditional, even stereotyped ways." In the remaining 11 percent, gender switching accounted for only about half, Susan Herring of Indiana University found.[17]

In the early 1990s, scholars documented the way that men and other high-status members of online groups dominated conversations on academic discussion boards. This was true when using full names and under conditions offering anonymity.[18]

In those early days of online conversations, evidence accumulated that women were also singled out for aggressive treatment in online conversations and were subject to unwanted sexual attention.[19] From the beginning, women turned to gender-neutral

Women

- Post shorter messages.
- Tend to drop out when they get no response.
- Express support of others.
- Look for common ground with questioners.
- Speak less in mixed groups.
- Are more aggressive in majority-male groups.
- Get more upset with violations of civility.
- Value social harmony.
- Apologize.
- Feel better when they know someone is enforcing rules.
- Tend to justify and qualify their positions.
- Use more endearing language, and use emoticons such as smiles three times more than men.
- Say the loss of privacy is the biggest problem of the internet.
- Do not control the topic of discussion except in groups where women make up a clear majority.

pseudonyms in chat and multiplayer games in an effort to avoid unwanted sexual attention.

The earliest days of online gaming, which revealed a deep strain of misogyny during the Gamergate episode in 2013 and 2014, also reflected women's and men's gendered styles. Players who used gender-neutral pseudonyms and players who chose virtual identities that did not match their gender actually played the game as themselves, rather than through the behavior of a fictional character, game creators noted and studies showed.

In those early days, women-presenting characters were found to use neutral or affectionate actions like "hugs" or "whuggles." Men used more violent verbs such as "kills," especially toward other male characters, in online gaming in the early 1990s.[20]

A long list of women's and men's characteristics in online conversations emerged when computing scholars Herring of the University

Men

- Write longer messages.
- Tend to begin and end discussions in mixed groups.
- Take an adversarial approach to questioners.
- Tolerate adversity.
- More commonly use crude or abusive language.
- Use three times as much challenging and insulting speech as women.
- Use violent verbs.
- Are less aggressive in majority female groups.
- Are less likely to value social harmony.
- Are more upset about threats to free expression.
- Say censorship is one of the biggest problems of the internet.

of Indiana and Sharon Stoerger, who directs Rutgers University's Information Technology and Informatics program, reviewed more than 100 studies of gender and online communication.

Generally speaking, men take a more adversarial approach to communication online. They feel the general parry and thrust of adversarial conversations are an ordinary part of the experience. They come to comment forums to have a say, and they're willing to engage in conversational pushing and shoving.

In contrast, women dislike environments with conflict, they seek common ground, and they speak less in mixed groups. Women don't get to set a conversational agenda until they're in the majority. The bottom line is that these communication behaviors function to recreate a gender regime that is at least as old as Homer. Yes, women can participate. But the cultural barriers to participation are prohibitive for many women.

Men's status as the default participants in the public square—created and promoted through millennia of legal privilege and political power—builds a cultural and conversational barrier that has the effect of excluding women's voices. The fact that men create and perpetuate an adversarial culture online in itself has the effect of excluding women's voices—and even the style of women's voices.

In *The Silent Sex*, coauthor Tali Mendelberg recounts her experience on a tenure and promotion committee at Princeton University that happened to be made up of five women. The committee was the same size as the experimental groups she and Christopher F. Karpowitz assembled to study gender and decision making in small groups. The culture she describes is uncanny in its resonance for many women in high-powered positions like those on the Princeton faculty. Long accustomed to being in the minority—women were only 25 percent of the political science faculty at the time—these women assembled and functionally created their own group norms.

"All were tenured. None was a shrinking violet. Yet in this group, unlike any of the other committees, the interaction took on what can only be described as a norm of niceness. The members affirmed each other's statements. They smiled and nodded. Each person spoke, and at length," Karpowitz and Mendelberg write. "How exactly did the group generate warmth, and how does that rapport lead to inclusion and genuine consensus?"[21]

Gender Domains and Efficacy

In addition to stylistic differences in conversations of all kinds, men and women also have vastly different responses to topics and settings for conversations. The social context matters. It's a difference that some scholars describe as a different "social logic" for men and women.[22]

In the same way that adversarial settings attract the competitive spirit of men and repulses the consensus-oriented focus of women, so, too, do different topics resonate with women.

Many different kinds of political acts remain deeply divided by gender. News comments are one of those domains. It's helpful to remember that silence did not begin with the internet. It has deep roots in women's experiences of trying to give and add a voice. It's been two millennia since Hortensia spoke of the unfairness of taxes imposed on women in ancient Rome, even though women had no political representation.

One of the key barriers to women's engagement is the fact that national and international politics remain largely a men's domain, decades of research shows.

Nowhere has this division of men's and women's labor been as stark as in opinion pieces submitted to newspaper op-ed pages. In 2005, the prominent feminist Susan Estrich, an author, political strategist, and law professor at the University of Southern California, engaged in a scathing debate with Michael Kinsley, who was then op-ed editor of the *Los Angeles Times*. Women's voices were missing in public debate, she said, with only 10 percent of op-eds at the *Los Angeles Times* being written by women.[23]

The Op-Ed Project grew out of that debate, executive director Catherine Orenstein has explained:

> About that time, I became curious why no one was talking about
> a more obvious and more solvable part of the problem, which is
> that women don't submit to front door forums—like op-ed pages
> or online commentary sites—with anywhere near the frequency
> that men do. These forums feed all other media and drive thought
> leadership, so an absence of women (or other diverse voices) in these
> forums predicts under-representation on a much larger scale—on TV,
> in business, in congress, for example. And I thought, why don't we
> just get more smart women submitting to these gateway forums?[24]

Among the things the group found was that 88 percent of op-ed submissions were from men. At first, Orenstein thought to attack the issue as a supply-side problem. The supply-side approach worked wonderfully—up to a point. When more women submitted op-eds, more women's op-ed pieces appeared.

Orenstein and the Op-Ed Project also found that supporting the supply side was more complicated than people imagined. In an interview, she described a scene from one of the group's training sessions, where facilitators coached people to develop opinion pieces: "We give people a form and ask them to fill in the blank. My name is _____. I am an expert in _____." While the questions might be obvious for people attending a session to prepare them to write opinion pieces, it is not so easy for participants, Orenstein said:

> We find intense resistance when we ask women and other underrepresented groups what they're expert in. People who are well represented in the media have an easy time with it. Women and others have a lot of resistance, which can explain why so few women submit op-ed pieces. Lean in arguments are true, but there are a lot of other truths. Underrepresented groups have a lot of conflicting commitments, and face a lot of cultural expectations that become internalized. In our seminars, we find ways to surface those internal conflicts and teach people to be able to deal with them.[25]

Numerous studies outline the way people respond to gender domains—the very essence of the gendered norms that comprise a misogynistic culture. In experimental settings, scholars continue to find the dynamic that Orenstein describes. People are unwilling to contribute ideas when the subject falls outside of gendered norms. Moreover, the hesitance comes from potential speakers themselves, not necessarily from people in the room that they believe will try to shut them down.[26] That kind of evidence is a data point that underscores how the issues are more systemic than situational. People respond to a wider cultural problem, not friendly or unfriendly group members.

Mary Beard's *London Review of Books* analysis about "The Public Voice of Women" provides one picture of the arc from official exclusion under the law to outward expressions of authority. In ancient literature, Beard explains, women could speak up to defend their homes, children, husbands, and women's interests. In one example of women's speaking by the Roman anthologist Hortensia, she is allowed to speak because she is speaking against a tax on women to support a war. "Women, in other words, may in extreme circumstances publicly defend their own sectional interests, but not speak for men or the community as a whole," Beard writes. "In general, as one second-century AD guru put it, 'a woman should as modestly guard against exposing her voice to outsiders as she would guard against stripping off her clothes.'"[27]

Political science scholars looking at women's participation have zeroed in on this fault line of men's and women's domains in acts of political participation among women. It is a primary factor that serves as a barrier to women's participation because they have far less confidence in their "personal information efficacy."[28]

Helpful Models

A number of institutions have crafted methods to improve women's representation and participation in areas that traditionally had been male-dominated or gender-coded in ways that inhibited women's participation. Harvey Mudd College, for example, increased women computer science majors from 10 percent to 50 percent of majors in five years. They remade the classroom environment, redirected heavy-handed communication behaviors, and created a beginner atmosphere in first-year courses so tech-savvy first-year students, who tended to be men, did not dominate. And they created women-centered programming challenges that inspired women to be problem solvers, not just demonstrate technical skills for skills' sake.[29]

In her seminal book, *Lean In: Women, Work, and the Will to Lead* (written with coauthor Nell Scovell), Facebook chief operating officer Sheryl Sandberg tells the story of a medical school professor who saw her TED talk. He went back to his rounds with medical students and realized that only men were speaking up in response to questions. So he devised a system where he noted who was present on a list, asked questions, and checked off each name. Since women are now the majority of medical students, women became the majority of voices in those pivotal conversations around the hospital. Within a short period of time, he told Sandberg, women were speaking up more freely, and they were often better prepared than their male classmates.[30]

Harvard Business School also made efforts much like those at Harvey Mudd College and boosted women's leadership and achievement. Though all the women there were already superstars, they were not emerging as leaders at the school. Through a thorough remake of the classroom atmosphere directed from the dean's office, with compulsory implementation by the faculty, the school changed the culture and hopes to influence business environments in the future.[31]

Now it is up to online media to restructure their conversational environments and fulfill their civic mission to engage people in a healthy democratic forum.

4

Women, Trolls, and Adversarial Culture Online

Trigger warning: This chapter includes depictions and language of extreme violence.

As a columnist in Florida, Michelle Ferrier went to work every day and wrote about her community. She wrote about her family and her neighbors and the ways people lived together.

Then the campaign of terror began.

"I got physical hate mail," Ferrier told the Online News Association meeting in 2015. "'How do you get an "N" out of a tree? Cut the rope.' And 'There's going to be a race war against you "N" people, and you're part of it.' After three years, I could not talk about what was happening to me in my column out of fear for my family and fear of my life. The terror these groups inflict on you is very deep and very powerful and very real."[1]

She got phone calls at home, information sent to her about her children, and threats about people with guns coming after her. Ferrier's employer's response: a colleague would accompany her to her car at the end of a work day.

She escalated her reports to more authorities. "I went to the police. I went to the FBI, CIA. The Committee to Protect Journalists took my case to the Department of Justice.[2] Nothing changed," Ferrier writes on the TrollBusters website. "But I did. I changed as a person. I became angrier. More wary and withdrawn. I had police patrolling my neighborhood. I gave up and quit my job to protect my family and young children.[3]

Finally, Ferrier moved and left journalism. She earned a PhD and went into academics. Now she's breaking new ground as a developer of TrollBusters, an assistance agency for women journalists and thought leaders who are victimized by internet antagonists.

For Ferrier and many other women leaders and women working online, vile, terrifying threats have become part of being a public figure. The campaign against Ferrier was sickening:

"BEFORE THIS WORLD ENDS, THERE WILL BE A RACE WAR . . ."
"ALL YOU PEOPLE DO IS CRY BITCH AND WINE [sic], BITCH."
"HAVE YOU PLAYED THE RACE CARD MICHELLE THIS WEEK"?[4]

That kind of abuse against women's voices online serves as a warning for all women: speaking out will put you in danger. It's a serious barrier for public affairs conversations on the internet that women cite in survey after survey.

For women online, cybermisogyny or gendertrolling harassment has become a powerful force to suppress women's speech and women's place in the public sphere. It has an intersectional impact on the voices of people of color or other marginalized groups such as transgender individuals. For women of color like Michelle Ferrier, the abuse is especially severe.

Ferrier writes about the hate mail in a chapter of one of the leading books that collects scholarship about cyberharassment, *Mediating Misogyny: Gender, Technology and Harassment*, edited by Jacqueline Ryan Vickery and Tracy Everbach. It came out in 2018 and features a wide range of topics from harassment, fan communities, presidential politics, "misogynoir," the use of technology in intimate partner abuse, as well as discussions about communities for resistance to misogynistic behaviors.

The broader message of cyberharassment of women and minorities is also immensely powerful: not only are public figures in danger, but everyone else is on notice, too. Speak out, and you'll be next. It's a classic and terribly effective new format for the misogynistic framework that has policed women's speech and political participation for millennia.

Ferrier explains in eloquent terms the importance of reshaping online spaces to make them safe for diverse voices: "We cannot continue to call ourselves journalists when we don't have a system in place that allows for diverse voices, gendered voices, people of different ethnicities able to speak out on issues that are important to them. If we as journalists don't fix this and understand the way it is suppressing speech, we're going to see ripple effects for many years to come."[5]

Ferrier's personal experiences and her deep understanding of the brutal intersectional impact of cyberhate led her to start TrollBusters, which assists journalists and other thought leaders with personal safety planning and reputation management after they are attacked.

Scholars have been examining misogyny expressed via the internet for more than a decade. Danielle Keats Citron's *Hate Crimes in Cyberspace* led the field with outlines of the terrible antagonism of revenge porn, the civil rights dilemma posed by those who objectify women against their will, and the women who are objectified. She outlines the way a few perpetrators have been charged with criminal threats, cyberstalking, cyberharassment, and bias intimidation. She describes the way, in an earlier era, the women's movement advocated for women's interests under the law with regard to violence, sexual harassment, and sexual violence. Eventually, she writes, legislatures and the courts recognized the harm done under color of law and adapted to new standards of law and social practice.[6]

Rather than accept an unregulated internet, Citron argues, legal remedies have to be found to prevent the serious emotional, professional, and financial harms that victims of cyberharassment experience. In particular, Citron describes the ways that women are disproportionately targeted for rape-related imagery and threats and the ways that the internet functions to aggregate antagonistic men and unleash their vitriol on selected targets. Often, those targeted have done nothing more than post a personal blog. Citron situates cyberharassment as a matter of civil rights law, and she provides a framework for how legal precedents and social norms of decency and civility can be leveraged to stop it.[7] Much of the feminist work around internet misogyny has sprung from the framework that Citron provided.

Adversarial Culture Online

While targeted misogyny and racism are one feature of digital culture, so, too, is a general tone of rancor and abuse in online forums. These oppressive characteristics of online conversation exist along a continuum. For anyone familiar with the sociology of race and gender, it's easy to see how gendered and racist attacks are an expected sociological outgrowth of a culture steeped in bullying. Donald Trump's tweets are an archive of these phenomena in themselves.

The comment spaces on news websites have almost always been understood to be places for bitter, attack-filled commentary, well beyond the point of civility—and they often have been. Comment spaces are regarded almost universally as "the bottom of the web," as Joseph M. Reagle Jr. describes in the subtitle of his 2015 book, *Reading the Comments: Likers, Haters, and Manipulators at the Bottom of the Web.*[8] Similarly, Whitney Phillips's amusing but painful 2015 book title illustrates a general understanding of the caustic nature of online conversations: *This Is Why We Can't Have Nice Things: Mapping the Relationship between Online Trolling and Mainstream Culture.*[9]

Cyberharassment is itself such a richly developed pastime that it's important to define some terms. Terms like *cyberbullying, flaming, trolling, cyberharassment,* and *cybermob* have developed in recent years to label particular brands of behavior in internet culture—from unpleasant to abusive. Here is how I mean them throughout the book.

Flaming   Flaming is leaving caustic, rude or abusive remarks on a site, often as personal attacks on an author.

Harassment, garden variety   Harassment online means a sustained pattern of aggressive or antagonistic behavior meant to hurt or demean an individual in online spaces or using online technologies. Harassment is a behavior in that it is used to "create an intimidating, annoying, frightening, or even hostile environment for the victim."[10] Harassment—in the legal sense—is different than occasional caustic remarks, which are more accurately described as "flaming."

This caveat is included in the Data and Society Research Institute's definition of harassment. It is key to understanding intimidation and threats as intrinsic features of violence against women. It is in keeping with legal definitions of harassment. It's the only way to understand the ways that online harassment is an extension of misogynistic aggression, characterized by sexualized talk, sexualized imagery, and sexualized violence.

Other common definitions of online harassment, however, include one-time name calling as a form of "harassment." This includes Pew Research Center's 2014 comprehensive survey of internet users. Thus, common usage of the term *harassment* is often far broader and can include behavior more accurately described as *flaming.*

Cybersexism and cybermisogyny   Cybersexism and cybermisogyny are online abuse of women and girls, including sexism and racism, often compounded by intersections with religion, sexuality, and gender identity. The abuse takes many forms and is meant to demean, degrade, insult, endanger, and silence women and girls.

This definition has been used by the Women's Media Center and by multiple authors, who also call it *gendertrolling*.

Manosphere   The manosphere is the collection of misogynistic websites and online communities dedicated to demeaning portrayals of women. Manosphere sites often function to aggregate internet users who thrive and bond over sexist resentment. Manosphere sites then redeploy antifeminist reaction to articles, incidents, and public figures in the form of cybermobs that generate threats and harassment targeted at individuals. This group is midway between garden variety trolls and subculture trolls.

Troll, garden variety   A common definition of a troll is someone who takes deliberately extreme positions or makes personal attacks to provoke reactions online. Such trolls frequently target those who already suffer from systemic bias due to race, class, gender, sexual orientation, and other characteristics.

This definition has been used by Andrew Losowsky of the Coral Project[11] and Karla Mantilla, author of *Gendertrolling: How Misogyny Went Viral.*[12]

Troll, subculture variety   A subcultural troll is someone who self-identifies as a troll and engages in a particular underworld of anonymous, stylized behaviors generally meant to disrupt, mislead, or satirize modern culture. Subcultural trolls generally reinforce gendered themes of dominance and success. This definition is from Phillips's ethnography, *This Is Why We Can't Have Nice Things: Mapping the Relationship between Online Trolling and Mainstream Culture.*[13]

Cybermob   A cybermob is a digital gathering of internet users who direct anger, derision, and threats to a single target to demean, intimidate, or silence the person.

The reason it's important to comprehend online harassment is that any one person sending an obnoxious or frightening message might be easily dismissed. However, a hundred internet users sending misogynistic messages in a semicoordinated attack is the digital equivalent of being physically surrounded by angry, hateful people pounding on your car as you try to escape an angry mob.

Superhighway of Hate

Sexism online is one important cultural force that reinforces and even magnifies women's disadvantaged status online. The impact is felt throughout culture.

Indeed, the pervasive role that the internet and smartphone technologies play throughout society must be understood as an integral feature of everyone's lives. Vast majorities of people are using internet technology and smartphones throughout their daily lives, and the internet is part of modern life, fundamental to personal and family relationships and to democratic and social conversations around the world. The Pew Research Center has tracked the adoption of online technologies since 2000 (see figure 4.1).

Like many women in public life, British author Laurie Penny talks about the reaction she got when she reported avalanches of rape and death threats to local police in the United Kingdom. Like many women receiving online threats, her fears were dismissed by local police. They often suggested: "Can't you just get off the internet?" Penny says,

> Sure, probably I can get off the internet. I would have no job, I
> wouldn't be able to talk to my friends, or to my mum, or be able
> to do anything other than sit in my house by myself. This is not
> about individual responsibility. It's about how society understands
> harassment of women and people of color and anybody who's not a
> white, cis, straight guy. We need to fight the backlash.[14]

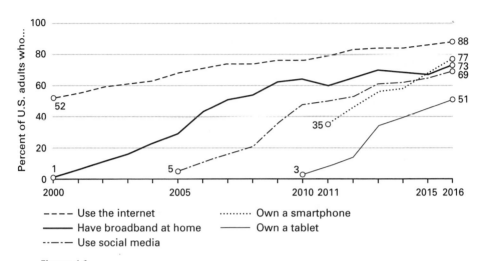

Figure 4.1

The evolution of technology adoption and usage.

Source: Aaron Smith, "Record Share of Americans Now Own Smartphones, Have Home Broadband," Pew Research Center, January 12, 2017, http://www.pewresearch.org/fact-tank/2017/01/12/evolution-of-technology. Surveys conducted 2000 to 2016. Internet use figures based on pooled analysis of all surveys conducted during each calendar year.

Like many women, Penny was experiencing the internet's remarkable ability to aggregate like-minded people and in turn direct hostility at individuals and institutions. The internet in essence builds cybermobs and provides a superhighway for age-old culture wars that Michelle Ferrier, Laurie Penny, and others describe.

"We have these huge cultural norms that are uncovered and amplified online in ways that we've never had to deal with before," says Soraya Chemaly, former director of the Women's Media Center's Speech Project and a prolific writer and activist for women's safety online. "Sometimes the law is a barrier in a big way."[15]

Online abuse is especially directed at women, often simply because they are visible online. It's the very definition of a policing function in a culture of misogyny that punishes women who choose to speak up. It's important to notice that the people who act out these absurd rules and punishments are often normal-looking people who are articulating misogynistic or racist themes because they can. The writer Lindy West chose to pursue a conversation with a particularly virulent and hateful man to see why he posted cruel things on the internet about her dead father. It was because she was a confident writer, he told her. He had no other reason, he said, and he apologized:

> Hey Lindy, I don't know why or even when I started trolling you. . . . I think my anger towards you stems from your happiness with your own being. It offended me, because it served to highlight my unhappiness with my own self. I have emailed you through two other Gmail accounts just to send you idiotic insults. I apologize for that. . . .
>
>   I can't say sorry enough. It was the lowest thing I had ever done. When you included it in your latest Jezebel article, it finally hit me: there is a living, breathing human being who's reading this shit. I'm attacking someone who never harmed me in any way and for no reason whatsoever. I'm done being a troll.[16]

In a context for Black women experiencing misogynoir, antagonists delight in being able to attack figures like Leslie Jones when she landed a role in a remake of the movie *Ghostbusters*. Jones was disparaged for failing to fulfill beauty standards of white men. "There is basically a large semi-organized mob of guys out there at all times looking for targets," one commenter wrote. "If they can combine racism with their misogyny, that's like Christmas for them."[17]

This chapter addresses several interrelated topics. First, a general picture of rancor and harassment online. Second, cybersexism as a particularly noxious vector of abuse toward women that directly and indirectly taints the atmosphere for conversations about public affairs and about women's place in society. Cybersexism is a particular method to enforce women's quiescence online, but much of internet culture fulfills many functions of misogynistic silencing behavior. And third, the tradition of subcultural trolls and a culture of online antagonism that poisons public discussions online in context as simply the workhorses of cultural oppression.

Harassment and Adversarial Culture Online

Basic facts are clear. "Harassment—from garden-variety name calling to more threatening behavior—is a common part of online life that colors the experiences of many web users," the Pew Research Center concluded in 2014. "Fully 73 percent of American adult internet users have witnessed online harassment and 40 percent have experienced it themselves."[18]

In the broadest strokes, the Pew research of the mobile device age illustrates the common experiences of adversarial culture online. Men and women both experience "abuse," including name calling, and most had witnessed it. It would be two years before another research institution probed the issue with gender-informed and race-informed survey that got to some of the issues for particular sets of people. That is explained in detail below:

> Online adults who witnessed harassment said they had seen at least one of the following occur to others online:
>
> - 60% of internet users said they had witnessed someone being called offensive names
> - 53% had seen efforts to purposefully embarrass someone
> - 25% witnessed someone being harassed for a sustained period of time
> - 24% had seen someone being physically threatened
> - 19% said they witnessed someone being sexually harassed
> - 18% said they had seen someone be stalked
>
> Internet users who have personally experienced online harassment said they were the target of at least one of the following online:
>
> - 27% of internet users have been called offensive names
> - 22% have had someone try to purposefully embarrass them
> - 8% have been physically threatened
> - 8% have been stalked
> - 7% have been harassed for a sustained period
> - 6% have been sexually harassed.[19]

The Pew research is one of a few surveys about of online harassment in recent years. All point to internet users' broad experience with name calling and hostile remarks and a narrower range of experience with severe behaviors like stalking or sexual harassment. All reflect marked differences in men's and women's experiences. Like several studies, Pew data show that young women are especially at risk of abuse online.

The Pew Research Center conducted its first look at online harassment in 2014, using a broad definition of the term. The center has long tracked the rise of social media and internet usage generally. The decision to examine patterns in harassment was a recognition that online abuse is a persistent factor in online spaces. The results provide a good baseline understanding of online rancor and abuse.

The 2014 research emerged just as many institutions began to understand and respond to the way violence against women is expressed online. It was the same year that Danielle Keats Citron's framework for understanding cyberharassment as a civil rights issue was published as *Hate Crimes in Cyberspace*.[20] Since then, the mainstream media, social media, and law enforcement officials at all levels have begun to understand the ways that aggression is expressed online, including depictions of sexual violence. Scholars are just beginning to discuss the role that aggression and violence online play in suppressing women's participation.

Women and men experience different kinds of harassment. Men are more commonly called names and purposefully embarrassed. Women are more likely to experience sustained and more serious types of abuse.

In 2016, research emerged from a new technology think tank that incorporated gender-informed and race-informed research paradigms about violence, much of it stemming from United States government-supported research. The Data and Society Research Institute, a foundation-backed group in New York founded by

Microsoft, had data that were remarkably similar to the 2014 survey by Pew but with added value. Insights from public health experts were incorporated, and the resulting survey incorporated a more nuanced view of the roles that gender and race play in culture—online and in real life.

Among the findings of the Data and Society study is the exposure that young people have to being hurt by partners or harassed over long periods of time. About four in every ten people between the ages of fifteen to twenty-nine reported seeing a romantic partner purposefully hurting their partner emotionally or psychologically. Almost half of internet users age fifteen to twenty-nine, 46 percent, said they had witnessed someone being sexually harassed or being harassed online over a long period of time. A third said they had witnessed someone being stalked.

Black internet users reported witnessing many forms of online abuse at higher rates than white or Hispanic internet users. Physical threats, mistreatment of romantic partners, and witnessing someone being harassed over a long period of time were all more common among Black users (see table 4.1).[21]

Women's trepidations about participating online are the result of real-world experiences that men have not experienced in the same degree.

Data about women journalists provide a picture of the kind of targeted threats that women face if they take part in civic affairs. An International Women's Media Foundation online survey of female journalists worldwide found that almost two-thirds of the 149 women journalists polled experienced intimidation, threats, or abuse in relation to their work. Many were online and included threats to family and friends.

In Norway, a survey found that men received more threats but that women were far more likely to receive sexualized threats. Young women in particular reported harassment.[22]

As women online had been saying for some years, the most serious types of harassment are targeted behaviors with recognizable

Table 4.1

The likelihood of witnessing online harassment varies by race and ethnicity.

Among all internet users, the percentage who say they have ever witnessed any of the following behaviors directed at a particular person online

	a	b	c
	White	Black	Hispanic
Someone being called offensive names	62	69[a,c]	60
Someone trying to embarrass another person on purpose	60	68[a]	60
Someone being physically threatened	31	46[a,c]	33
A romantic partner purposefully hurting their partner emotionally or psychologically	26	38[a]	32[a]
Someone being sexually harassed	24	29	31[a]
Someone being harassed online over a long period of time	19	27[a]	22
Someone being stalked	18	22	19
Any of these	71	78	69

Notes: Columns marked with a superscript letter indicate a statistically significant different at the 95 percent level between that column and the column designated by that superscript letter. Statistical significance is determined inside the specific section covering each subgroup. *Source:* Data & Society / CiPHR Measuring Cyberabuse Survey, May 17–July 31, 2016, https://www.pewresearch.org/internet/2014/10/22/online-harassment. Interviews were conducted in English and Spanish ($n = 3,002$ U.S internet users age fifteen and older).

features of gendered violence and abuse (see figure 4.2). Younger women in particular are targeted for extreme harassment.

Consistent with those results showing women more likely to be subject to extreme abuse, Pew Research also showed that women are singled out for particular persistent forms of abuse, young women especially. The Pew Research defined young women as those ages eighteen to twenty-four. As with data from other institutions, in figure 4.3, young people are experiencing adversarial and abusive online behaviors at a rate more than twice that of older men and women.

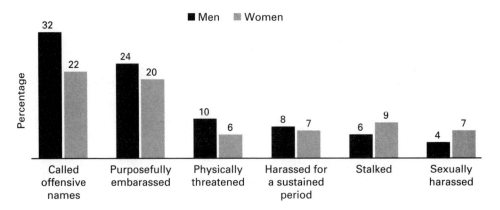

Figure 4.2
Men and women experience different varieties of online harassment.
Source: Pew Research Center, American Trends Panel (wave 4), survey conducted May 30–June 30, 2014, *n* = 2,839.

In 2016, two years after the Pew results were released, Australian research commissioned by the software company Norton/Symantec found similar patterns. Half of Australian women reported experiencing online harassment, and 76 percent of women under age thirty did so.

Women in Australia were twice as likely as men to experience "sextortion, graphic sexual harassment, threats of sexual violence and cyberstalking." About six in ten women reported bullying online, compared to a little more than a third of men.[23]

"This survey uncovers the prevalence of harassment against women in the online world, and sheds light on the extent of the problem in our society," said Melissa Dempsey, senior director of the computer security software firm Norton, which commissioned the survey. "It also exposes the high emotional toll online harassment is having on Australian women and brings to light the uncomfortable truth that some Australian women are feeling violated, abused and frightened by their online experiences."[24]

Follow-up research about Australian men in 2016 had similar results, with name calling and bullying common experiences. Gay,

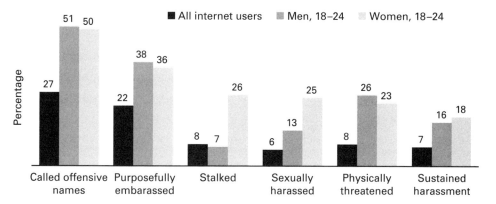

Figure 4.3
Young women experience particularly several forms of online harassment.
Source: Pew Research Center, American Trends Panel (wave 4), survey conducted May 30–June 30, 2014, *n*=2,839.

bisexual, and transgender men were more often targeted for severe forms of abuse. And 6 percent of men were targeted because of their sports team affiliation, compared to women at 3 percent.[25] Again, online abuse displayed the dynamics of gendered abuse.

Cybersexism in Context with Violence against Women

While women in public life were early targets for cyberharassment, something far more dangerous has been happening in many women's personal lives. Many women also began to experience digital extensions of intimate partner violence, such as stalking and surveillance assisted by the Global Positioning System (GPS), as I wrote for Women's eNews in 2006.[26]

Suddenly, batterers could sit at home or use a smartphone at any moment to check the location of a partner or former partner, simply because the person carried a smartphone or a perpetrator had hidden a GPS device in a car. In fact, advocates at domestic violence assistance centers have said that one of a batterer's favorites gifts to give for Christmas is a smartphone because it makes a victim's location easy to monitor. It's a device built for stalking.

In a 2012 survey financed through the U.S. Department of Justice, three-quarters of domestic violence agencies said that abusers were accessing victims' online accounts, and two-thirds said that abusers were monitoring victims' online activities. Similar numbers of women had their photographs posted online without their consent.

Clearly, the visceral dynamics of violence against women in private and the disdain for women's place in the public sphere have been remixed in digital culture. Misogyny has met with digital technologies and taken shape in new and different ways. Online culture and technologies propel sexist backlash into the public and also project violence against women into the online lives of individual women.

Things began to change in 2011 and 2012. Feminists, women writers, law enforcement leaders nationally and internationally, internet legal experts, and others involved in the architecture of the internet began to talk about legal solutions to problems in the functionally lawless Wild West atmosphere of the cybersphere. Meetings and workshops at Harvard University's Berkman Center for Internet and Society and at the United Nations all sought testimony and formed working groups to address various aspects of sexism online.

The Women's Media Center in New York was involved and developed strategies to change public perceptions of gendered abuse online. A key part was adapting a time-honored domestic violence tool called the power and control wheel to digital technologies.

The Women's Media Center Speech Project director Soraya Chemaly and Debjani Roy reconceived the power and control wheel as the online abuse wheel[27] to encompass digital technologies. The model of intimate partner violence and control has been used for decades to educate women and communities about the spectrum of attitudes and behaviors that comprise and enable intimate partner violence.

In the online abuse wheel, online abuse tactics, impacts, and legal issues are portrayed in concentric circles, with the result being abusive impact on individual victims in the center. Like the Data & Society Research Institute's survey, it incorporates decades of research and legal history on violence against women into its portrayal of the way abusive practices are deployed online.

The purpose of such abuse, according to the center, "usually includes wanting to embarrass, humiliate, scare, threaten, silence, extort, or, in some instances, encourage mob attacks or malevolent engagements."[28]

Part and parcel of the online abuse wheel are a range of tactics, including sending rape threats, publishing home address information, promoting harassment (doxxing), defaming, and sending nonconsensual pornography. All of these tactics comprise a taxonomy of online abuse, giving shape to the range of intimidation tactics used in gendered harassment online.

Some of the tactics are used, author and activist Sarah Jeong has noted, to "crowdsource domestic abuse."[29] The techniques spill over into mob-based harassment of women who are in the public eye (see figure 4.4).

To understand the ways that women's speech and political participation are expressed online, it's vital to understand the dynamics of violence against women throughout societies. The issues of cybersexism, cybermisogyny, revenge pornography, stalking, threatening, and cybermob harassment campaigns are part of a continuum that women understand in that context, even if individuals making caustic remarks on a news website do not understand the impact they are having. Perpetrators do not even need to understand that they are engaging in a long tradition of abusive behavior against women or that in *The Odyssey*, Telemachus told his mother to "shut up."

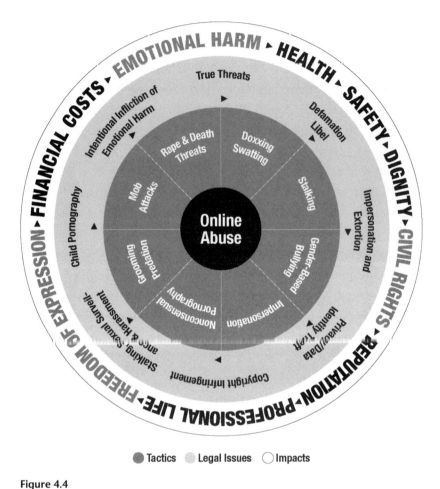

Figure 4.4
Online abuse wheel.
Source: Women's Media Center, "Online Abuse 101," https://www.womensmediacenter
.com/speech-project/online-abuse-101.

For well documented reasons, the internet can be a scary place for women, as many young women explained when my research team conducted an online convenience survey at the Missouri School of Journalism's Reynolds Journalism Institute in 2015. While 84 percent of respondents said they never commented in news comment sections, three-quarters said they commented on news articles within their own circles on social media.[30]

Revenge Porn

To understand the ways that online culture perpetuates old patterns of gender-based abuse and aggression toward women, it's helpful to turn back the clock to an episode in cultural history—the Miss America Pageant's treatment of Vanessa Williams.

In 1984, Miss America Vanessa Williams was dethroned when nude images of her were published in *Penthouse* magazine without her consent. It was not until 2015, after "revenge porn" came to be understood as an abusive practice and was finally prosecuted in a few cases, that the Miss America organization publicly admitted that its punitive actions were wrong and restored Williams's title. "I want to apologize for anything that was said or done that made you feel any less the Miss America you are and the Miss America you always will be," the executive chair of the Miss America pageant said in an onstage apology.[31]

The fact that the apology finally came in 2015 was less a reflection on the Miss America organization than it was a reflection on maturing public understanding of revenge porn and other ways that sexism is expressed in digital culture.

Among the biggest beneficiaries of the expanding internet were the perpetrators and profiteers who published and traded pornography and sexual images essentially free from financial cost or legal consequence.

What's more, average young women were being victimized the same way that Vanessa Williams had been thirty years earlier. But now it was happening at fiber optic speed, and many more competitors were making space available for sexualized images. The cottage industry came to be known as "revenge porn," an abusive practice where mostly men post nonconsensual photographs of women engaged in sex acts, posing nude in private settings, or photoshopped onto images of other women in lewd settings.

Revenge porn became a tactic soon adopted by batterers worldwide.

Internet sites such as "isanyoneup.com" thrived with images shared by users, sometimes obtained by illegally taking images from another person's computer—or hacking. Chat room forums like 4chan and reddit served as digital meeting places for sharing abusive images, including child pornography.

Like Williams, the victims of revenge porn are often publicly humiliated and suffer career damage, often by design of a malicious partner or former partner. It is one digital manifestation of domestic violence and stalking, though perpetrators can also be strangers. Commonly, these images were shared myriad times and often reported to employers as evidence of a woman's poor image and unbecoming behavior outside of work.

Kayla Laws's case and a handful of other examples of egregious cybermob threats in 2012, 2013, and 2014 eventually came to change public understanding of the way sexism is expressed with digital means. In Laws's case, the hacking group Anonymous got involved, and the Federal Bureau of Investigation ultimately prosecuted the website administrator. The prosecution came only after the Laws family collected evidence of interstate invasion of privacy involving multiple victims and gave the evidence to the FBI.

When it happened to Kayla Laws in 2012, her family's appeals to local, state, and federal officials fell on deaf ears. The website's administrator, Hunter Moore, apparently had hacked into Kayla's email account or received hacked information. Kayla had shared photographs with no one.

But Hunter Moore had messed with the wrong woman. Kayla's mother, Charlotte Laws, a former private investigator, politician, and television personality, pursued legal action against the website. Charlotte Laws contacted the website and asked Moore to remove Kayla's picture under the Digital Millennium Copyright Act. Within a short time, Charlotte was on the receiving end of a torrent of violent threats and abuse, all ignored by law enforcement. A contact at the shadowy hacking group Anonymous warned her to beware of strange cars sitting outside her house because that would be one way malevolent hackers would try to infect her computers.

And then the cars appeared.

Charlotte Laws recounted her odyssey in a 2013 magazine story and later a book:

> Moore . . . called himself a "professional life ruiner" and described his website as "pure evil." He threw legal letters in the trash, addressed his followers as "my children," taking a page from the Charles Manson handbook; and regularly taunted victims, encouraging them to commit suicide. People claimed to be afraid of him. He had no fear of lawsuits; he knew a victim would be unlikely to sue because a civil suit would cost $60,000 . . . and forever link a woman's name with the image she hoped to hide.
>
> Moore maintained that his victims were sluts, asked to be abused and deserved to lose their jobs, embarrass their families and find themselves forever ruined. Below photos on the site, his followers posted crude and misogynistic remarks. Victims were taunted as "fat cows," "creatures with nasty teeth," "ugly whores," "white trash sluts" and "whales." One commenter said, "Jesus, someone call Greenpeace and get her back in the water." The website was not about pornography; it was about ridiculing and hurting others.[32]

Rape Threats Are Daily Occurrences

While the movement to rein in revenge porn was growing, a number of women involved in computer gaming began to take on sexism in the computer gaming industry.

Apparently nothing is as threatening to many male computer gamers as a woman blogger or a woman developer who wants to create games and a gaming culture with less cleavage, rape, violence, and objectification of women, according to Anita Sarkeesian. Sarkeesian had developed a video outlining a range of sexist tropes in video games. The radical notion that women might deserve access to more egalitarian images and characters in video games spawned a backlash in an episode of intimidation and threats that came to be known as Gamergate, when resentful game developers coalesced under the hashtag #Gamergate.

One such free thinker was game developer Brianna Wu. During a nine-month period in 2014 and 2015, an online mob of angry gamers issued more than a hundred threats against Wu. During the same period, blogger Anita Sarkeesian was serially threatened with rape and death. A game was created where "players" could punch and cut Sarkeesian, leaving virtual scars and bruises on images of her face. People mailed her photographs of her own image covered in what was purportedly their ejaculate:[33]

> During those months, much of the video game world—which is massive—became obsessed with the idea that women might ruin the future of games by persuading game studios to abandon sexy female characters or tone down the default machismo of male characters.[34] It is difficult to estimate just how big the Gamergate movement really was, but at its height 2 million tweets were sent using the term "Gamergate."[35] About 10,000 users discussed Gamergate on Reddit.[36]

In the end, the U.S. Attorney's office in Boston declined to prosecute four men identified as sources of the threats against Wu, despite the fact that prosecutors had videotaped confessions.[37]

Random Rape Threat Generator

The type of rape and death threats that characterized Gamergate have become such a ubiquitous global phenomenon to women in the public eye that two women in Australia developed the "Random Rape Threat Generator."[38] It uses the text of actual language directed at women in the public eye to develop standard-issue rape threats.

Some sample random threats:

- "A bomb with a trigger is outside your home, you subnormal ballbuster."
- "I killed a woman like you who made fun of guys cocks. You out-to-get-men child."
- "I'd rape you if you weren't so unrapeable. You man-hating gay cunt."
- "I hope you get raped in your *sshole and eyeballs. You whorish douchebag.
- "I hope you get raped with a chainsaw. You disgusting frootloop."

Women have real reasons to feel fearful of threats that a man in a similar position might more easily shake off, writer Chemaly notes. One in five women will be sexually assaulted in her lifetime, and about one of every ten women worldwide first experiences intercourse through sexual violence. On the other hand, only one in seventy-one men will be sexually assaulted during his lifetime.[39] Sexual violence and threats of sexual violence are very realistic fears that many women live with on a daily basis.

That's one reason that women journalists and especially women of color remain on edge about targeted campaigns of abuse or even the steady arrival of hate mail. In response to a study of comments in the *Guardian* in 2016, Amanda Taub recognized the themes in the comments, tweets, and other messages that she now expects when she writes about the Israeli-Palestinian conflict, feminism, or rape. Taub is now a journalist at the *New York Times*:

> The most disturbing ones are the elaborate fantasies for how I should be raped or maimed or killed in order to "teach me a lesson" about why whatever I've written is so wrong. I've received recommendations that I should be sodomized with a gun, that I should be raped by a thousand men, that I should be raped and murdered by terrorists, and that I should be handed over to ISIS to become another journalist murdered on camera—and those are just the ones I happen to remember off the top of my head, not a complete list.[40]

Taub was responding to the results of an analysis in the *Guardian* of the publication's own comments. A 2016 study of 70 million comments submitted to that site illustrated how the gender and race of opinion writers influenced the level of abusive comments. The results confirmed what women journalists and journalists of color have long experienced: articles they write attract more abuse. "Although the majority of our regular opinion writers are white men, we found that those who experienced the highest levels of abuse and dismissive trolling were not. The 10 regular writers who got the most abuse were eight women (four were white and four non-white) and two black men," the *Guardian* staff wrote:[41]

> Here are some examples: a female journalist reports on a demonstration outside an abortion clinic, and a reader responds, "You are so ugly that if you got pregnant I would drive you to the abortion clinic myself"; a British Muslim writes about her experiences of Islamophobia and is told to "marry an ISIS fighter and then see how you like that!"; a black correspondent is called "a racist who hates white people" when he reports the news that another black American has been shot by the police. We wouldn't tolerate such insults offline, and at the *Guardian* we don't tolerate it online either.[42]

Sites such as the *Guardian* and the *New York Times* long ago recognized the value of supporting civil conversations around their news and opinion products. Social media sites and wiki-based platforms, however, have relied mostly on users to report bad comments and otherwise police the space themselves until the last few years.

The point is that misogynistic violence is very much with us. It may be expressed online, but its purpose is to disrupt public conversations and silence women who speak up.

Trolls and Online Abuse

The word *troll* has many connotations in conversations about online abuse and harassment, so I want to make clear how I'm using it here. Every serious discussion of inflammatory behavior on the internet uses the term *troll*—either as a noun or as a verb—in a general way, as described by Andrew Losowsky above. There's a range of trolls: organized trolling, spontaneous trolling, and garden-variety nastiness.

But disruptive trolling behavior is a spectrum of disruption. Sometimes, people goad others just for fun. Others leave comments on a YouTube video of a woman being beheaded by a Mexican drug cartel talking about her buttocks or how they might enjoy fornicating with the stump.[43]

The *Guardian* columnist and author Lindy West has a useful definition of a troll that draws a line across a trolling continuum from random person leaving inflammatory comments to people who are antagonistic for fun. West, author of the memoir *Shrill: Notes from a Loud Woman*, is a prominent feminist writer and fat activist who was among the earliest public figures to take on misogynist harassment in public:

> Trolling is recreational abuse—usually anonymous—intended to waste the subject's time or get a rise out of them or frustrate or frighten them into silence. Sometimes it's relatively innocuous (like asking contrarian questions just to start an argument) or juvenile (like making fun of my weight or my intelligence), but—particularly when the subject is a young woman—it frequently crosses the line into bona fide, dangerous stalking and harassment.[44]

In any nuanced discussion of inflammatory and abusive behavior, however, it's important to understand the particular digital subculture of the capital-T Trolls.

Trolls are a distinct underworld of anonymous internet users who meet in online chat rooms like Reddit forums, /b/, and 8kun (formerly 8chan). They see themselves as Trolls, proper, and endeavor to create disruption for *lulz*, a Troll word for laughs. They self-identify as both avengers and revengers. These are people whose lives revolve around disrupting social order, insulting people, and causing pain just for the joke value, Whitney Phillips writes in *This Is Why We Can't Have Nice Things.*[45]

As a global troll movement thrived, one branch broke off to become Anonymous, the shadowy group of hacking activists whose work is often purposefully political. One example is their coordination with Julian Assange of Wikileaks to distribute stolen diplomatic data and documents. They have also hacked into child sexual abuse pornography sharing sites to shut them down.

Indeed, during Kayla Laws and Charlotte Laws's investigation and campaign to shut down Hunter Moore's isanyoneup.com revenge porn site, a member of Anonymous reached out to Charlotte Laws. Ultimately, the hacktivists shut down the isanyoneup site through a denial of service attack (a hacking technique that is also used against victims of violence, as the Online Abuse Wheel reflects).

Mostly, though, trolls thrive on being antagonistic as a leisure activity, Phillips writes in *This Is Why We Can't Have Nice Things.* One such "hilarious" pastime is called RIP trolling. In that vein, individuals post fake tribute pages to people who have died for the express purpose of gathering vulgar, obscene, or demeaning fake "memories." One such incident became a global phenomenon in 2010 when SeaWorld trainer Dawn Brancheau was killed by Tilikum, a 12,000-pound killer whale, during a performance: "Within minutes of Brancheau's death, trolls began uploading macros on /b/ featuring a homicidal whale as well as variations on rule 34, an unofficial rule of the Internet declaring that whatever 'it' is, there is porn of it. With the invocation of rule 34, Dawn Brancheau the person was thus transformed into Dawn Brancheau the meme—that is to say, a dehumanized, sexualized object of lulz."[46]

This particular subculture of trolls has cultivated a stylized brand of misogynistic harassment everywhere the internet is in use. The trolling culture has been apparent since the beginning of chat rooms and has been widely chronicled.[47] These troll subcultures are part of internet reality. If you don't understand how or why a dead, whale-loving marine biologist might become the object of hateful porno-graphic jokes, it's impossible to understand a lot of cyberharassment. On the one hand, it's a misogynistic form of policing women. But it's important to understand the extent of the truly pointless vengeance and demented and disordered behavior that is wildly popular, often among otherwise ordinary people who have normal lives.

As public understanding of cybersexism and cyberharassment grew in 2015 and 2016, a campaign to get some of the ugliest misogynistic violence off of Facebook, Twitter, and YouTube began to bear fruit.

For a long time, however, activists had difficulty persuading web-site officials that bloody photos of dead women's bodies with head wounds and "humorous" statements like "I like her for her brains"[48] violated their terms of service. Feminists gained traction only after including advertisers in their strategy. Women, Action & the Media, working in a global coalition with the Women's Media Center, doc-umented the images that were appearing next to advertiser images, along with websites' reasons for keeping material posted.

"We had graphic representations, horrible images we couldn't share—beheadings and live rapes being filmed," Chemaly said. "We asked Facebook to recognize violence against women as a legitimate form of hatred. We weren't asking them to change their guidelines or suppress other people's free speech. We wanted them not to label hatred as 'controversial humor.'"

Platforms were not supportive until advertisers became involved and started pulling out their financial support. "What constitutes safety, harm, true threat is as monstrously androcentric as anything else," Chemaly said. "We would send them threats, tell them 'I feel threatened,' and say 'this is against your policy.' Facebook would say, 'We don't think that's a serious threat.'"[49]

Figure 4.5
"I like her for her brains." Facebook posting.
Source: Women, Action & the Media, http://www.womenactionmedia.org/examples
-of-gender-based-hate-speech-on-facebook.

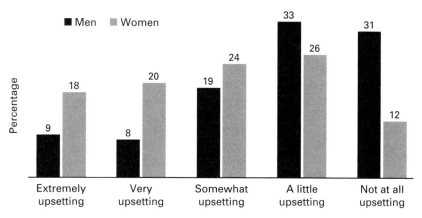

Figure 4.6
Women more likely to be upset by online harassment.
Source: Pew Research Center, American Trends Panel (wave 4), survey conducted May 30 to June 30, 2014, *n*=932.

Finally, Facebook agreed to be more responsive to hateful materials after a campaign in 2013. By 2017, Facebook and Twitter had begun to take steps to keep abuse off the network, however incomplete their enforcement.

Still, violent threats are not being prosecuted by law enforcement, as in Brianna Wu's case. Active campaigns to silence women are still part of the landscape.

It should have come as no surprise when the Pew Research Center found that more than a third of women found online harassment "very upsetting" or "extremely upsetting," compared to just 17 percent of men. In contrast, nearly two-thirds of men found online harassment either "a little" upsetting or "not at all upsetting."

Given women and men's differing experiences with harassment, it's not surprising that women are reluctant to speak up online. Between an internet culture that has given bullies free rein, coordinated terror campaigns against prominent women, and women's aversion to conflict in online spaces, the barriers to women's participation are manifest.

Online Abuse 101

Tactics

Tactics are wide ranging. They are sometimes legal but harmful and consequential. They may legal but violate a particular platform's guidelines and terms of service. Some, but not all, are illegal, including, but not limited to child pornography, copyright infringements, data theft, defamation, extortion, intentional infliction of emotional harm, libel, privacy infringements, sexual harassment, sexual surveillance, stalking, and true threats.

cross-platform harassment: When a harasser or group of harassers deliberately sabotages or invades multiple online spaces for the purposes of harassing a target. Cross-platform harassment is very effective because users are currently unable to report this scope and context of the harassment when they contact platforms, each of which will only consider the harassment happening on their own sites.

cyberexploitation, nonconsensual photography, or "revenge porn": The distribution of sexually graphic images without the consent of the subject of the images. The abuser obtains images or videos in the course of a prior relationship or hacks into the victim's computer, social media accounts, or phone. Women make up more than 95 percent of reported victims. The unauthorized sharing of sexualized images is still not illegal in the majority of U.S. states. Twenty-two states now have laws on the books, and proposed national legislation is being drafted. (You can check your state here.) It is defined as the nonconsensual distribution and publication of intimate photos and videos.

deadnaming: A form of direct harassment in which a target's former name is revealed against their wishes for the purposes of harm. This technique is most commonly used to out members of the LGTBQIA community who may have changed their birth names for any variety of reasons, including to avoid professional discrimination and physical danger.

defamation: Coordinated attempts at defamation take place when a person or, sometimes, organized groups deliberately flood social media and review sites with negative and defamatory information.

DOS: DOS stands for "denial-of-service," an attack that makes a website or network resource unavailable to its users.

doxing: The unauthorized retrieving and publishing, often by hacking, of a person's personal information, including, but not limited to, full names, addresses, phone numbers, emails, spouse and children names, and financial details. *Dox* is a slang version of *documents* or *.doc*. Causing fear, stress, and panic is the objective of doxing, even when perpetrators think or say that their objective is "harmless."

electronically enabled financial abuse: The use of the internet and other forms of technology to exert financial pressure on a target, usually a woman involved in intimate partner abuse. This might include, for example, denying access to online accounts, manipulating credit information to create negative scores, and identity theft.

false accusations of blasphemy: Women face online threats globally, but they run a unique risk in conservative religious countries where blasphemy is against the law and where honor killings are a serious threat. Accusing someone of blasphemy can become, itself, an act of violence.

flaming: A flood of vitriolic and hostile messages including threats, insults, slurs, and profanity.

gender-based slurs and harassment: Name-calling is common online. Gendered harassment, however, involves the use of words, insults, profanity, and often images to communicate hostility toward girls and women because they are women. Typically, harassers resort to words such as *bitch, slut, whore,* or *cunt* and include commentary on women's physical appearances.

Google bombing: The deliberate optimization of malicious information and websites online so that when people search for a target, they immediately see defamatory content. In 2012, for example, Bettina Wulff, the wife of Germany's then president, sued Google because the company's autocomplete search function perpetuated rumors that she was once a prostitute.

grooming and predation: Online grooming is when a person using social media to deliberate cultivates an emotional connection with a child in order to sexually abuse or exploit that child.

hate speech: Hate speech has no uniform legal definition. Online, this means that every social media platform has its own unique definition. As a baseline, however, hate speech is language or imagery that denigrates, insults, threatens, or targets individual or groups of people on the basis of their identity—based on gender, race, color, religion, national origin, sexual orientation, disability, or other traits. There is no hate speech exception to the First Amendment. Hate speech usually has specific, discriminatory harms rooted in history and usually employs words, action, and the use of images meant to deliberately shame, annoy, scare, embarrass, humiliate, denigrate, or threaten another person. Most legal definitions of harassment take into consideration the intent of the harasser. This, however, fails to translate usefully in the case of cyberharassment, the use of the internet, electronic, and mobile applications for these purposes. In the case of technology-enabled

Online Abuse 101 (continued)

harassment and abuse, intent can be difficult to prove and diffuse. For example, most laws do not currently consider third-party communications to be harassing. So whereas the law understands sending someone a threatening message for the purposes of extortion, it does not understand the nonconsensual sharing of sexual images to someone other than the subject of the photograph illegal or hateful.

identity theft and online impersonation: As defined by the Department of Justice, identity theft includes "crimes in which someone wrongfully obtains and uses another person's personal data in some way that involves fraud or deception, typically for economic gain." The law applies to any person or entity who impersonates another person on the internet with the "intent to obtain a benefit or injure or defraud another." Many states distinguish this from impersonation, in which a person creates an account, website, or ad using a person's name and address with the intention of harming another person. In 2013, for example, a jury convicted thirty-two-year-old Michael Johnson of more than eighty counts related to his having impersonated his ex-wife online. He had purchased online ads and connected with would-be johns posing as his wife. He posted rape fantasies inviting men to kick down her door and have sex with her. In addition to sharing prices for sex with her, he also included sex with her three daughters and with the toddler boy that the couple had together. The abuse continued when he contacted one of the daughters' school, posting a message to the school's website in her name, reading, "I will have sex with the teachers in return for passing grades." As many as fifty men a day showed up at the woman's home. She eventually moved her family to another state. Other cases similarly involving impersonation, involving false fantasies of violent gang rape, are commonly used as part of ongoing intimate violence. The difference between these two tactics is that identity theft benefits the perpetrator, while impersonation results in a distinct harm to another person.

IRL attacks: In-real-life attacks are incidents where online abuse either moves into the "real" world or is already part of an ongoing stalking or intimate partner violence interaction. IRL trolling can also mean simply trying to instill fear by letting a target know that the abuser knows their address or place of employment.

mob attacks and cybermobs: Hostile mobs include hundreds, sometimes thousands of people systematically harassing a target. #Slanegirl, a hashtag that was used for the trending global public shaming of a teenage girl filmed performing fellatio, is one example. Attacks on public figures like Anita Sarkeesian or Caroline Criado-Perez have been conducted by cybermobs.

rape videos: Videos of rapes in progress that are subsequently used to shame or extort or are sold as nonconsensual porn. These images are sometimes used to populate online spaces created for sharing them, cybercesspools whose sole purpose is to deprive people of dignity by humiliating and harassing them. In India, rape videos are part of what law enforcement has described as a thriving "revenge porn economy." They are used to blackmail, shame, and extort. The United States and United Kingdom have seen multiple publicized cases of teenage girls whose rapes were filmed and shared commit suicide.

retaliation against supporters of victims: Online abusers will often threaten to or engage in harassing their target's family members, friends, employers or community of supporters.

sexual objectification: Harassers frequently objectify their targets, including through the use of manipulated photographs and sexually explicit descriptions of their bodies. Girls and women's photographs are often used without their consent and manipulated so that they appear in pornographic scenes or used in memes.

shock and grief trolling: Targeting vulnerable people by using the names and images of lost ones to create memes, websites, and fake Twitter accounts or Facebook pages. Feminist writer Lindy West has described how harassers set up Twitter accounts using a stolen photograph of her recently deceased father. The name on the account was a play on his name and a reference to his death. "Embarrassed father of an idiot," the bio read. It cited his location as "Dirt hole in Seattle."

spying and sexual surveillance: Most people think of spying and surveillance in terms of governments spying on citizens; however, women are frequently illegally (and legally) surveilled. This happens in their apartments; in changing rooms, department stores, and supermarket bathrooms; on public stairways and subway platforms; in sports arenas and locker rooms; in police stations; and in classrooms while they teach. The minimizing expression "Peeping Tom" is particularly insufficient given the impact of the nature, scale, and amplification of the internet on the power of stolen images and recordings to be used in harmful ways.

stalking and stalking by proxy: Justice Department records reveal that 70 percent of those stalked online are women and more than 80 percent of cyberstalking defendants are male.

sexting and abusive sexting: Sexting is the consensual electronic sharing of naked or sexual photographs. This is different, however, from the

Online Abuse 101 (continued)

nonconsensual sharing of the same images. While sexting is often demonized as dangerous, the danger and infraction are actually resident in the violation of privacy and consent that accompanies the sharing of images without the subject's consent. For example, while teenage boys and girls sext at the same rates, boys are between two and three times more likely to share images that they are sent.

slut-shaming: A form of gender-based bullying often targeting teenage girls. Slut-shaming, stalking, the use of nonconsensual photography, and sexual surveillance frequently overlap, amplifying impact on targets. Amanda Todd, Rehtaeh Parsons, Audrie Potts, Felicia Garcia, Tyler Clementi, Rachel Ehmke, and Steubenville's Jane Doe and Jada are people who were targeted by combinations of these tactics.

swatting: Deliberately tricking authorities into responding to a false emergency situation at a specific address. The term comes from SWAT (Special Weapons and Tactics), a branch of the U.S. police that uses militarized techniques, equipment, and firearms to breach targeted sites. Harassers will report a serious threat or emergency, eliciting a law enforcement response that might include the use of weapons and possibility of being killed or hurt.

threats: Rape and death threats frequently coincide with sexist, racist commentary. While online threats may not pass current legal tests for what constitutes a "true threat," they do generate anxiety and alter the course of a person's life.

trafficking: While not traditionally thought of as a form of online harassment and abuse, trafficking involves multiple types of electronically enabled abuse. Social media is used by traffickers to sell people whose photographs they share without their consent, often including photographs of their abuse of women as an example to others. Seventy-six percent of trafficked persons are girls and women, and the internet is now a major sales platform.

unsolicited pornography: Sending unsolicited pornography, violent rape porn gifs, or photographs in which a target's photograph has been sexualized. Women politicians, writers, athletes, celebrities, and more have their photographs electronically manipulated for the purposes of creating nonconsensual pornography and of degrading them publicly.

Source: Women's Media Center, Taxonomy of Online Abuse, http://wmcspeech project.com/online-abuse-101.

For news sites and other public forums, the problems are less about violent imagery and more about the clear message from the wider internet: women beware. The solution to engaging women has to be about platforms creating safe, lawful places where women's voices are engaged, supported, and affirmed.

Cybermisogyny, trolling, and semicoordinated internet-fueled harassment are new tactics, but they're merely tactics—new ways of silencing women in the public sphere that are slightly less messy than cutting out a woman's tongue, as in the classics literature. Until publishers and digital consumers recognize them as basic elements of silencing women in the broader culture, women will stay away from civic forums. For decades, feminists have marched to "take back the night" from rape. New movements will need to tackle the new public square before women will use their voices in equal measure to men.

5
Women and News

A New Paradigm in the Digital Era

"If the *Financial Times* were a person, it would be a man."

—Readers in a focus group

Hanne Jalborg noticed something remarkable as she reviewed data about users on *Expressen*, the online news site of one of Sweden's two national evening newspapers. Parsing segments of readers, Jalborg saw that the site was in striking distance of being the number one source of news among Swedish women.

Three years into an innovative audience strategy with gender-informed reporting and analysis, the director of audience insights at *Expressen* saw an achievable goal. In November 2017, Jalborg presented the data to editors and management and proposed a short timeline to reach it—a hallmark of *Expressen*'s digital strategy.

"The managers were really excited about the goal," Jalborg said. "We've found that if we write more about stories and topics that women read—not just in stereotyped topics but across all the verticals—we get more female readers."[1]

Within a month, *Expressen* had claimed its national leadership goal. It is now the largest news site for Swedish women.

As *Expressen* had increasing success, other editors in Europe took note. Swedish software developer Olga Stern, who created the GeNews software that tracked the gender metrics of sourcing at *Expressen*, made presentations at meetings such as the Online News Association annual meeting in London. The BBC's Elinor Shields also appeared and led further efforts at the BBC.

In 2017, editors from the *Financial Times* and others visited the *Expressen* newsroom to learn about its digital strategy. Ben Preston of the *Financial Times* tweeted about the gender statistics displayed on monitors throughout the newsroom. "In the newsroom of *Expressen*, a mighty Swedish tabloid, a running score of men vs women interviewed in stories each day," he wrote.[2]

In the few years before 2020, global news media increasingly began building the foundation of a data-driven strategy to increase women's readership and engagement. At the heart of this strategy is the metrics of gender representation in news stories, conversations, and images. The goal is to fix one of the news media's most persistent business problems. Women historically have never been nearly as engaged in news media as men.

"Our readers told us, 'If the *Financial Times* were a person, it would be a man,'" said Renée Kaplan of the *Financial Times*. "The rise of audience metrics means we're inexorably aware of who we're reaching and who we're not. And sourcing is an issue."[3]

Around the world, news product teams looking at growth opportunities are coming to the same conclusions that feminists have been articulating for decades. If news media want to have a robust audience among women, leading publications have realized, they have to do a much better job including the voices and images of women experts. What's more, they need to avoid stereotypes and cover women's areas of interest in politics and business more prominently.

In 2018, more than six hundred teams at the BBC signed up for a program to monitor the representation of women in their content.

This initiative—50:50: The Equality Project—was expanded across all content divisions, including news, entertainment, sports, and science by 2019. By March 2020, two-thirds of the teams were producing content that included half women as contributors and content experts. According to Nina Goswami, the creative product lead on the 50:50 Project:

> At the BBC, we were looking for ways to make our diversity goals more effective. We improved the diversity of the workforce, but we needed a way to connect diversity goals to the content creators who were creating programs. We tallied gender, and then started looking at what in the U.K. we call BAME—Black, Asian, Minority or Ethnic. We're looking at intersectionality and will be able to report that in the future. The real beauty of 50:50 is the public perception that we are creating more interesting stories and programs. We have more women consuming the content; they're noticing what we're doing, and they're liking what they see.[4]

Businesses like the *Financial Times*, where just one in five subscribers was a woman in 2018, and other global networks like Bloomberg News and the BBC are developing content metrics tools designed to track and boost the representation of women in stories, images, video, and live events. The *New York Times* and the *Financial Times* are using open-source software called GenderMeme that was developed at Stanford University. The *Financial Times* has also joined the BBC's 50:50 initiative, which has launched a global program to improve the representation of women, minority groups, and people with disabilities throughout the news and in other parts of public life.

Technically, it is not too complicated to produce a stream of content analytics by gender. Stern, the software entrepreneur in Stockholm, created a basic version of GeNews at a weekend hackathon focused on news, she says. Essentially, what software developers do is build a bridge between two sets of data—a content stream and a reference list of names by gender. The software bridge links the content of a news site with databases of names and pronouns. What reporters and editors can see on their screens as a result is a rough count—before a story, audio, or video goes live—of the proportion of women sources included in any given story or set of stories. According to Stern, "It's kind of like a Fitbit for your gender balance. If your deadline is approaching, you can check the tool, and it tells you you have to go do some more steps to reach your goal."[5]

At Bloomberg, editors work by hand to tag stories that include at least one woman as a source, and they then track how various publications and programs are performing, down to the level of editors and reporters, said Laura Zelenko, senior executive editor at Bloomberg. The BBC is using a similar approach of coding digital content as it is produced.

"Having more women as sources helps inform what stories we tell and how we tell them for fairness, balance, and for limiting our own biases," Zelenko said. "Including women is a competitive necessity for every business, and especially media businesses."[6]

At the BBC, programs are generating gender metrics about who is referenced, who is pictured, who tells the story, and who's speaking on video, said Ros Atkins, host of the TV news program *Outside Source*, who led the BBC's 50:50 effort in the early days. The BBC launched its 100 Women project on women in the twenty-first century in part to expand the accessibility of women sources in newsrooms around the world that were accustomed to looking to familiar experts. Bloomberg is creating databases of women sources as well, Zelenko said.

In Sweden, *Expressen*'s process of building its audience among women was much more methodical than setting a one-month goal. The effort followed three years of transformation and a focused effort to add more women sources, Jalborg said. *Expressen* also made efforts to tell important stories in ways that engage women users—with storytelling structures that emphasize women's voices, women's bylines, and a clear relevance of an issue to people's lives.

The *Expressen* newsroom, by using the GeNews content analysis tool, was able to learn in real time how many women's voices were reflected in their stories and columns. As might be expected, by using a gender-informed analysis of topics, sources, and images, *Expressen* boosted its readership by treating women with respect in their coverage.

Who knew?

The New Business Paradigm in Digital Media

What's remarkable about the boost in women reading and consuming news at the BBC and *Expressen* is what it represents in the news industry—a fundamental shift in the way newsrooms define their products and their relationships with audiences.

At the BBC, the impact was profound. BBC Audiences surveyed people who use any BBC online service, including BBC websites, iPlayer, and BBC Sounds. The impact was dramatic. Of the two thousand people surveyed, 39 percent said they noticed a shift toward more women. Among young people ages sixteen to thirty-four, 40 percent said they enjoyed the content more. For young women ages sixteen to twenty-four, two-thirds said they enjoyed the content more. A third of women ages twenty-five to thirty-four said they now consume more BBC online content.[7]

As the BBC's research indicates, cultivating the audience among younger people is a serious focus. As one pundit put it, the digital era has created a special generation: "The Young and the Newsless."[8]

Throughout their histories, news organizations have been content to have audiences dominated by men. In fact, some strategists and journalists are going so far as to describe their publications *as* men.

"Most newspapers are men," NiemanLab's Laura Hazard Owen wrote in 2018 in an article about the *Financial Times*. "And for a long time, no one really thought that was a problem."[9] Now the revolution in data analytics is driving a fundamental reassessment of what defines news and who should be in news audiences. The change is shaping how newsrooms decide whose priorities, voices, and images will be reflected in print, online, and on broadcasts and videos. Indeed, the changing dynamics of gender and digital metrics are shifting how society is portrayed throughout the internet.

At the same time, the transition to digital news distribution and the decline of print media offer a third wave of feminist opportunity for women to seize their public voices. It's possible that the business-based decisions driving the portrayal of women in news media and throughout entertainment media could help build a foundation to strengthen the place of women's voices throughout society.

Like the sixty-year growth curve in women's voting in the United States from universal suffrage in 1920 to equal participation in 1980, bringing women's voices to equality in national and international affairs will take at least a generation, perhaps two or three. News organizations with a long view and a business model that understands how to reach and engage women's audiences will lead the way.

First, however, traditional news organizations have a deeply rooted legacy as male-focused products to overcome.

As the next chapter on news and technology products discusses, newsrooms need to address the interlocking facts of staffing, news values, and product assumptions to unfurl the promise of digital engagement among women. Here's where the legacy products stand.

Legacy News Organizations Have Traditionally Focused on a Mostly Male Audience

Up to the present day, mainstream print, broadcast, and online news organizations have almost always had more men than women engage with their streams of hard news—the news about powerful institutions in society such as Congress, industry, and civic affairs. These are the stories that frame how people and institutional powers look at their places in society as it functions. The natural result is that men in institutions and men in newsrooms have been reiterating the gender bias of everyday life and in powerful institutions in news media every day. For journalists, this has been called "accurately reflecting the work of powerful institutions."

For women, however, the news values that reflect the work and priorities of institutions controlled by overwhelming majorities of men leave them disconnected from news media that do not connect as well with their interests and priorities. Women's lack of enthusiasm for hard news has left news businesses with a smaller audience overall. Only in recent years are these businesses recognizing the market opportunities they have left untapped.

Similar patterns were evident among Black and Hispanic news consumers in a survey conducted by the Media Insight Project in 2014 for the American Press Institute and the Associated Press-NORC at the University of Chicago. The survey showed that these consumers were continuing to be avid consumers of news as news shifted to mobile devices but had less trust in how their communities were portrayed.[10]

To get a clear picture of the way things are shifting, it's helpful to look at a baseline snapshot of reader behavior from 2012. That was the final time the Pew Research Center conducted a comprehensive News Consumption Survey in the United States. The data are particularly interesting because the survey was taken just as legacy news organizations were grappling with the pivot to digital media consumption and the decline of print (see figure 5.1).

In the years since the Pew data were collected, digital news distribution has shifted from a mostly free service to a monthly subscription-based industry standard in the United States. Print subscriptions and print advertising revenue are plummeting,

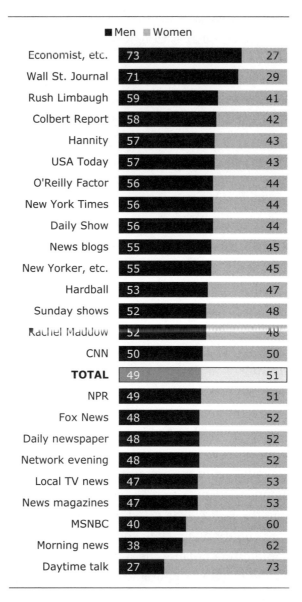

Figure 5.1
Readership in major U.S. news sources, 2012.
Source: Pew Research Center, "Demographics and Political Views of News Audiences," in "Trends in News Consumption, 1991–2012: In Changing News Landscape, Even Television Is Vulnerable," September 2012. Figures may not add up to 100 percent because of rounding. Based on regular readers, viewers, and listeners of each news source.

continuing a much longer trend.[11] Digital subscriptions have been one of a few bright spots in an industry where revenues have devastated small publications especially.

As a point of reference, the *New York Times* established its paywall in March 2011, charging frequent readers to see articles and other features online. Setting up the paywall was a remarkable event for a general-interest publication at the time. General-interest news sites had been distributing content for free. At the same time, digital startup publications like BuzzFeed, the Huffington Post, and AOL were disrupting the power dynamics of news distribution.

When the *New York Times* paywall was instituted, casual readers were initially allowed twenty free articles a month.[12] Readers who wanted to read more articles needed to make a commitment to a subscription or buy articles individually. After cutting back the number of free articles to ten per month for several years, the number of free articles declined to five per month in late 2017.[13] Financial news agencies like Bloomberg News and publishers like the *Financial Times* and the *Wall Street Journal* had online paywalls for some time, reflecting their mission to serve a high-income, specialty audience with a need for deep knowledge of financial and economic affairs.

Across the same time period of the late 2010s, the news industry shifted entirely to a digital-first strategy. In past decades, news organizations often held stories until the morning paper or until a story aired on a regularly scheduled broadcast. The shift to digital first and the intense competition to refresh websites, phone apps, and email news feeds on a continuous basis upended old concepts about morning and evening news cycles for newspapers and broadcasting.

For all the disruption in the news business, a variety of data shows that the same stable gender gaps in news audiences have carried over from print publications to digital content and digital audiences. This is not surprising to feminists. Critics of male-dominated media content didn't expect a sea change because the medium changed.

However, the rise of data analytics insights into audience demographics is having a dramatic influence on news businesses. Suddenly, gender gaps in news audiences appear as market opportunities that are ready to be developed. While hardly based on a dedication to equality for women and girls, news organizations now understand in a whole new light the imperative of covering issues of interest to women and girls. It is undoubtedly a factor that will boost the public confidence of women that their voices matter in local, state, national, and international affairs.

The advent of online news as the most important measure of a news organization's reach and audience engagement means that a news business knows virtually everything about what a reader does on its site. It knows how readers clicked into a story—whether from the home page, a newsletter, a link on social media, or a search on Google. Sometimes readers come from a technology company's news curation service, like Google News, Apple News, or Flipboard.

News companies also can track, or sometimes deduce by linking databases, the gender of people who use their sites.

As Renée Kaplan described in an interview with NiemanLab in 2018, editors at the *Financial Times* began looking at the gender of their audience only in 2016. "That's when we discovered that our subscribers were 80 percent male and 20 percent female," Kaplan said. "That's just not good. It wasn't necessarily a reflection of the content, it wasn't a reflection of what we wanted, and in a world in which 50 percent or more of people are women, it was also a business opportunity. We didn't have enough women, and suddenly we knew it, incontrovertibly."[14]

Women and Men Have Long Shown Different Interests in Types of News

Surveys of readers in the United States have always reflected a significant gap between men's and women's interest in various news topics and sources. The differences also track other ways where women are less engaged in national and international affairs and more engaged in some other topics like education and community news. For example, women are a small minority of leaders in national government, but they are increasingly well represented in local offices.

Looking back to the Pew Research Center's U.S. news consumption survey from 2006 provides a useful historical yardstick of gender gaps across sections of newspapers. In digital terms, the legacy print sections are now referred to as *verticals* because of the way content is organized in technology terms. That year was just before digital circulation began its ascent and when internet usage became a standard in many homes in the United States.

As the data show, men have traditionally dominated audiences for national, international, and financial news, following only the male-focused sports sections of legacy news organizations (see figure 5.2).

Subsequent surveys of news audiences have shown almost seamless persistence in the legacy gender gaps in patterns of readership and viewership across topic areas.

In 2014, the Media Insight Project, an initiative of the American Press Institute and AP-NORC, surveyed men and women and found these significant differences. They reflect other data and surveys showing similar gaps.[15]

First, women are not as keen as men on keeping up with the news, but they are just as likely to report reading, watching, or hearing an in-depth news piece in the previous week. While 60 percent of men say they like keeping up with the news "a lot," only 51 percent of women say that—a 9-point gap. About a third of women say they enjoy following the news "some"—37 percent of women compared to 27 percent of men.

Second, women report much stronger interests in some areas of news than men and less interest in other areas. The same gender role influences that shape primary and secondary education and occupational segregation are reflected in news consumption, too.

Gender Profile of News Audiences

	Percent who are...	
Of those who	Men	Women
closely follow:	%	%
Sports news	74	26
Science and technology	69	31
Business and finance	65	35
International	63	37
Washington news	59	41
Local government	55	45
Consumer news	51	49
National population	**48**	**52**
The weather	47	53
Crime news	46	54
Culture and the arts	44	56
Community news	42	58
Entertainment news	39	61
Health news	37	63
Religion	36	64

Figure 5.2

Gender profile of news audiences.

Source: Pew Research Center, "Where Men and Women Differ in Following the News," February 6, 2008, http://www.pewresearch.org/2008/02/06/where-men-and-women-differ-in-following-the-news, data from Pew Research Center, "Online Papers Modestly Boost Newspaper Readership," July 30, 2006.

National news is one area where women and men report a relatively small 5 percentage-point gap in reported interest, with 74 percent of men and 69 percent of women saying they follow the news. Interest in science and technology news is similar, with a 6 percentage-point gap, according to the Media Insight Project's data from 2014.

A 2017 Pew Research Center study showed a larger gap in interest in science news, especially among those who follow science news most closely. While 55 percent of men are active or casual readers of science news, just 42 percent of women reported following science news. Most of that gap came in the "very interested" category, where 22 percent of men and just 12 percent of women identified themselves.[16]

Men are more likely to report following foreign and international news, with 75 percent of men and 61 percent of women saying they were interested, a 14 percentage-point gap. More than two-thirds of women, 69 percent, report following news of education and schools, compared to half of men. (This interest is also reflected in women's relatively robust participation in elected school positions, as illustrated in chapters about women in public office.) Women also outpace men in following news about health and medicine, with about 74 percent of women and 56 percent of men.

Women also follow news of lifestyle more than men, with 58 percent of women and 30 percent of men. Women show much more interest than men in following news about entertainment and celebrities, with a 44 percent to 28 percent gap.

A 2015 data set from the Media Insight Project about people ages eighteen to thirty-four showed some important differences from older readers. Even so, gender gaps remain in the groups who most actively seek out news. Among millennials ages eighteen to twenty-four who "actively seek out news and information," many more are men: 56 percent are men, and 44 percent are women. That gender gap holds in people in the twenty-five to thirty-four age group, who were identified by the Media Insight Project as "activists." Forty-eight percent of men that age say they follow national news compared to just 38 percent of women, a gap of 10 percentage points.[17]

Not surprisingly, gender gaps in readership and interest in different topics bear a striking resemblance to the kind of coverage a news organization is providing. And like other major power institutions, mainstream news organizations have long reflected a decidedly, verifiably male perspective on news.

The Reuters Institute for the Study of Journalism at Oxford University has been tracking digital news consumption. Its 2020

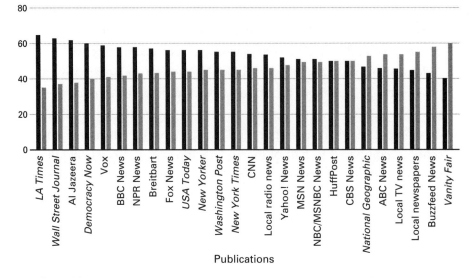

Figure 5.3

U.S. digital news audiences by gender, 2020.

Source: Data based on Nic Newman et al., "Reuters Institute Digital News Report 2020," Reuters Institute for the Study of Journalism, June 2020.

report shows a persistent male majority among news consumers of national daily news media and a more female-heavy audience for local news and select others, such as *National Geographic*. The data do not reflect only subscribers but show when survey responders said they had read news in that publication that week through free access, a social media link, or link sharing (see figure 5.3).[18]

Gender Segregation in Coverage of News

In the twenty-first century, women and minorities, especially women of color, remain remarkably underrepresented in newsrooms throughout the world. For decades, surveys have documented this continuing pattern in the United States and more recently throughout the world.

Sometimes, people expect news organizations to mount challenges to fundamental injustices. Despite some mythology about journalism, however, traditional news media largely reflect powerful institutions as they already exist and naturally reflect the priorities of those institutions.

For women, that has meant being portrayed in media as secondary figures in society. Feminists have long criticized this approach as failing to represent the whole society. Since 2010, those criticisms have most powerfully taken shape on the global stage through UN Women, the United Nations Entity for Gender Equality and the Empowerment of Women.

Good journalism has always challenged institutional powers—within the framework of legacy institutions. But mainstream journalism has never fundamentally challenged the legacy and the legitimacy of male dominance of powerful institutions.

UN Women describes women's representation in media in a much different frame. Women's representation in media is fundamental to the well-being of society, as Phumzile Mlambo-Ngcuka, UN under-secretary-general and executive director of UN Women, wrote in the introduction of a 2015 global study: "The media are a powerful force in shaping how we see the world, what we think, and often how we act. They should be an example of gender equality, depicting women in diverse jobs and situations and representing women in all areas of coverage. Women and girls are half of humanity. Giving equal time and weight to their stories is an important part of creating a better, freer world for all of us."[19]

The underrepresentation of women in media is remarkably consistent worldwide, according to the Global Media Monitoring Project. The project, financed through UN Women and the nonsectarian World Association for Christian Communication, has been conducted every five years since 1995. In 2015, teams in 114 countries monitored more than 22,000 stories and tweets from 2,030 media sources. The results showed no improvements in the representation of women as sources or presenters overall, though there were pockets of improvements in some regions.

The bottom line is that media minimize the portrayal of women's roles in public life and continue to portray both women and men in stereotypical occupations and roles, according to the 2015 results. According to the report, "The journalistic gender lens in source selection is not only male centred, but is also skewed to a certain kind of masculinity when selecting interviewees for all types of views, from 'expert' opinion to 'ordinary' person testimonies."[20]

Here are some of the key points of women's representation in media around the globe, according to the 2015 study:

- Worldwide, women make up only 24 percent of the people heard, read about, or seen in newspaper, television, and radio news, exactly the same level found in 2010.

- Women's relative invisibility in traditional news media has crossed over into digital news delivery platforms. Only 26 percent of the people in internet news stories and media news tweets combined are women.

- There is a global glass ceiling for female news reporters in newspaper bylines and newscast reports, with 37 percent of stories reported by women, the same as in 2005.

- Women are featured as experts only 19 percent of the time in the news, virtually the same as their representation as spokespersons. Women have seen an increase to 38 percent of sources of personal experience in 2015.[21]

The portrayal of women's occupations and roles is one vital piece of the Global Media Monitoring Project data. The studies detail the way women are portrayed as sources of news, looking at their presence in news topics, their functions in the news, the occupations they are portrayed as holding, the age of individuals represented, their rendering as merely victims or survivors of events, and the descriptions of men's and women's family status in ways that are relevant to the news.

One bright spot is the leading role that women journalists are taking in selecting sources for stories. Women are 33 percent of sources in stories by online news female reporters, compared to 23 percent in stories by men.[22]

One remaining challenge in global news is elevating issues of human rights in coverage of politics and economics, according to the Global Media Monitoring project. Even when policy makers understand that poverty and political disempowerment are imbued with gender bias, issues of equality and economic and human rights were present in only 8 percent of political stories and only 7 percent off economics news.[23]

Historical Representation in Newsrooms and News Products

The Women's Media Center, founded in 2005, has been publishing comprehensive analyses of women's representation in media and women's representation as producers of news and entertainment in the United States since 2012. Year after year, women's representation in bylines and on newscasts has remained stubbornly unequal.

The 2017 report includes these stark statistics. Men continue to dominate with 62 percent of bylines in print and online (see figure 5.4). In national television in the United States, women's representation has declined significantly before 2017, to just 25 percent of reporting and producing credits on national newscasts.[24]

People of color are barely represented in U.S. newsrooms, in bylines, and on air, according to 2018 data from the Women's Media Center. While people of color make up about 40 percent of the United States population, more than 80 percent of journalists in an American Society of Newspaper Editors survey were white (see figure 5.5). White men held half of all print journalism positions, and white women held 32 percent.

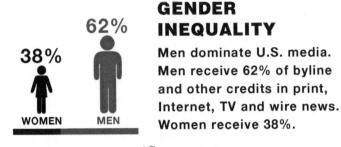

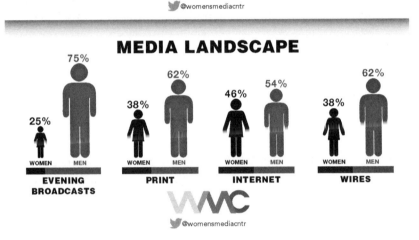

Figure 5.4
Gender inequality in the U.S. news landscape, 2017.
Source: Women's Media Center, https://womensmediacenter.com/reports/the-status
-of-women-in-u.s.-media-2017.

Visualizing the Old Newsroom Dynamic

To get a sense of the way things are changing in newsrooms, it's important to understand how newsrooms have approached their work in the past.

Like other powerful institutions throughout the world, mainstream, general-interest news organizations have always been male dominated. Mainstream news reports have reflected that fact in

Women are more than half of the U.S population and people of color nearly 40 percent.
But those who staff the nation's news organizations hardly reflect that diversity.

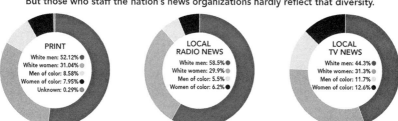

PRINT
White men: 52.12% ●
White women: 31.04% ●
Men of color: 8.58% ○
Women of color: 7.95% ●
Unknown: 0.29% ●

LOCAL RADIO NEWS
White men: 58.5% ●
White women: 29.9% ●
Men of color: 5.5% ○
Women of color: 6.2% ●

LOCAL TV NEWS
White men: 44.3% ●
White women: 31.3% ○
Men of color: 11.7% ○
Women of color: 12.6% ●

Figure 5.5

Women of color are underrepresented in U.S. news media.

Source: American Society of Newspaper Editors: Print numbers are based only on the fraction of newsrooms that responded to ASNE's survey. The chart shows white and minority percentages of overall workforce, including both newsroom leaders and all others. Radio Television Digital News Association: Percentage estimates based on random sample.

Note: There is no data for both the race and gender of online-only news staff. Unknown: The race of a very small number of employees at some organizations is listed as "unknown" because those persons desired not to provide the information.

two important ways. First, news organizations have covered powerful institutions without questioning their control by men. Second, news reports have almost always been framed by men who interpret and report public life as news.

Outside of public uprisings like the feminist wave in the 1970s and a select few women who have risen to public attention, news coverage in mainstream news organizations has reflected little attention to fundamental questions about women's empowerment.

I had a personal and professional experience with lack of newsroom interest in issues of women's empowerment—indeed, in the vital role of gender equality in economic and national development—when my family spent six months in China in 2000. In 1995, five years before I went to China, the United Nation's historic Fourth World Conference on Women was held in Beijing. When I went to China in 2000, women all over the world were reconvening in their home countries to assess the progress made in the intervening five

years, in preparation for the Five-Year Review of the Implementation of the Beijing Declaration and Platform for Action (Beijing +5)
global meeting at the United Nations in New York in June 2000.

In the spring of 2000 in a foreigner's apartment in central China,
I learned that Chinese women would convene in Beijing in May
to assess Chinese women's progress ahead of the Beijing +5 global
meeting in New York in June. These activists—including physicians,
women officials, and leaders of nongovernmental organizations—
would come from every province and county.

I applied for journalist credentials to attend the May 2000 meeting of Chinese women in Beijing. Then I pitched a story about the
political future of women in China to six newspaper editors in the
United States whom I knew well enough to address by first name.
I received one reply: an editor in Texas offered to forward the idea
to the features page. I ended up writing only for Women's eNews,
a feminist news site that debuted that year, and told the story of
Chinese women's progress and the barriers to progress to a feminist
audience.

A story about the political advancement of half a billion women
in China was either ignored or relegated to the section that talked
about lifestyle issues.

Fortunately, times are starting to change. Much of the change is
being driven by the business priorities of media companies, and the
revolution in a field known as technology product development.

The BBC's 50:50 Project is signing up its own global news services
to boost women's representation around the globe. It's also signing
on partners such as TVNZ, TV New Zealand. Sophie Baird, executive producer, says the project has changed the way two of their
news programs think about representation on their broadcasts.
"The Breakfast and Fair Go teams have changed the way they think
and work since starting the 50:50 Project. Female representation
has very much become part of the conversation when talking about

talent, stories and experts. We think this is pretty amazing given we've only been taking part since June 2019,"

Journalists in Indonesia have signed on, too. "We believe that our coverage has to reflect the reality of society," Wahyu Dhyatmika, the editor-in-chief of Tempo magazine said. "Not only in terms of the issues and values, but also in the diversity of genders that we highlight in news reports."[25]

More and more, the voice in news is female.

6

Implicit Bias in the Design of Technology

It's really difficult to overstate how gender, racial, and ethnic biases have quietly but thoroughly dominated the development of new technology products. Comments are one example. To understand how women's voices and the voices of people of color have been overlooked for years, it is vital to understand the software and technology development environments that gave birth to these new products. The oversights have profound implications for the future of democracy in technological societies.

Consider one example of unintentional but absurd bias from one of the world's most successful technology companies: the Apple Health app.

When the Apple Health app was released, Apple pronounced it a "comprehensive tracking system for human health." It allowed users to track blood pressure, steps, blood alcohol content, sleep patterns, respiratory rate, the intake of calories, fiber, fat, iodine, and magnesium, as well as other aspects of health.

There was one little oversight. "Back when it launched, the company seemed to have forgotten about the humans who have periods," Davey Alba wrote at Wired.[1]

The women's health oversight is huge and obvious—to women, at least. Any man who waited with bated breath for news about a possible pregnancy will understand, too. Unintentional bias ruled. The oversight was fixed after other period trackers had time to penetrate the market.

The menstruation oversight is a great example of how "brogrammer" culture in Silicon Valley can lead to failures in product development. It's not because all the brogrammers are antagonistic. It's because the technology sector has been dominated by a particular type of engineer, entrepreneur, and venture capitalist—white guys—and they have as many implicit biases as anyone else.

The combination of a lack of diversity and the product development frameworks used throughout the technology sector has had damaging implications for many technology companies. That is because the start-small business methods tend to reinforce the assumptions of a lopsided workforce to the point that a company as big and smart as Apple can release a "comprehensive" health program that ignores women of reproductive age. Such women, after all, are a big part of their target market.

A small number of gender-analysis evangelists have been working on the issues for a few years. In addition, a growing coalition of engineers, data technologists, and designers is driving a new conversation about inclusive design principles.

To understand the cost to Apple, consider that reproductive health, contraception, and periods are top concerns among sexually active young women. Menstrual history is important for health-care providers, too. "Menstrual history is definitely a key health measure for women," Lynn Marie Westphal, an associate professor in obstetrics and gynecology at Stanford University Medical Center, told San Jose's *Mercury News*: "A lot of diseases will manifest as abnormalities of menstrual cycles."[2]

Apple's oversight wasn't absurd just because it overlooked women's health. It was commercially absurd because the company essentially assumed a man as the model of its consumers. It failed to consider half of its potential market, even though other products like the iPhone had been designed as unisex tools with all types of users in mind. (In fact, several generations of iPhones were biased against left-handed people because displays and controls were out of reach for lefties.[3] Unexamined assumptions can be costly in all different directions.)

The financial implications for Apple were equally mind-boggling. Such health and fitness apps are among the most popular among women and teens especially.[4] Women's global earning power at the time was valued at $18 trillion, according to the global capital investment and consulting firm Frost & Sullivan.[5] Even though Apple updated the Health app to include a period tracker, numerous other period trackers emerged. By 2019, websites for women's magazines like *Marie Claire* and *Fitness* were rating period trackers like "Spot On" and "Aunt Flo." The Apple Health app is conspicuous by its absence from these lists.

Technology Startup Culture, Product Development, and "Lean" Business Practices

The story of Apple's Health app illustrates some of the fundamental barriers to realizing gender, racial, and ethnic equality in any technology offering. It shows some of the ways that silent but profound biases unintentionally manifest themselves in technology products. The Health app also shows how business methods in common use can result in unintended self-sabotage for technology companies, whose focus is on building and selling products.

Sometimes, the start-small technology ethos has catastrophic consequences for democracy and for women's safety. In the case of social media, technologies can even facilitate genocide by helping connect extremist groups worldwide. The implications are much bigger than whether a technology product has a wide market.

Catherine Buni and Soraya Chemaly write that these unintended consequences of bias are risks that technology companies must be held accountable for:

A daily flood of stories about security breaches,[6] surveillance risks,[7] weaponized data,[8] voter manipulation,[9] disinformation,[10] algorithmic biases,[11] conspiracy theories,[12] hate,[13] and harassment[14] attests to the infinite volume and variety of possible failures. The internet of things, already enmeshed in our day-to-day lives, is rife with profound security risks.[15] From glitchy voting-related apps[16] hastily designed and released, to concerns about dangerous[17] vaping pods, self-driving cars,[18] exploding smartphones, and supposedly revolutionary blood tests,[19] companies routinely release untested, unverified, unregulated, and, sometimes, fraudulent products.[20]

A growing movement for inclusive design and "design justice" is working to resolve some of the problems with gender and race bias and the many ways those systems of social power can reverberate through a technological society.

A lot is at stake when a company or an industry develop products like comments sections that functionally exclude many of the people that designers might have hoped to serve and engage. The designer Kat Holmes set out to articulate how to remedy such problems by using inclusive product design in her 2018 book, *Mismatch: How Inclusion Shapes Design*:

> What happens when a design object rejects us? A door that won't open. A transit system that won't service our neighborhood. A computer mouse that doesn't work for people who are left handed. A touch-screen payment system at a grocery store that only works for people who read English phrases, have 20/20 vision, and use a credit card.
>
> When we're excluded by these designs, how does it shape our sense of belonging in the world? This question led me from playgrounds to computer systems, from Detroit public housing to virtual gaming worlds.
>
> Ask a hundred people what inclusion means and you'll get a hundred different answers. Ask them what it means to be excluded and the answer will be uniformly clear: It's when you're left out.[21]

Part of the reason that the technology sector so often develops exclusive technological products is because it is steeped in a start-small-and-work-up culture that historically has given implicit bias free rein in product design. These methods are great for building new technologies fast. They are good to get started, for example, by adapting old newsprint companies and turning them into technology companies. But the start small and move fast approach is also a central cause of comment sections having been designed with men's communication values in mind. People are excluded, not on purpose but because these methods did not account for a variety of users.

Fortunately, businesses are beginning to realize they promote business success when they use gender and race to inform their product development. Building diverse workforces that reflect a variety of life experiences is a key part of excellent product development practices.

Many of the biggest barriers to gender-informed and racial-diversity-informed thinking in the technology field are obvious (see figures 6.1, 6.2, and 6.3). First, the field is hugely dominated by white men—the "brogrammers." That male-centric atmosphere reflects layers of bias such as inequality throughout educational systems worldwide and finance decisions about who receives startup funding, for example. Consider these numbers provided by leading technology companies. Among employees in technological work, women are outnumbered by men three to one or four to one. The numbers roughly match the continued male domination in computer science and engineering departments in U.S. colleges and universities. The higher representation of women at Pinterest, for example, reflects that platform's popularity as a destination among women users.[22]

Second, prevailing business management methods in software and technology development are based on models that prize small goals that focus on releasing what is known as a minimum viable product (MVP), often without nuance about users.

Third, software developers and technology designers have as many unconscious biases as anyone else. Those biases frequently result in discriminatory outcomes for potential users. Worse, existing

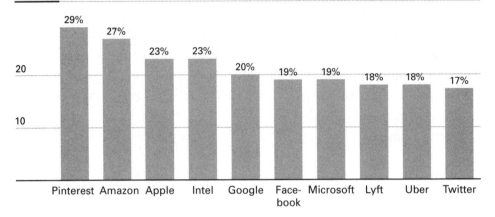

Figure 6.1
Global representation of women in tech positions in ten major companies.
Source: Sara Harrison, "Five Years of Tech Diversity Reports—and Little Progress," *Wired*,
October 16, 2019, https://www.wired.com/story/five-years-tech-diversity-reports-little
-progress.

research about known barriers to women's inclusion in technology
designs is routinely ignored. One of the barriers to women's entry
into technology fields and to successful product development is the
male-dominated atmosphere itself. For example, a study of barriers
to open-source software communities showed that 71 percent of the
tools and infrastructure available were gender biased, and the vast
majority of those biases were known issues.[23] In other words, the
solutions were available, but the communities did not care enough
to use them.

When Workers Lack Diversity and Start with an MVP Mindset, They Miss Big Things

For a clear illustration of how these characteristics of the technology industry collide with business success, consider the Snapchat

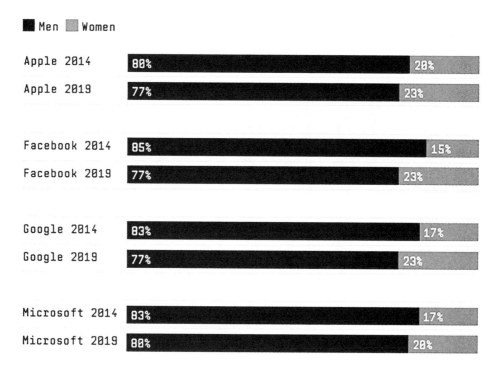

■ Men ▨ Women

Apple 2014	80%	20%
Apple 2019	77%	23%
Facebook 2014	85%	15%
Facebook 2019	77%	23%
Google 2014	83%	17%
Google 2019	77%	23%
Microsoft 2014	83%	17%
Microsoft 2019	80%	20%

Figure 6.2
The share of women in tech jobs has grown, 2014.
Source: Sara Harrison, "Five Years of Tech Diversity Reports—and Little Progress," *Wired*, October 16, 2019, https://www.wired.com/story/five-years-tech-diversity-reports-little -progress.

experience of technology consultant and entrepreneur Y-Vonne Hutchinson.

"My boyfriend convinced me to use Snapchat," Hutchinson wrote in the *MIT Technology Review*. "He was taking goofy pictures and wanted me to join him. When I tried, the app would map my face, and—nothing. We changed positions. We tried improving the lighting. Nothing worked. I started to get that familiar sinking feeling in my stomach, the flush of heat to my face. Growing up in Texas, I received many negative messages about my dark skin. Now here I was, 20 years later, too black for Snapchat."[24]

Overall representation

Women

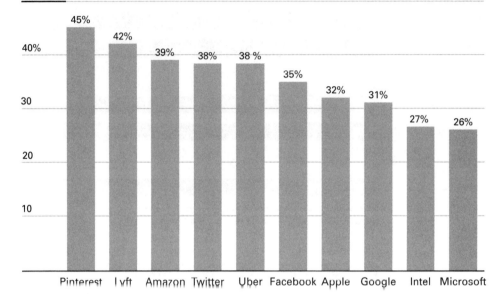

Figure 6.3
Overall representation in tech jobs.
Source: Rani Molla, "How Facebook Compares to Other Tech Companies in Diversity: It's Just as Diverse—or Not—as Other Tech Companies," Recode, April 11, 2018, https://www.vox.com/2018/4/11/17225574/facebook-tech-diversity-women.

Now movements in Silicon Valley and in Europe are working to embed gender and racial diversity analysis at the conception of new products. If Apple had considered gender before it released its Health app and called it "comprehensive," the company might have boosted early acceptance of the product and made a lot of their male users happy as well. Men have a stake in contraception, pregnancy, and the health of women in their lives, after all.

A growing coalition of scholars, government agencies, and businesses in the United States and Europe is driving change. These

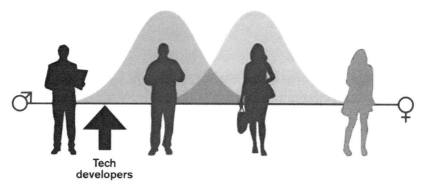

Figure 6.4
Behavioral differences in relation to technology.
Source: design-people, "We Are Product & Experience Designers," https://www.design
-people.com.

people are working to uncover the roots of bias in all aspects of
the technology industry. To succeed among women, the goal is to
embed gender analysis into existing business methods.

The design-people studio and consultancy in Denmark offers
an important illustration of men and women users as overlapping
bell curves of motivations and expectations in their approaches
to technology (see figure 6.4). The company has been at the heart
of European research into gender-informed product development. The female interaction strategy summarizes the research
on technology developers to illustrate that the engineers thinking up new products fall on the heavily "male" end of the user
spectrum—people naturally thinking systematically about a product's features.

In the engineering world, products have traditionally emerged
from engineers who are focused on the features of a technology and
then created products based on those features. With that illustration, it's easy to see why many technology products have fallen flat
with a lot of users.

Business Methods in Product Development

A few widely accepted management principles that became popular during the technology boom in the early 2000s have come to dominate product development in software and technology design. They emphasize quick, short cycles of software and product creation and release. This "do something small and release it" culture is naturally in tension with the idea that product developers first should take a wide view of users to maximize product acceptance. In this culture, start small and make some progress is an ethos.

A new wave of reformers is offering new frameworks for collaborative design. These will mostly be addressed in the next chapter on methods. For the purpose of this chapter, I am simply introducing the methodologies that have gotten much of the technology sector to the place it is today.

While many product development workplace models exist, four of the most influential provide a quick view of how engineers and product developers approach their work. All emphasize a continuous process of development, reassessment, and testing to keep businesses in line with consumers and financial rewards:

- Agile software development,
- Design thinking,
- Lean startup business principles, and
- The business model canvas.

Agile Software Development

Among the most influential concepts in technology product development is a workplace organization framework known as the Agile software development method, published online in 2001 as the "Manifesto for Agile Software Development."

Agile and its principles—developed by seventeen men, as it happens—are influential in software circles, including career-enhancing professional certifications, and are used throughout the world. The principles prioritize creating a starter product and then "iterating" or continually providing updates in subsequent versions. The release of a minimum viable product (MVP) is embraced as a necessary beginning, with updates an expected part of the process.

If you ever see the technologists in your workplace gathering in a circle, standing up, you're witnessing a "scrum," a project management method used by Agile teams. Standing meetings are used to emphasize brevity, activity, and a culture of teamwork. The emphasis in Agile is providing a business-focused methodology that avoids wasting staff time and financial resources on ideas or products bound for failure. The idea is continuous improvement and managing the creation of value for the company.

This culture of "iterating" is what Apple did with its Health app within a year of the product's first release. Indeed, the flurry of media coverage about menstrual health was, in a way, a huge affirming message for Apple: women consumers expected Apple to take them seriously and saw the Apple Health app as a failure. To a product manager, that's a sign of huge market demand.

As the tech boom took hold in the Silicon Valley in the early years of the twenty-first century, many Agile principles were popularized in business schools and in startup culture and eventually became embedded in established institutions such as news organizations. Adoption accelerated in news after the financial crash in 2008, as publishers faced the imperatives of their futures as technology companies.

A few years after the Agile manifesto was published, Silicon Valley also became increasingly influenced by a systems way of thinking from the Hasso Plattner Institute of Design at Stanford University.

Design Thinking

Design thinking is a methodology for creativity in institutions, problem-solving, and product development—among many other specific applications. It has been embraced in the technology field as a way of thinking about innovation. The idea is to challenge people, institutions, and businesses to think holistically about problems in an empathic way and to continually revisit users, technologists, and products in a process of continuous innovation.

The five stages of design thinking process are shown in figure 6.5, an illustration from the Interaction Design Foundation.

Design thinking is now widely taught in business schools as a foundation of innovation management. Although it is not a business method, design thinking's model of continuous change, continuous evaluation and reevaluation, and the continual release of prototypes and new products has become central to thinking about technology product design. It provides a cultural foundation to all technology-driven businesses, especially since methods specific to technology are based on the process of continuous innovation.

Some critics of corporate and institutional design thinkers have launched a challenge to these concepts in the design justice movement. These designers challenge product and institutional leaders to center those people who are too often marginalized by design. Sasha Costanza-Chock has articulated new processes in *Design*

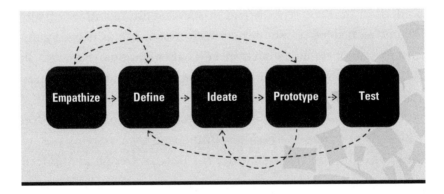

Figure 6.5
Design thinking: A five-stage process.
Source: Rikke Friis Dam and Teo Yu Siang, "5 Stages in the Design Thinking Process," Interaction Design Foundation, July 13, 2019, https://www.interaction-design.org /literature/article/5-stages-in-the-design-thinking-process.

Justice: Community-Led Practices to Build the Worlds We Need.[25] A network of organizers has posted principles in the Design Justice Network.[26]

Design thinking emphasizes having empathy with consumers and users, clarifying a problem with human interaction, creating prototypes, and testing how they work in the real world. Design justice proponents push for a complete rethinking about how societies are built, how decisions are made, and whose perspectives shape an environment entirely. Readers who know something about user experience will recognize the process of creative iteration that defines success with consumers in an online environment.

The principles of design thinking demand that creators have empathy for a broad variety of users from the outset and that each idea is tested to make sure it actually performs as intended. The design justice movement's criticism is that design thinking focuses too much on creators' projections and not enough on community priorities. In terms of women's voices in public forums, the question is whose voices are designed to be heard?

Lean Startup

The lean startup method for businesses emerged in 2009, just as the world experienced a historic stock market crash that wiped out many young technology businesses. In 2011, Eric Ries published a book detailing the method, *The Lean Startup: How Today's Entrepreneurs Use Continuous Innovation to Create Radically Successful Businesses.*[27] It became a *New York Times* bestseller and a leading business textbook and guide for corporate and startup culture. At its heart, it takes the Agile philosophy and frames it in a business context. The continuous innovation process at the heart of design thinking is also embedded in Ries's method.

The "lean" concept is to bring a product to market or a test market in a bare-bones form to test its validity. The alternative is spending too much on an unworkable idea, Ries explains:[28]

Too many startups begin with an idea for a product that they think people want. They then spend months, sometimes years, perfecting that product without ever showing the product, even in a very rudimentary form, to the prospective customer. When they fail to reach broad uptake from customers, it is often because they never spoke to prospective customers and determined whether or not the product was interesting. When customers ultimately communicate, through their indifference, that they don't care about the idea, the startup fails.[29]

Since the lean concept unfolded in the early 2000s, it has been adapted for startups and legacy institutions like news organizations as well. It is widely accepted as a framework for how to introduce new products—releasing them a little at a time and then improving them with updates over time.

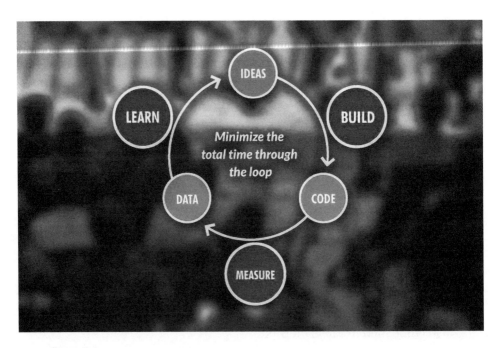

Figure 6.6
The lean startup.
Source: Eric Ries, "The Lean Startup Methodology," TheLeanStartup.com.

The lean startup process is illustrated as a process of continuous innovation. Start with an idea, build a minimum viable product, test the product, measure its successes and opportunities for improvement with quantifiable metrics, learn about how to make it better, and release new and better products that build on early successes.

The Business Model Canvas

The business model canvas[30] is another popular tool for entrepreneurs and technologists (see figure 6.7). It begins as a one-page planning document. Developed by Swiss entrepreneur Alex Osterwalder, it has become a standard reference in the technology field. Osterwalder is coauthor with Yves Pigneur of the book *Business Model Generation: A Handbook for Visionaries, Game-Changers, and Challengers*.[31] He lectures widely and often speaks at conferences of engineers and entrepreneurs.

The business model canvas for a project outlines key partners, activities, resources, value propositions, customer relationships, delivery channels, customer segments, cost structure, and revenue streams. In a one-page document, the canvas gives a striking overview of how these vital aspects of business success relate to each other. No business plan is complete without a lot more development, but if one of these categories fails, it spells the collapse of a business—even with a brilliant product.

To understand how the business model canvas works, it's useful to consider a popular case study in business and engineering schools. In a talk to engineering students at Stanford, Osterwalder explained how Nestlé's popular Nespresso coffee makers failed their early market tests, even though consumers loved them. Product testers liked the coffee makers, he said, but the sales force didn't want to sell small machines to businesses, which were the original target market. There's much less profit on the sale of an inexpensive system than an elaborate one, so the original sales strategy failed. The

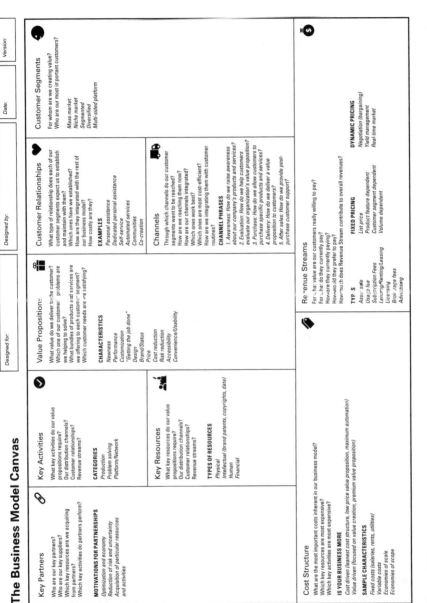

Figure 6.7

The business model canvas.

Source: Strategyzer, available at https://commons.wikimedia.org/wiki/File:Business_Model_Canvas.png.

technology-consumer relationship was successful at the end-user level, but the company couldn't get the product to its office-based market.

Ultimately, Nestlé pivoted its Nespresso coffee-making product strategy to an internet-based market, with continuous subscriptions for coffee pods as the primary source of continuing revenue. The technology stayed the same, but its path to being a market success was completely different than what had been envisioned by its creators.

When "Lean" Principles Collide with Bias

When these start-small principles of technology development are operating in a workplace that is not diverse, the principles collide with unconscious biases and skew product development. The results can be discriminatory for users and function as a form of business self-sabotage.

Product developers and designers who fail to anticipate biases routinely offer technologies and services that amplify, perpetuate, or solidify biases in disturbing ways.

Ideally, an iterative process would provide opportunities to reconceive minimum viable products as widely viable products. Unfortunately, that often has not been the case.

The dearth of women's voices in news comments sections is one example that results in a disturbingly lopsided picture of public voices. However, comments are just one representative point in a much wider picture.

Often, as in news comments, a product design that may be gender- or race-neutral on its face is nevertheless problematic in the real world. On the other hand, putting a product onto a platform like news sites opens the floodgates that concentrate and amplify the biases, exclusions, and power systems in society.

Some well-known examples of the discriminatory effect of open platforms is the cyberharassment and cybermisogyny inherent on Twitter and in chat communities on websites like Reddit and 8kun (called 8chan until November 2019). (For a fuller discussion, see chapter 4 on hate on the internet.)

To their creators, those platforms were created simply as places to communicate, with features that supported the development of like-minded communities. Yet all serve to amplify invidious stereotypes and discrimination. Facebook ended up being used as a tool of genocide against Rohingya Muslims in Myanmar in 2018, as the company acknowledged months after thousands of people were killed.[32] Certain features of these platforms—the aggregation of like-minded people on internet platforms, using algorithms that help like-minded people find each other, and the frictionless way that hate can be redeployed toward particular targets—are baked into their design. A decade into the social media society, platforms like Twitter and Reddit are still in the early phases of addressing the hate speech and hate campaigns they have fostered.

Advocates for targeted communities have long identified these problems as features, not bugs, of internet technologies. The collision of monocultural product design cultures with social bias is inevitable, they say.

If any proof were needed about the way Twitter has developed as a conduit for hate speech, consider the artificial intelligence tool that Microsoft designed to learn about conversations. Though the tool was never intended to behave offensively, the bot learned to tweet like a neo-Nazi within twenty-four hours.[33]

Another well-known example of a platform that enabled and amplified racial and gender-based discrimination is Airbnb, the successful home-sharing business. The company offered its service on an open platform without planning for the kind of bias and hostility that people of color and transgender, gay, and lesbian people experience every day. The company didn't plan for the risk of sexual assault that hosts and guests might experience when they let a stranger into their homes or when they went into a stranger's home for the night. Women understood that booking a stay in someone's home would pose a risk. Black consumers understood that some white Airbnb hosts would not want them in their homes. LGBTQ consumers knew the kind of reception they would get with white evangelical Christians and other conservative religious homeowners. Airbnb, however, did not account for the obvious problems that would arise.

Airbnb is also a textbook case of the business consequences of having work forces that are lacking in diversity and developers who often haven't experienced the kinds of biases that users will inevitably experience. It resulted in hurtful discrimination against users, civil rights lawsuits against the company, and an international public relations failure that is likely to be treated as a case study for years to come. As a 2016 *New York Times* headline put it: "As Airbnb Grows, So Do Claims of Discrimination."[34]

Airbnb became the subject of the hashtag movement #AirbnbWhileBlack after treating several individual instances of discrimination as if problems were simply the result of a few nefarious individuals. Consumers had been telling the company they were experiencing blatant racial, religious, and homophobic bias, according to news coverage in 2016, but the company did not address persistent bias as a systemic issue.

By the time the social media campaign reached its nadir, a Harvard Business School study had confirmed that black users were 16 percent less likely to find accommodation than white users.[35] Only when the issue flooded onto the public stage did the company hire former U.S. Attorney General Eric Holder to help it address discrimination in a comprehensive way.[36]

The company's response reflected an insular perspective on corporate responsibility. A travel industry analyst described the discrimination problem as not inherent in the product. "Airbnb wasn't the one who discriminated; it was the homeowner who exhibited ugly behavior," said Henry H. Harteveldt, the founder of Atmosphere Research Group. "It does show Airbnb didn't think to include a stated policy or training about nondiscrimination."

The result was not inevitable, however. The company might have considered the risks. In fact, it's basic business practice to conduct a "SWOT analysis" of a potential product to assess a product's strengths, weaknesses, opportunities, and threats.

Some experts on technology and bias talk about bias as implicit parts of technology products. Y-Vonne Hutchinson describes the problem in a more holistic way. The idea is to have product developers anticipate biases and prevent them from being baked into a product or service in the first place. "Biases can become embedded in a product during any period of the development process," Hutchison wrote. "If the people making the products happen to come from a group that rarely experiences discrimination, those people will have a harder time predicting how bias will manifest itself."[37]

As technology work forces remain notoriously dominated by white men, industry will need to make systemic changes. Part of the solution is to fix the monocultural work forces and boards of directors leading their businesses. The other is to incorporate gender, race, and ethnic analysis into their product design processes.

Tools for designing products empathically, as the design thinking model already theoretically incorporates, can perform better by incorporating more diverse workforces and truly collaborative design processes. Iterative processes like that foreseen in the lean startup model can also use wider lenses to support wider product acceptance.

Fortunately, tools for gender, race, and ethnic analysis are emerging.

7
Tools to Fight Bias in Technology

The fundamental idea for creating gender-informed and race-informed technology products such as online comments forums comes down to two simple rules.

First, include gender, race, and intersectional analysis at the beginning of product development because men, women, and white and racial minorities comprise very different sets of user experiences. If gender is not considered at the beginning of designing a minimum viable product, then it needs to be systematically considered throughout the iterative product development frameworks that are now standard in the technology industry.

Second, use diverse, gender-informed, multifaceted user templates to create innovation, promote product acceptance, and broaden the base of consumers.

These two steps sound simple. The problem is that gender and race biases are so deeply woven into our concepts of ourselves in the world that overcoming the bias requires a profound paradigm shift.

An outline for an ideal paradigm change has taken shape at Stanford University's Gendered Innovations program, the German Ministry of Research, and some European think tanks and industry groups. Stanford has emerged as a global clearinghouse for gender-informed innovators after promoting gender-informed scientific and medical research for years.

As the work outlined in this chapter shows, the vocabularies of scholars and designers vary when they describe the varying user experience facets and the preferences of men and women users. For general purposes, it's clearest to understand that gender categories exist as two overlapping bell curves. Outdated gender binary definitions are no longer scientifically accepted, and yet the terms remain in use.[1]

Some of the most exciting early work in active business cases for gender-informed user experience profiles and product development was from a design firm in Denmark, design-people.[2] Klaus Schroeder, the company's chief executive officer and strategic innovation director, has worked closely with business leaders and European grant agencies to promote gender-informed product development strategies that are good for business.

The insights are both simple and profound. "We think women's needs are different from men's," Schroeder said at a conference at Microsoft headquarters. "We think we can use this difference to make better user experiences for all users."[3]

Schroeder's remarks about women, men, and user experience encompass all of product design, just as biases shape untold parts of our lives. They include all kinds of hands-on products, from cell phone headsets to home heating and cooling systems, as well as media platforms like MSN.

Because the biases that influence technology are legion throughout society, it's vital to understand the ways that gender bias has hidden implicit meanings throughout everyday life. Only by understanding the insidiousness of bias can a window open that will display how to create new experiences.

Gender biases are so universal that they distort many market choices, with life and death consequences for consumers, as Londa Schiebinger of Stanford University's Gendered Innovations program outlines in encyclopedic detail.

Gender bias . . . leads to missed market opportunities. In engineering, for example, considering short people (many women, but also many men) "out-of-position" drivers leads to greater injury in automobile accidents.[4] In basic research, failing to use appropriate samples of male and female cells, tissues, and animals yields faulty results, such as in stem cell transplants.[5] In medicine, not recognizing osteoporosis as a male disease[6] delays diagnosis and treatment in men. In city planning, not collecting data on caregiving work leads to inefficient transportation systems.[7]

These biases also hurt companies' performance and lead to costly and embarrassing business failures, such as the ones at Apple and Airbnb that were described in the previous chapter. They result in deep distrust like the distrust of mainstream news organizations by Black and Hispanic consumers. For news organizations, it means that women are less likely to comment on news articles and thus spend less time on-site. People involved in comment sections are also among the most loyal news consumers, so it's beneficial to engage people in this way.

The point in the context of boosting women's representation in civic discussions is that gender bias is simply a feature of designs of all kinds of products, experiences, and services. Biases are so embedded in the way we actually see the world around us that they shape everything in ways that are unintentional but still grievously wrong.

Without a more complex perspective, designers and technologists end up with what Caroline Criado Perez calls "One Size Fits Men."[8]

News, Implicit Bias, and the Emergence of Online Conversations

Given the pervasive impact of implicit bias in product design, it would be wrong to point to news comments as a particularly egregious example. Bias is there, but this bias reflects the state of the technology field in which news businesses operate, as chapter 6 on implicit bias illustrates. The next step is engaging potential users in designing a new vision, identifying opportunities, biases, and short-comings, adjusting development methods to be truly inclusive, and preventing future biased results.

In news, gender historically has been underappreciated or actively ignored as a matter of business practice, as illustrated in earlier chapters. Most often, the implicit biases of mostly male editors have ruled the design of products.

When print news organizations began making a transition to the digital sphere, editors and software developers naturally looked for ways to distribute news stories, photographs, and features on the growing network known as the World Wide Web. At the time, in the 1980s and 1990s, there was growing interest in digital content known initially as the Weblog (blog)—freewheeling posts and streams of information and writing shared by small audiences of fans. Though younger readers will not remember the internet before beautiful, HTML based web pages, the early web was a patchwork of text features that followed a vertical, one-way kind of logic.

In those spaces and in the online chat rooms for computer enthusiasts and interest groups, people engaged in conversations in a linear series of exchanges. First one, then another, then another, in a bare-bones progression that in essence moved out like the end of a straight line.

News editors naturally adapted to the form. They posted news stories and created branded blogs with featured journalists, with a comments section at the end of an article.

The design did follow an obvious logic. First, people read a news story, and when they reached the end of it, they could post their thoughts. If readers wanted to exchange ideas, they could address each other in a natural linear flow.

Voilà! Or maybe not so much. The conversation worked for some people, who turned out to be mostly men. It was an excellent first step in creating interactive conversational spaces.

The problem with the approach for news comments is that it was largely a failure among women, and no one really tried to figure that out until about 2015, as research in the United States and Australia began to show these patterns. Because profile photos of commenters are unusual on news sites, race was invisible. As the news industry is beginning to understand, the linear blog comment formula was actually based on some deeply gender-biased assumptions, however unintentional the bias may have been.

Designing technology offerings such as article comments based on the assumption that people are motivated to freely share their views has fundamental gender and race bias baked into the software and graphic design. In that way, the news business is like any other legacy business.

On the other hand, social networks like Facebook that women have embraced were originally designed so that college students like Mark Zuckerberg could connect with buddies and cruise for dates. Focusing on social connections turned out to be useful for young men in college but also strikes the heart of women's communication values.

One good illustration of the contrast between a product designed by a technologist and the same product redesigned by someone attuned to women's preferences for social and real-life use of a product is the programmable thermostat.

If you think like an electrical engineer, you may have loved the original programmable thermostat. But you would still need to study the instruction manual and have it in hand while you programmed the thermostat. This is how technologists thrive—with logical steps focused on the commands you need to give the machine to make the heat come on at the time you wake up and to cool things off when you ordinarily go to bed.

Technologists might even enjoy the puzzle-solving challenge of working through the technical steps. Everyone else, not so much.

If you have technology preferences like average homeowners, your product needs are more like the kinds of command you might give Alexa or Google Nest: "Hey Google, turn down the heat to 62 at 9 p.m." "Hey Google, set the heat to 68 at 6 a.m." "Hey Google, set the thermostat to that schedule on weekdays."

In the news comments space, listening to women's concerns might have identified and helped eliminate an obvious problem far earlier. A study conducted at the Reynolds Journalism Institute at the University of Missouri reflected some of the ways that social media work better for young women when it comes to talking about issues in the news. Young women were asked survey questions about whether they ever comment on news articles. One said, "I think overall commenting is great among people you can trust, but among the general public commenting is horrible to the point of scary."[10] Another respondent said the open, anything-goes culture of news comments is off-putting, but smaller groups are more acceptable. "I don't mind commenting on Facebook where only my friends will see something," she said.[11]

Women are telling news sites that they have a problem they need to fix. So, too, with people of color. "Specifically, Black women were not as interested in such a hostile space," said Meredith Clark, the University of Virginia professor who surveyed marginalized audiences for the Coral Project. "It's part and parcel of the silencing of women of color that this country has made quotidian."[12]

These themes echo many of the data that have come back about news commenting, generally.

The solution lies in embedding the process-oriented values of gender and communication outlined in chapter 3. Already, some forms of media that have a high level of engagement from women illustrate what works. Facebook, for example, allows users to limit who sees their posts, encourages crosstalk by allowing users to tag each other's names when permitted by the other user, and allows users to delete, mute, or reply to anyone who violates their own standards. These themes arose in the women surveyed at the

Reynolds Journalism Institute and in the University of Texas's Center for Media Engagement study of news commenting.

Using social media is a workable approach for people who can construct their own circles of conversation. But these small circles do not normally represent a community forum. And that is where the particular civic role of local journalism comes in.

Making connections between future users and the designers of technology products is the new frontier for people who care about the social justice implications of technology. Making connections is also a new frontier for businesses that want broader consumer bases.

For people who care about realizing women's potential in technology fields and in public life, uncovering biases, and using tools to prevent their harmful effects, it's a revelation.

Now a growing set of tools is emerging to make it happen.

Tools for Gender-Informed Product Design

A number of tools are available for fighting bias in products like the comments sections on news sites. The GenderMag (Gender Magnifier) software analysis tool tests software for hidden biases, and the Gendered Innovations Project's "Engineering Checklist" from Stanford University asks key questions for incorporating sex and gender analyses into engineering. Danish research offers some insights on gender and product design that can guide any new product development.

In addition to these two product testing and development tools, the European Union's RRI Tools project promotes responsible research and innovation (RRI) in all of science, technology, policy, and industry, from designing curricula for schools and universities to legislators and corporate boards. The RRI Tools project includes Stanford's Gender in Design Toolkit and is required reading for anyone interested in systemic change.[13] Many of its principles are reflected in the design justice movement, which seeks inclusive community consultation in building institutions. The RRI principles are embodied in the other toolkits discussed here.

The basic idea behind these three sets of tools is simple: technologies designed with a broad base of end users in mind are more successful and beneficial than any brilliant technology designed by assuming that people are all the same. Heart stents are ingenious; designing heart stents as one-size-fits-all are less so. Likewise, programmable thermostats are ingenious; expecting consumers to think like a computer programmer in order to make them work is less so.

A key insight to these tools is that they are based on a model of considering user experience first. In fact, user experience (UX) is a specialty in the technology field. But gender is not always used to companies' best advantage, and UX personas are not always grounded in evidence-based data.

The idea is to move engineers from a default focus on technology features to a new approach to creating technology with users in mind first.

Technology Design Is Gender Sensitive

European research into the design of technology rests on two key insights—first, that men and women have different motivations and interactive relationships with technology products[14] and second, that product designers have traditionally worked based on their own cognitive styles, which turn out to work not very well for everyone else. That's where problems develop when engineers begin with minimum viable product strategies.

These two ideas turn up across the literature about gender, technology development, and human-computer interaction strategies.

The results suggest that businesses and organizations that want to reach a maximum market need to adopt a paradigm shift toward designing products for multiple user groups. For complex reasons, that has not often been the case.

As recently as 2004, the Consumer Electronics Association found that only one percent of women believed that electronics manufacturers had them in mind when developing products. To put that in context, 2004 was the same year that nineteen-year-old Mark Zuckerberg and his friends created TheFacebook.com as a social network for students.

Gender Magnifier

Computer scientist Margaret Burnett of Oregon State University has developed a software review and user-experience persona creation method called GenderMag (for Gender Magnifier) to eliminate bias in software development and deployment. It's an open-source software kit available for free.[15]

As a specialist in human-computer interaction (HCI), Burnett came to understand that a lot of software was failing its intended users because of the way developers looked at their goals. Software engineers were essentially writing software that performed the desired tasks, but the tools were working well only for people who looked at technology the same way they did.

Burnett realized that users have various styles of thinking and processing information and that those differences influence the way that users perceive a computer interface—the human-computer interaction. She and her colleagues combed the research across disciplines to find evidence for building meaningful user-experience personas that could be used to test software designs. Those information processing styles are clustered by gender, even though they cross genders and cultures.

Burnett travels widely to explain and spread the word about the gendered aspects of computing through a fellowship with the Association of Computing Machinery. At a computer science conference, she displayed a presentation slide on "risk aversion" as a facet of software users and explained that different personas respond differently, depending on the way they process information and interact with computers: "Imagine if there were software that was built in such a way that it was really only supportive of people to the left of that black line. It turns out there *is* a lot of software like that, because it turns out a lot of the people who are building a lot of software historically have had a lot of facets in common with this persona."[16]

Burnett's colleague Anita Sarma described the way that gender influences the way users interact with products: "Certain problem-solving styles are more favored by men than by women (and vice versa). Software tools often support the tool developers' preferred style of problem-solving. When those tools are developed by male-dominated teams, they can inadvertently create gender bias."[17]

The GenderMag review process identifies five key problem-solving facets that users display when they engage with software products. The problem-solving facets are not explicitly about gender. In fact, men and women are present across the styles. However, women and men do tend to cluster on different ends of the problem-solving spectrum, much like the Danish examples.

Burnett and her colleagues found that the user's approach to software-based problem solving depends on the user's

1. motivations for using the software,
2. style of processing information (does the user do comprehensive research first or dive in?),
3. sense of computer self-efficacy,
4. attitudes toward technological risks (is the user worried about breaking something?), and

5. preferred styles for learning technology (does the user follow directions carefully or just do it?).[18]

From research into these nongendered user facets, Burnett developed three user personas in the user-experience model. Their names are Tim, Abi, and Pat. These personas are then used to test a software interface.

Looking at the user experiences according to a user's aversion to risk-taking with learning and using software, the Tim, Pat, and Abi personas fall along a continuum from being comfortable with risk to being averse to risk (see figure 7.1). That is, are they willing to click here or there and tinker with parts of an interactive process to see if it will work in the way they expected?

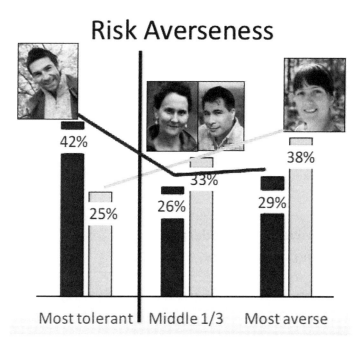

Figure 7.1

Source: Margaret Burnett et al., "Finding Gender-Inclusiveness Software Issues with GenderMag: A Field Investigation," 2016.

So in the risk-aversion facet, 42 percent of male users will present like Tim, but another 55 percent of men will present like Pat and Abi. For women, about 25 percent of women are very tolerant of risk in problem-solving: "That means that about 75 percent of the females are not being very well supported on the risk spectrum, and at least half of the males, on this facet. Anything that we do to support the people who have these facet values help everybody, but it also levels the playing field on gender inclusiveness."[19]

Even software developers who are skeptical about appeals to gender equality can easily see that their software is going to fail with more than half of the men using it. As all of the bias-prevention tools show, screening for gender bias in Burnett's example is clearly a benefit to all kinds of users. Without that kind of testing, only software developers and users like them will naturally adapt to many designs.

Fortunately, testing software and other digital products for gender bias is also a terrific way to ensure that they are acceptable among the widest possible audiences.

An interesting side effect of using the GenderMag personas, Burnett says, is that they inspire a greater diversity of views in work groups. "Some people found Abi very empowering," Burnett said. "Women felt they could advocate their own values and had the framework to support their views."[20]

Stanford University's Gendered Innovations "Engineering Checklist"

For more than a decade, scholars have been exploring the many influences of biological sex and cultural aspects of gender in technology design. Researchers in Germany, working with funding from the German Ministry for Research, outlined the ways that diverse workforces can support innovation and broaden the base of knowledge that is captured in the early stages of product development

The Gendered Innovations "Engineering Checklist" is available on Stanford's Gendered Innovations website, which is periodically updated as more research emerges.[21] The following questions about any given product have been selected from the checklist's twenty-five items:

1. Do potential consumers have different characteristics by gender, age, profession, or income?

2. What role do sex and gender play with regard to the developing technology?

3. What are the potential areas for using the technology that might be influenced by whether the user is a man, a woman, or nonbinary?

4. Might different groups of users have different expectations for the user interface, features and functions, or exterior design? Do some features (for example, willingness to speak to strangers) reinforce gender inequality?

5. Would it be more cost-effective to engineer for gender differences before or after the initial product comes out?

6. Would some designs reinforce existing social roles like gender-segregated work forces? For example, does software in healthcare settings have greater adoption by men or women?

7. Are test groups diverse by age, sex, gender identity, and physical characteristics like height?

8. Do your internal and external teams include the needed gender expertise? Could you expand your business opportunities if they did?

9. Is there anything about gender that you might need to know that you don't know now? Does your team understand how to incorporate gender expertise and innovation into existing design engineering and quality methods?

10. Are there anatomical differences (voice pitch for voice-activated technology, for example)?[22]

The Gendered Innovations program has outlined four common problems to avoid in designing products:[23]

Four Warnings about Gender

1. Critically examine your assumptions about women as a group and men as a group. Each group and transgender people are each diverse sets of users with varying attitudes, preferences, needs, behaviors, and levels of knowledge.

2. Critically examine if you think men, women, and transgender people are different, and how.

3. Critically question whether any observed differences in women, men, and transgender people are solely biological in origin rather than the result of a lifetime of learning.

4. Question whether gender differences in one culture are also present in other cultures.[24]

In 2009 and 2010, the European Union adopted a framework for science and technology innovation that embeds gender equality and social justice priorities into decision making for all kinds of research and development. The resulting Responsible Research and Innovation (RRI) tools provide a clear guide to innovation in a variety of fields.[25] The purpose of a continental framework of responsible research and innovation is neatly summarized:

> It is the duty of all science and technology decision makers, researchers and innovators to act responsibly to ensure their work does no harm. But RRI goes beyond this, to strive for a shared responsibility on research and innovation that does good—addressing the key issues facing society in an ethically and environmentally aware manner.[26]

First, the RRI Tools website outlines a wide view of the institutions that have a stake in the research and development process:

• Policy makers,

• The research community (including managers, technicians, and support staff),

- The education community (from primary grades through universities, including teachers, students, families, and science centers and museums),
- Business and industry (from small and medium-sized businesses to transnational companies, including networks, incubator hubs, and other supporting organizations), and
- Civil society organizations (including individuals and organizations such as trade unions, nonprofits, and the media).[27]

RRI Tools also outline six essential themes for policy makers:

- *Ethics:* Research integrity should embrace accountability, fairness, and good stewardship as core principles of research integrity.
- *Gender equality:* Research should include the perspectives of both men and women in research and innovation, including considering the relevance of outcomes to the whole population. This includes having balanced representation on teams and decision-making bodies and embedding gender-related methods into the research and innovation process and content itself.
- *Governance:* Responsible research and innovation methods should be embraced as part of the core values of decision-making bodies.
- *Open access:* Scientific research results should be open and have few barriers to access, especially if it is publicly funded. Designing data access for open sharing encourages collaborations, catalyzes innovation, and improves research quality. Results and data should follow the FAIR principle: it's findable, accessible, interoperable, and reusable.
- *Public engagement:* Research and innovation should engage early with policy makers, businesses and industry, and educational institutions to ensure that the results match the values, needs, and expectations of society.
- *Science education:* Science education needs to be embraced as a national and international goal, with the wide perspectives of responsible research and innovation at its center.[28]

For community builders who are focused on social change at a community level, the design justice movement offers a more extensive set of tools that goes to a goal of reshaping the dynamics between technology, institutions, and society. The underlying theory is to remake the exclusionary systems that critical race theory scholar Patricia Hill Collins calls the matrix of domination: the intersecting structures of white supremacy, heteropatriarchy, capitalism, and settler colonialism. The principles and tools are outlined in detail in Sasha Costanza-Chock's book *Design Justice: Community-Led Practices to Build the Worlds We Need.*[29]

For product developers, the tools described in this chapter provide product-focused lines of inquiry to interrogate product ideas across disciplines and to interrogate the design of interactive forums and technology itself. All of the tools can help guide those who are thinking about or developing technology that serves society.

The principles developed by design-people in Denmark can be helpful in answering the questions proposed by Stanford's Gendered Innovations tools. For instance, in the comments context, thinking from a user-experience perspective and conducting meaningful user research could save a lot of false steps. Mostly, though, product developers need to become familiar with general user motivations like those in the GenderMag software. It will shed light on why people choose to use or not use any particular product.

How to Shift toward Inclusion

The design justice movement and inclusive design rules have basic questions for designing products. Kat Holmes offers themes that are a brief takeaway:

- Consider diversity in terms of human interactions and the ways people change over time.

- Identify ability biases and mismatched interactions that are related to your solution.
- Create a diversity of ways to participate in an experience.
- Design for interdependence, and bring complementary skills together.
- Build a basic literacy in accessibility and grow a depth of expertise in the specific accessibility criteria that are relevant to your solutions.
- Adopt a more flexible definition of a designer. Open up processes, and invite contributions from people with relevant but nontraditional skills.[30]

A lot of people might be surprised by their own answers to the basic questions in this chapter and the pictures that emerge from a more open process. Using GenderMag's Tim, Pat, and Abi personas has improved software in virtually every team that has used them to test the inclusive design of their products.

For news comments, the answer is that women users generally want to be involved with give-and-take conversations with other people in their communities. They're waiting for news sites to offer the opportunity.

Conclusion

Overcoming Mensorship

The first day I clicked to open the back end of the *New York Times*'s debut online comments content management system in 2007, I felt I was opening a hallowed space to give people a voice. Open comments, I thought, and people will come.

Then reality set in. The conversation did not begin to reflect the voices of the people. Little did I realize that my early impressions moderating comments would lead me on a path of discovery to the historical depths of gender segregation throughout society.

My search for explanations and a more robust democratic forum became an archaeological excavation in the middle of the digital public square. It turns out the fossils of historic race and gender segregation have functioned as the new bones of the digital public square. The rules and the shapes and the technology of the forum have changed—at least at a superficial level—but the public conversations have not caught up.

In the digital world, we are all La Brea Woman, the hominid whose bones were preserved in the La Brea tar pits in California. We are still shouted down, interrupted, and underpaid. Sometimes people confront us on the front steps at work. Sometimes they gather in a chat room and target an outspoken woman for abuse. So many hurdles remain, but it's important to remember that the forces silencing women are the forces of millennia. It may be the internet age, but we still need to find our way out of the tar pit.

In the twenty-first century, men still tell women to shut up. Most often, this is indirectly achieved with an interruption, as the research behind "the Silent Sex" proved. Too many people miss the historical relevance of the devastating sexism.

This must change.

From one computer screen over more than a decade, I've come to see clearly the way that millennia of history and legal discrimination against women have functioned to suppress women's voices. The suppression remains in effect through the wider culture, even as women scroll the news on their tablets, phones, and computers.

I've come to understand the way that sociological "gender frames" have pushed historic bias into even the newest technology and into digital forums.

The fossils of gender segregation continue to give shape to daily life through a range of vectors that serve to suppress women's voices online and in public:

- Women are interrupted more frequently when we speak.
- Women are disparaged when we advocate for our own interests.
- Women are dismissed when we explain the public benefits of a society that works well for women, children, and families.
- Women are told their voices, their tones, and their approaches are unacceptable, even when women win a majority vote in elections and go to Congress—when they have earned the highest elective offices in a democratic system.
- Women are systematically subjected to rape and death threats when they assert their views in public—even about topics as lighthearted as characters in video games.

- Women are denied protection of the law when they are threatened for speaking and ask law enforcement to hold offenders accountable for criminal threats.

All for the audacity of acting on our legal rights in the public square.

Women have learned from experience, then, that their voices really do not have a welcome place in public life, especially in settings where men are in the majority. The barriers are not palpable or even visible to many people who have been immune from interruptions and the public doubt cast on nonwhite speakers and women. People will say they don't feel the need to correct a problem they do not perceive. But people do not need to experience the social consequences of misogyny to create inclusive systems.

Is it any wonder that women volunteer less to speak in public and submit comments at one third the rate of men?

All of these things must change.

The next great benchmark for women's equality is claiming equal speaking time throughout society. Only then will women's voices naturally be reflected equally in the digital sphere.

I believe deeply in the news comments space. As a lifetime proponent of participatory democracy, as a feminist devoted to a living democracy with equal voices, as a journalist, I believe deeply in the role of civic media in creating community forums. Even as media splinter societies into ever more disparate audience segments and as social media algorithms push people into like-minded communities with self-reinforcing communication loops, I believe deeply in the role of news organizations to host inclusive communities.

Not everyone will agree that news communities can be a solution. They will certainly not be a cure-all. But the tools and the deeply engaging methods such as those developed by the Coral Project are showing the way that using empathic tools for community inclusion can build toward community conversations that overcome some of the barriers in oppressive systems.

Discuss Spotlight part one: Does Boston deserve its racist
reputation?

Figure 8.1
Source: Patricia Wen, Akilah Johnson, Liz Kowalczyk, Todd Wallack, Nicole Dungca,
Adrian Walker, and Andrew Ryan. "Boston. Racism. Image. Reality," *Boston Globe*,
December 10, 2017.

In Boston, journalists using the Coral Project's Discuss tool
reached out to ask whether Boston deserves its racist reputation.
The result was the kind of probing picture of community experi
ence that design justice advocates envision (see figure 8.1). And
the team that created the project was a finalist for the Pulitzer
Prize.[12]

Journalism has the tools. The media more generally have the
tools. Now the challenge is to put the tools to use, and breathe new
life into democracy itself.

Overcoming Mensorship

Overcoming mensorship will require systemic change and action at
many levels. It will require change in public meetings. It will require
change in the dynamics of large group conversations. It will require
change in two-way conversations and inclusive frameworks for work
meetings, public meetings, and public planning and administration.
It will require news and entertainment media that portray women as

fully equal citizens and as individual agents. It will require new ways of framing injustice and inequality as problems that need to be solved.

Overcoming mensorship means laying the bricks in a foundation away from the institutions that historically excluded women and toward a welcoming reality where women are regarded as equally entitled to public space and speaking time.

This is a book about women, the web, and the future of a diverse, inclusive democracy. My recommendations for the future are my recommendations for a technological society—a society where conversations online are the new public square.

At a purely technical level, giving diverse women's voices equal time and space on the web is theoretically achievable in short order. The BBC has already accomplished this goal in more than four hundred programs by using a simple product tool and establishing gender as a key performance indicator. Metrics in news are a far better guidepost for newsworthiness than the implicit biases that rest on systematic underrepresentation of powerful women across media for centuries.

Bringing diverse women's voices to equality in a technology society could happen quickly if that were the only priority.

Life is messier than that.

Realizing a vision of an equal voice for women on the web is much more than a goal for the technology sector. Technologists can power gender equality on the web. Realizing a vision of an equal voice for women means fixing gender exclusion and creating gender equality throughout society, centered on understanding women at the intersections of race and gender. I believe deeply in journalism's civic mission to create that reality in the media we produce and that people consume every day. Every day.

My prescriptions for the future of democracy have many spokes. But the basic idea is clear. Media must adopt gender and racial representation as key performance indicators for their own coverage and for the behavior of the institutions they cover. This means media must embrace equal speaking time as a benchmark for women's equality and as a measure of democracy.

Benchmarks for Women, Men, and Conversation in Democracy

1. Embrace equal time and equal voice as benchmarks of democratic society, and challenge institutions to meet the benchmark.

As news comments reflect, women's voices remain vastly underrepresented in democratic society. Women are indeed "the Silent Sex," and this is a sign of an unhealthy democracy—an unrealized vision of democracy.

Feminists in the 1970s and 1980s often portrayed the goal of women's power as having a seat at the table. In subsequent decades, women argued for more seats at the table.

Fifty years later, we know that equality is also a matter of women having the floor, having the microphone, and speaking about issues and concerns without fear or favor.

Public bodies, public officials, and citizens can adopt equal time standards, encourage a range of participants, and create welcoming public spaces designed for inclusion for women to raise issues and concerns. Public boards can be asked to assess their own performance using a 50:50 tool as they go as part of an assessment of every meeting. Until every forum measures up, women and men will continue to receive the clear implied message that women's voices are not valued or not entitled to a hearing.

2. Include gender, race, and ethnic analysis at the heart of business tools and planning rubrics.

Embedding gender, race, and ethnic analysis tools into business planning references such as the lean startup, the business model canvas, design thinking, and Agile software development is a prerequisite of ethical business architecture. In a world where technologists are literally building the architecture of society online, building products that reflect all would drive business culture changes across the board.

In a technology society, technology creators are at the heart of building virtual cultures. Tools such as GenderMag and the Gendered Innovations "Engineering Checklist" are prerequisites for successful business planning, period. No view of business analytics or business planning is complete without this kind of analysis. It's about the foundations of digital culture, yes, but it's also good for business.

The rise of business data analytics, with its attendant ability to parse consumer segments and habits, has already begun to push gender analysis into broad use in business planning. The rise of diverse user-experience profiles as tools for building business strategy also points to a more inclusive culture. It's still true that startup culture requires the spark of imagination and the ability to think about what's small and attainable. However, there's no reason that any venture capital should ever go to products whose creators are designing products only for people like themselves. Successful businesses are built on broader visions, if only for the bottom line.

3. Include gender, race, and ethnic bias assessment tools at the earliest stages of software and product development as fundamental aspects of product management.

Technology product developers and data scientists and have an obligation to prevent gender, race, and ethnic bias. They have an obligation to prevent the perpetuation of bias and an obligation to avoid creating new vectors for bias. Doing gender, race, and ethnic analysis is unarguably good for business, creating bigger markets and greater opportunities for businesses.

Businesses and developers have tools available such as the Gendered Innovations "Engineering Checklist," the GenderMag software testing system, the European Responsible Research and Innovation tools, and the tools from the design justice movement. Improving the culture of business institutions through gender analysis contributes to an institution's expectations of its relationship with the public. In this way, technologists can drive change from within institutions such as media organizations simply by influencing assumptions of who an institution is meant to serve.

Inclusive design has begun to take root in academic computer science departments and in business schools. Carrying it forward into businesses will require some time, but curbing bias in technologically driven businesses can be driven by changes in technology departments.

4. Create meaningful criminal and civil penalties for cyberharassment, violent threats, and online mobs as fundamental threats to free speech.

A society where women reasonably fear to speak or write in public is a terror society, not a free society with the rule of law.

Ensuring free speech for women in the online age is one of the great challenges for free speech in the twenty-first century and requires a law enforcement response equal to those for in-person mobs and verbal threats (there is a paucity of criminal sanctions for verbal threats). In a society where women who speak in public routinely receive violent threats and are pervasively portrayed as victims of rape, anything less than criminal sanctions is a sign of deep bias in law enforcement methods and mechanisms.

Twitter, Facebook, and YouTube have taken some steps in recent years to deplatform certain forms of violent behavior. Facebook broadened its definition of *terrorism* in 2019 to help eliminate some of the most extreme voices on its platform, for example.[3] Advertisers have pushed platforms toward social responsibility by withdrawing their business. Procter & Gamble, one of YouTube's biggest advertisers, pushed YouTube in the right direction after it found one of its ads alongside an ISIS video. Some web services, such as Cloudflare, have withdrawn their services from violent channels of communication like 8kun (previously called 8chan), especially after a series of neo-Nazi mass shootings from Christchurch, New Zealand, to El Paso, Texas, in 2019.

Global aggregation of hate organizations and a more connected world for white supremacists and other violent ethnic and misogynist groups may have been an inevitable product of digital communication. But technology companies can take responsibility for preventing it, and some are showing how it can be done.

5. Elevate and surface women's voices in online conversations so that women's voices have an equal rank with men's voices, using simple technological tools to bring women's comments higher in their display.

That is all. It is a simple solution that can be fixed and automated.

6. Identify and call out interruptions as a primary tool of a sexist history of exclusion.

"The Silent Sex" experiments conclusively proved that interruptions are the primary method that silences women in small group settings. This was proved empirically by the Brigham Young and Princeton team in an experimental setting and confirmed empirically in meetings of public officials from school boards from small towns to the largest cities.

Understanding and calling out the interruption as a primary example of overbearing and inappropriate behavior is a central part of the cure for democracy. Interruptions mostly function now in their hidden status as an expression in implicit bias. Giving interruptions their name as an antidemocratic and counterproductive sexist expression can help make them as scarce as a supervisor calling a woman staff member "sweetheart."

7. Technology leaders and civic and corporate boards of directors must take primary responsibility for creating, displaying, and cultivating equal voices and influence for women.

Tools like GenderMeme, which tallies the representation of women and men in a given text, can be used to boost women's representation as experts and leaders and the voices of authority in the news.

These kinds of tools do raise a circular question about the origins of bias, but that is no reason to accept the status quo. When is unequal representation creating bias, and when is it merely conveying inequality as a fact of life? In the end, however, the answer to the question doesn't matter if creating an equal voice is embraced as a threshold of democracy. The issues can and must be addressed if institutions value this vital benchmark of democratic society.

8. Overcoming women's silence is primarily an institutional responsibility.

Frameworks promoting diverse women's voices and women's authority derive from the top of organizations, as they have at the Harvard Business School and Harvey Mudd College's computer science program. Institutional frameworks also include training for women participants. Women are trained to assert themselves, to ask questions, to demand respect, and to reclaim the floor when interrupted. And that is the source of my final recommendation.

9. Speak up. Silence is not inevitable.

Silence is an issue where the personal is the political and the political is the personal.

Though women's silence is primarily a systemic issue, it is still incumbent on women and their allies to insist on change. Overcoming systemic barriers must also be, to borrow a phrase from Gloria Steinem, a revolution from within.

Silence is personal, yes. But silence is also political. And the political aspect of women's silence shapes every individual woman's expectation of her efficacy in public. If just one in four members of Congress or Parliament are women, then silence becomes an expectation. It's a circular pattern. Representation reflects the systemic silencing of women. And the women's minority in public office hedge their voices.

To break the patterns of millennia, individual women must summon courage, empower each other, and work steadily toward claiming an equal voice throughout their lives. It is essential to claiming the legacy of the diverse array of suffragists, and it's something every woman and every daughter and granddaughter deserves.

Women, the Web, and the Future of Democracy

This book has been about the political, media, and cultural institutions that reflect, create, and reinforce women's silence and the projected silence of underrepresented minorities on the internet. Truly, it's a global issue.

Women's silence has been the foundation of many injustices. Indeed, the prevailing perceptions and implicit biases that rob women's voices of their authority are predicated on the history of women as excluded from the public forum. Overcome the implicit silencing, and women's voices will naturally rise.

The #MeToo movement is one clear example. The wave of women's demonstrations that swept the world in 2017 as the Women's March and that gave rise to a surge of women running for office in the United States flamed to life like a wildfire. The causes of the two phenomena were similar, too.

Like a wildfire, the #MeToo movement was fueled by a long accumulation of debris on the forest floor of the criminal and civil justice system. Like a forest floor collecting twigs, branches, and fallen trees over a long period of years, individual women over millennia have had to endure harassment and assault in silence, without legal or moral consequences for perpetrators. This is still the case in many fields.

Sometimes, sexual abuse and harassment were tolerated because the only institutions designed to address injustice were themselves mired in historic indifference to women's concerns. Sometimes, it was because a man formerly had a right to sexually assault his wife, as a matter of law. Sometimes, it was because women did not have a right to hold a job after becoming pregnant. Sometimes, it was because women spoke up but were penalized for doing so. Women still often face the choice of seeking to hold an offender accountable at the cost of her career.

All of these experiences have primarily been addressed as institutional failures, and they are institutional failures. However, silence is the basis of them all. The civil justice and criminal justice systems were never designed to hold offenders accountable for sexual assault.

Sexual harassment and sexual assault, long understood by feminists and labor scholars as occupational safety hazards, had been lying around waiting for a spark. The digital aggregation of like-minded women has begun to change that equation.

Raging infernos seeking justice for victims of sexual assault and sexual harassment roared through the entertainment industry in 2017, leading to the arrest of serial sexual abusers and the rightful shame of many more. The hashtag #MeToo was born and entered common parlance for sexual abuse and sexual harassment.

More alleged offenders lost their reputations and their professional standing, as women and men came forward to describe experiences that had long been suppressed under the weight of the legal insulation and credibility that many abusers enjoy. Sometimes it was a long history of actresses alleging assault and manipulation in the casting rooms of entertainment mogul Harvey Weinstein or opera singers and actors alleging harassment by Placido Domingo, the famous tenor. Sometimes, it was young men alleging that actor Kevin Spacey had groped them or manipulated them into sexual situations. The criminal case against Spacey was dismissed, but the number of allegations that became public left his reputation tattered and the loss of his lead role as President Frank Underwood on the television show *House of Cards*.

Almost as suddenly, like a wildfire, the Women's March came to life in 2017, sparking millions of women into the street from

Argentina to the Arctic to demand a voice and justice for women in public life. The movement and the political fallout around the world since the march were fueled by the debris of millennia of discrimination, millennia of exclusion, millennia of institutions shaped by the misogyny that has limited women's influence in supposedly democratic societies.

In politics, new growth is emerging, too. Recent numbers in the United States reflect equality in the odds of women and minorities winning elections, once they are on the ballot.[4]

After a century of women voting, finally bringing women's voices to equality in the public forum is the next great quest. Leaders in technology fields must be the leaders in making this a reality throughout the information society.

The diverse suffrage leaders Alice Paul, Ida B. Wells-Barnett, Carrie Chapman Catt, and Mabel Ping-Hua Lee would expect nothing less, and with haste.

Acknowledgments

So many people have inspired my journalism and my vision for this book that I scarcely know where to begin. When all is said and done, the core of my "stop talking, start writing" support came from my Maine writing group. Bill Trippe was instrumental. Amy Farrell, my intellectual touchstone and doppelgänger, read early drafts and provided important direction for the finished manuscript. Jim Ellefson brought us together. Philip Kinsler, Kate Seeley, John Bloom, and Francesca Elms cheered me. A younger generation inspired me. Valerie Carter, Michael Howard, and Emma Howard provide a year-round sounding board.

Gita Manaktala, my editor at the MIT Press, helped germinate the seed of the book and bring it to full expression. The MIT staff were unfailingly supportive and helpful.

The Journalism & Women Symposium has been vital to my developing a feminist journalist's voice with the support and reflection from myriad women over the course of two decades. My late editors, Rita Henley Jensen of Women's eNews and Mary Thom of the Women's Media Center, showed interest in my work through this network. Both died too young, but both provided early validation and a commitment to publishing women's voices long before commercial journalism came to the realization that women like news, too. They affirmed my deep belief and commitment to informing public policy priorities for women voters. I miss them. My inspiration from this group is endless, but I cherish the support of Rachel Jones, Jackie Spinner, Dawn Garcia, Becky Day, Dan Day, and every writer and editor who has believed in my work.

The ideas for this book were born from a fellowship at the Reynolds Journalism Institute at the Missouri School of Journalism at the University of Missouri. Mike McKean's friendship and support were crucial in the early stages. Randy Picht ran the show, Esther Thorson provided needed academic perspective, and Amy Simons coordinated campus resources and student work. Kristin Rohlwing and Humera Lodhi were vital research support while students at the University of Missouri. They are thriving professionals now, and I thank them for their inspiration and continued support. Steve Weinberg and Janine Latus each provided lasting friendship and inspiring examples as authors.

At the *New York Times*, I have enjoyed wide support and benefited from the reflections from many colleagues and a workplace where people are inspired to truly, deeply think in global terms. Marcia Loughran, Bassey Etim, Kari Haskell, Eric Copage, Lisa Tarchak, Rachel Harris, Erin Wright, Marie Tae McDermott, Jesse Pennington, Wadzanai Mhute, Rita Levine, Sean Lee, Lisa Letostak, Kevin Hayes, and Robin Frost all offered wisdom and support. Nancy Wartik and Dennis Overbye were special sources of support, hospitality, and coaching. The long arc of my research and writing would have been completely different without them. Phoebe Lett, Francesca Donner, and Joe Hart have been inspirations. The staff of the Coral Project provided immeasurable insight into technology and civic discussion. The internet would be less intelligent without the genius of Andrew Losowsky, Sydette Harry, and David Erwin.

I have also drawn on a wide circle of friends and colleagues closer to home and hearth whose conversation and perspective added shape to my life and my thinking. Sandip Wilson, Anne Hayes-Grillo, and Michael Grillo are my extended family. Paul Grosswiler, through the course of decades, helped me become the thinker I am. I've enjoyed the support of my children's circles of friends, including Matthew Romer, Elene Imnaishvili, Cristiana Dabija, Aimee Ouelette, Ellie Macmillan, Sarah Keene, Serena Wallace, and Ashley Stone.

Louis Tessier, my brother, is my rock; his wife, Julie, is a gift. My father, Vern Tessier, has come to embrace women's voices in leadership, and he has embraced my role as a journalist, too. I would be a different person without his personal commitment to the *CBS Evening News*. My late mother, Kathleen Freidhoff Tessier, was my original social justice warrior.

My children, Leif and Simone Grosswiler, always believed in me. This book is for them.

Notes

Introduction

1. Mark Leibovich, "For A.O.C., 'Existential Crises' as Her District Becomes the Coronavirus Epicenter," *New York Times*, May 4, 2020, https://www.nytimes.com /2020/05/04/us/politics/coronavirus-alexandria-ocasio-cortez.html.

2. Mike Lillis, "Ocasio-Cortez Accosted by GOP Lawmaker over Remarks: 'That Kind of Confrontation Hasn't Ever Happened to Me,'" *The Hill*, July 21, 2020, https:// thehill.com/homenews/house/508259-ocaasio-cortez-accosted-by-gop-lawmaker -over-remarks-that-kind-of.

3. Alexandria Ocasio-Cortez, Statement on the floor of the House of Representatives, July 23, 2020, quoted in Nicholas Wu, "'I Am Someone's Daughter Too.' Read Rep. Ocasio-Cortez's Full Speech Responding to Rep. Ted Yoho," https://www .usatoday.com/story/news/politics/2020/07/24/aoc-response-ted-yoho-read-text-rep -ocasio-cortezs-speech/5500633002.

4. Luke Broadwater and Catie Edmondson, "A.O.C. Unleashes a Viral Condemnation of Sexism in Congress," *New York Times*, July 23, 2020, https://nyti.ms/2RFBrJQ #permid=108304920.

5. Broadwater and Edmondson, "A.O. C. Unleashes a Viral Condemnation of Sexism."

6. Alexandria Ocasio-Cortez (@AOC), "I Never Spoke to Rep. Yoho before He Decided to Accost Me," Twitter, July 21, 2020, https://twitter.com/AOC/status /1285574615910227968?s=20.

7. A definitive catalog of the ways that misogyny thrives and resisted online is provided in Jacqueline Ryan Vickery and Tracy Everbach, eds., *Mediating Misogyny: Gender, Technology and Harassment* (Palgrave MacMillan, 2018).

8. Kate Manne, *Down Girl: The Logic of Misogyny* (Oxford University Press 2018), 19.

9. Christopher Karpowitz and Tali Mendelberg, *The Silent Sex: Gender, Deliberation & Institutions* (Princeton University Press, 2014).

10. Donald J. Trump (@realDonaldTrump), "So Interesting to See 'Progressive' Democrat Congresswomen," Twitter, July 14, 2019, https://twitter.com/realDonaldTrump /status/1150381394234941448.

11. Mary Beard, *Women & Power: A Manifesto* (Liveright Publishing, 2017).

12. Natalie Jomini Stroud, Emily Van Duyn, and Cynthia Peacock, "Survey of Commenters and Comment Readers," Center for Media Engagement (Center for Media Engagement, University of Texas at Austin, 2016), https://mediaengagement.org /research/survey-of-commenters-and-comment-readers.

13. Emily Van Duyn, Cynthia Peacock, and Natalie Jomini Stroud, "The Gender Gap in Online News Comment Sections," *Social Science Computer Review*, July 26, 2019, doi: 10.1177/894439319864876; Natalie Jomini Stroud, interview with the author, September 30, 2020.

14. Alan Rappeport, "Gloria Steinem and Madeleine Albright Rebuke Young Women Backing Bernie Sanders," *New York Times*, February 8, 2016, https://www .nytimes.com/2016/02/08/us/politics/gloria-steinem-madeleine-albright-hillary -clinton-bernie-sanders.html.

15. Rappeport, "Gloria Steinem and Madeleine Albright Rebuke Young Women Backing Bernie Sanders."

16. "New Hampshire Primary Results," *New York Times*, September 29, 2016, http:// www.nytimes.com/elections/2016/results/primaries/new-hampshire.

17. Josh Hafner, "Here's How Badly Clinton Lost among Women in New Hampshire This Week," *USA Today*, February 10, 2016, https://www.usatoday.com/story /news/politics/onpolitics/2016/02/10/new-hampshire-hillary-clinton-women -voters-bernie-sanders/80198302.

18. Madeleine Albright, "Madeleine Albright: My Undiplomatic Moment," *New York Times*, February 12, 2016, http://www.nytimes.com/2016/02/13/opinion/madeleine -albright-my-undiplomatic-moment.html?comments#permid=17555102.

19. Albright, "Madeleine Albright: My Undiplomatic Moment."

20. Albright, "Madeleine Albright: My Undiplomatic Moment."

21. Albright, "Madeleine Albright: My Undiplomatic Moment."

22. Joy Jenkins and J. David Wolfgang, "A Space for Women: Online Commenting Forums as Indicators of Civility and Feminist Community-Building," in *Mediating*

Misogyny: Gender, Technology, and Harassment, ed. Jacqueline Ryan Vickery and Tracy Everbach (Palgrave Macmillan, 2018), 247–268.

23. Karen Desborough, "The Global Anti-Street Harassment Movement: Digitally-Enabled Feminist Activism," in *Mediating Misogyny: Gender, Technology, and Harassment,* ed. Jacqueline Ryan Vickery and Tracy Everbach (Palgrave Macmillan, 2018), 333–351.

24. David Brooks, "Why Trump Soars," *New York Times*, April 18, 2011, http://www.nytimes.com/2011/04/19/opinion/19brooks.html.

25. Christopher Buskirk, "Barr Is Right about Everything. Admit You Were Wrong," *New York Times*, April 18, 2019, https://www.nytimes.com/2019/04/18/opinion/barr-media-trump.html.

26. Joseph M. Reagle Jr., *Reading the Comments: Likers, Haters, and Manipulators at the Bottom of the Web* (MIT Press, 2015).

27. Allan M. Siegal and William G. Connolly, *The New York Times Manual of Style and Usage* (New York Times, 2016).

28. Katharine Q. Seelye, "Molly Ivins, Columnist, Dies at 62," *New York Times*, February 1, 2007, http://www.nytimes.com/2007/02/01/washington/01ivins.html.

29. Antonis Kalogeropoulos and Rasmus Kleis Nielsen, "Social Inequalities in News Consumption," Reuters Institute for the Study of Journalism, University of Oxford, October 2018, https://reutersinstitute.politics.ox.ac.uk/sites/default/files/2018-10/Kalogeropolous%20Social%20Inequality%20in%20News%20FINAL.pdf.

30. Emily Bell, "Silicon Valley and Journalism: Make Up or Break Up?," video presentation, Reuters Institute for the Study of Journalism, University of Oxford, November 21, 2014, reutersinstitute.politics.ox.ac.uk/risj-review/emily-bell-silicon-valley-and-journalism-make-or-break, transcript at Nick Tjaardstra, "Emily Bell's Seminal Speech on the Relationship between Journalism and Technology: It's Time to Make Up or Break Up," WAN-IFRA, November 26, 2014, https://blog.wan-ifra.org/2014/11/26/emily-bells-seminal-speech-on-the-relationship-between-journalism-and-technology-its-time.

31. Brent Staples, "How the Suffrage Movement Betrayed Black Women," *New York Times*, July 18, 2018, https://www.nytimes.com/2018/07/28/opinion/sunday/suffrage-movement-racism-black-women.html.

32. Janet Shibley Hyde et al., "The Future of Sex and Gender in Psychology: Five Challenges to the Gender Binary," *American Psychologist* 74, no. 2 (February 2019): 171–193, https://doi.org/10.1037/amp0000307.

33. Some of the standards for gender and research have been changing with the leadership of a few people in media think tanks, especially Andrew Losowsky at the

Coral Project, which is now part of Vox Media. It began as a joint project of the Mozilla Foundation, the *New York Times*, and the *Washington Post*.

34. "Sex and Gender," Gendered Innovations in Science, Health & Medicine, Engineering, and Environment, Stanford University, http://genderedinnovations.stanford .edu/terms/distinct.html.

35. Manne, *Down Girl*.

36. Kate Manne, *Entitled: How Male Privilege Hurts Women (Crown, 2020)*.

37. Those who are interested in inquiring further about race, genetics, and discrimination have numerous sources to draw from. *Scientific American* offers a summary of current research and efforts to excise invidious discrimination that shapes all manner of science to this day. Megan Gannon, "Race Is a Social Construct, Scientists Argue," *Scientific American*, February 5, 2016, https://www.scientificamerican .com/article/race-is-a-social-construct-scientists-argue/. *The New England Journal of Medicine* has current conversations about how race-based research is warping medical decisions in ways that harm people of color. Darshali A. Vyas, Leo G. Eisenstein, and David S. Jones, "Hidden in Plain Sight: Reconsidering the Use of Race Correction in Clinical Algorithms," *New England Journal of Medicine*, August 27, 2020, https://www.nejm.org/doi/full/10.1056/NEJMms2004740.

38. Kimberlé Crenshaw et al., eds., *Critical Race Theory: The Key Writings That Formed the Movement* (The New Press, 1995), 357.

39. Patricia Hill Collins and Sirma Bilge, *Intersectionality*, 2nd ed. (Polity Press, 2020), 15.

Chapter 1

1. Thomas Fuller and Christopher Flavelle, "A Climate Reckoning in Fire-Stricken California," *New York Times*, September 10, 2020, https://www.nytimes.com/2020 /09/10/us/climate-change-california-wildfires.html.

2. Fuller and Flavelle, "A Climate Reckoning," https://nyti.ms/3mPfF4Z#permid =109066109.

3. Fuller and Flavelle, "A Climate Reckoning," https://nyti.ms/3i7R5bY#permid =109066921.

4. Aaron M. McCright, "The Effects of Gender on Climate Change Knowledge and Concern in the American Public," *Population and Environment* 32, no. 1 (2010): 66– 87, http://www.jstor.org/stable/40984168.

5. Fuller and Flavelle, "A Climate Reckoning," https://nyti.ms/2S8C8vr#permid =109071713.

6. Fuller and Flavelle, "A Climate Reckoning," https://nyti.ms/3cGXYjq#permid =109071219.

7. Fuller and Flavelle, "A Climate Reckoning," https://nyti.ms/32jB2D2#permid =109071864.

8. Comparative data are from a web site that draws gender identification from birth records, proprietors say, https://www.babynameshub.com/gendercompare.cfm?Name =Shelby.

9. Media Insight Project, "The Personal News Cycle: A Focus on African American and Hispanic News Consumers," American Press Institute and AP-NORC Center for Public Affairs Research, September 16, 2014, http://www.mediainsight.org/Pages /focus-on-african-american-and-hispanic-news-consumers.aspx.

10. Meredith D. Clark, "Marginalized Voices and the Comments," Coral by Vox Media, October 2, 2018, https://guides.coralproject.net/survey-marginalized-voices/.

11. Meredith D. Clark, interview with the author, September 24, 2020.

12. Dawn Fallik, email to the author, April 21, 2016.

13. Jon Pareles, "Prince: An Artist Who Defined Genre, Is Dead," *New York Times*, April 21, 2016, https://www.nytimes.com/2016/04/22/arts/music/prince-dead.html #permid=18285560.

14. Alan Mislove et al., "Understanding the Demographics of Twitter Users," in *Proceedings of the Fifth AAAI International Conference on Weblogs and Social Media, Barcelona, Catalonia, Spain, July 17–21, 2011* (AAAI Press, 2011), establishes a methodology to assess demographics when possible.

15. Pareles, "Prince," https://www.nytimes.com/2016/04/22/arts/music/prince-dead .html#permid=18285671.

16. Emma Pierson, home page, https://cs.stanford.edu/~emmap1.

17. Emma Pierson, "Outnumbered But Well-Spoken: Female Commenters in the *New York Times*," in *CSCW '15: Proceedings of the 18th ACM Conference on Computer Supported Cooperative Work & Social Computing* (ACM, 2015). https://dl.acm.org/doi /10.1145/2675133.2675134.

18. The OpEdProject, "The Byline Survey Report, 2012: Who Narrates the World?," *The Byline Blog* (blog), May 29, 2012, June 29, 2012, https://theopedproject.wordpress .com/2012/05/28/the-byline-survey-2011.

19. Andrew J. Perrin, "'Since This Is the Editorial Section I Intend to Express My Opinion': Inequality and Expressivity in Letters to the Editor," *The Communication Review* 19, no. 1 (January 2, 2016): 55–76, https://doi.org/10.1080/10714421.2016 .1128188.

20. Joseph Lichterman, "*New York Times* Editor: 'We Have to Treat Comments as Content,'" NiemanLab, October 2, 2015, http://www.niemanlab.org/2015/10/new-york-times-editor-we-have-to-treat-comments-as-content.

21. Fiona Martin, "Getting My Two Cents Worth In: Access, Interaction, Participation and Social Inclusion in Online News Commenting," *#ISOJ* 6, no. 1 (April 15, 2015), https://isojjournal.wordpress.com/2015/04/15/getting-my-two-cents-worth-in-access-interaction-participation-and-social-inclusion-in-online-news-commenting.

22. Fiona Martin, interview with the author, October 10, 2016.

23. Martin Langeveld, "*Texas Tribune* Is Ramping Up," NiemanLab, July 20, 2009, http://www.niemanlab.org/2009/07/texas-tribun/.

24. Susan Chira and Catrin Einhorn, "How Tough Is It to Change a Culture of Harassment? Ask Women at Ford," *New York Times*, December 19, 2017, https://www.nytimes.com/interactive/2017/12/19/us/ford-chicago-sexual-harassment.html.

25. Dylan Farrow, "An Open Letter from Dylan Farrow," *On the Ground* (blog), *New York Times*, February 1, 2014, https://kristof.blogs.nytimes.com/2014/02/01/an-open-letter-from-dylan-farrow.

26. Farrow, "An Open Letter," http://kristof.blogs.nytimes.com/2014/02/01/an-open-letter-from-dylan-farrow/?comments#permid=11072054.

27. Farrow, "An Open Letter," http://kristof.blogs.nytimes.com/2014/02/01/an-open-letter-from-dylan-farrow/?comments#permid=11072127.

28. Farrow, "An Open Letter," http://kristof.blogs.nytimes.com/2014/02/01/an-open-letter-from-dylan-farrow/?comments#permid=11072148.

29. Farrow, "An Open Letter," https://kristof.blogs.nytimes.com/2014/02/01/an-open-letter-from-dylan-farrow/#permid=11085123.

30. Farrow, "An Open Letter," http://kristof.blogs.nytimes.com/2014/02/01/an-open-letter-from-dylan-farrow/?comments#permid=11072225.

31. Farrow, "An Open Letter," http://kristof.blogs.nytimes.com/2014/02/01/an-open-letter-from-dylan-farrow/?comments#permid=11072013.

32. Farrow, "An Open Letter," http://kristof.blogs.nytimes.com/2014/02/01/an-open-letter-from-dylan-farrow/?comments#permid=11072190.

33. Emma Pierson, "How to Get More Women to Join the Debate," *On the Ground* (blog), *New York Times*, January 6, 2015, http://kristof.blogs.nytimes.com/2015/01/06/how-to-get-more-women-to-join-the-debate.

34. Bret Stephens, "The Smearing of Woody Allen," *New York Times*, February 9, 2018, https://www.nytimes.com/2018/02/09/opinion/smearing-of-woody-allen.html.

35. Maureen Orth, "10 Undeniable Facts about the Woody Allen Sexual-Abuse Allegation," *Vanity Fair*, March 6, 2020, https://www.vanityfair.com/news/2014/02 /woody-allen-sex-abuse-10-facts.

36. Kimberly Probolus, "A Woman's Plea: Let's Raise Our Voices," *New York Times*, January 31, 2019, https://www.nytimes.com/2019/01/31/opinion/letters/letters-to -editor-new-york-times-women.html.

37. Thomas Feyer and Susan Mermelstein, "The Editors Respond: We Hear You," *New York Times*, January 31, 2019, https://www.nytimes.com/2019/01/31/opinion /letters/letters-to-editor-new-york-times-women.html.

38. Catherine Sanderson, "Homage to a Dying Breed: Stick-Shift Cars," letter to the editor, *New York Times*, March 31, 2019, https://www.nytimes.com/2019/03/31 /opinion/letters/stick-shift-cars.html.

39. Roxana Robinson et al., "A Plea from 33 Writers: Words Matter. Stop Using 'Quid Pro Quo,'" *New York Times*, November 8, 2019, https://www.nytimes.com /2019/11/08/opinion/letters/quid-pro-quo.html.

40. Thomas Feyer and Susan Mermelstein, "Women, Please Speak Out," *New York Times*, February 14, 2020, https://www.nytimes.com/2020/02/14/opinion/letters /letters-editor-nytimes-gender.html.

41. Marie T. Tessier, "Seeking More Women's Voices in the Digital Public Square," *New York Times*, May 10, 2019, https://www.nytimes.com/2019/05/10/opinion /letters/women-voices.html.

42. Perrin, "'Since This Is the Editorial Section I Intend to Express My Opinion.'"

43. Center for American Women and Politics, Rutgers University Eagle Institute of Politics, New Brunswick, New Jersey. *Facts: Facts and Historial Data on Women Candidates and Officeholders*. https://cawp.rutgers.edu/facts.

44. Cristal Williams Chancellor, Katti Gray, Diahann Hill, Faye Wolfe, Tiffany Nguyen, "The Status of Women in the U.S. Media," Women's Media Center, February 21 2019. https://womensmediacenter.com/reports/the-status-of-women-in-u-s-media-2019.

45. Sheryl Sandberg and Nell Scovell, *Lean In: Women, Work, and the Will to Lead* (Alfred A. Knopf, 2013).

46. Martin, "Getting My Two Cents Worth In."

47. Martin, "Getting My Two Cents Worth In."

48. Pew Research Center, "Perceptions of Online Environments," in "Online Harassment," October 22, 2014, 8, http://www.pewinternet.org/2014/10/22/online -harassment/pi_2014-10-22__online-harassment-04.

49. Catherine Buni and Soraya Chemaly, "The Risk Makers: Viral Hate, Election Interference, and Hacked Accounts. Inside the Tech Industry's Decades-Long Failure to Reckon with Risks," Type Investigations, September 21, 2020, https://www.typeinvestigations.org/investigation/2020/09/21/the-risk-makers.

50. Jessica Megarry, "Under the Watchful Eyes of Men: Theorising the Implications of Male Surveillance Practices for Feminist Activism on Social Media," *Feminist Media Studies* 18, no. 6 (2017): 1070–1085, https://doi.org/10.1080/14680777.2017.1387584.

Chapter 2

1. Toni Carter, interview with the author, September 2, 2016.

2. Christopher F. Karpowitz and Tali Mendelberg, *The Silent Sex: Gender, Deliberation and Institutions* (Princeton University Press, 2014).

3. Kelly Ditmar, interview with the author, August 30, 2016.

4. Lori D. Ginzberg, *Elizabeth Cady Stanton: An American Life* (Hill and Wang, 2009). Chapter 4, "War and Reconstruction (1861–1868)," provides extensive writings from Elizabeth Cady Stanton promoting the worst kinds of stereotypes about Black men. It's a part of the history that Stanton, Susan B. Anthony, Matilda Joslyn Gage, and Ida Husted Harper left out of *The History of Woman Suffrage* (6 vols., 1881–1922), which had been the standard reference of the age. As one friend puts it, "Biography is journalism; autobiography is public relations." The suffragists' public relations held up well for generations, until contemporary scholars reviewed the record.

5. National Park Service, "1913 Woman Suffrage Procession," https://www.nps.gov/articles/woman-suffrage-procession1913.htm.

6. Frank M. Bryan, *Real Democracy: The New England Town Meeting and How It Works* (University of Chicago Press, 2004).

7. Tali Mendelberg, interview with the author, April 22, 2016.

8. Karpowitz and Mendelberg, *The Silent Sex*, 16–19. For a deeper dive, the authors summarize decades of research throughout the world and across different aspects of policy and politics.

9. Bryan, *Real Democracy*, 3. As indicated in the title of the book, Bryan believes citizens voting in live meetings is the pinnacle of democratic expression.

10. See Bryan, *Real Democracy*, 226–231, for a detailed statistical assessment of variables influencing and not influencing women's participation.

11. Frank M. Bryan, interview with the author, August 31, 2016.

12. Marie Tessier, "Speaking While Female, and at a Disadvantage," *New York Times*, October 27, 2016, https://www.nytimes.com/2016/10/27/upshot/speaking-while -female-and-at-a-disadvantage.html#permid=20297956.

13. Bryan, interview with the author, August 31, 2016.

14. Tessier, "Speaking While Female, and at a Disadvantage," https://www.nytimes .com/2016/10/27/upshot/speaking-while-female-and-at-a-disadvantage.html.

15. Bryan, *Real Democracy*, 216.

16. Karpowitz and Mendelberg, *The Silent Sex*, 298–300.

17. Karpowitz and Mendelberg, *The Silent Sex*, 298–300.

18. Karpowitz and Mendelberg, *The Silent Sex*, 3.

19. Frederick M. Hess and Olivia Meeks, "School Boards circa 2010: Governance in the Accountability Era," table 1, National School Board Association, https://cdn-files.nsba .org/s3fs-public/SBcirca2010_WEB.pdf?Piya0hP.hbJ4QXagUmzbETjNuhDB__kM.

20. Karpowitz and Mendelberg, *The Silent Sex*, 288.

21. Center for American Women and Politics (CAWP), "Women in Elective Office" and "Facts on Women of Color in Office," Rutgers University, September 23, 2020, https://cawp.rutgers.edu/women-elective-office-2020 and https://cawp.rutgers.edu /fact-sheets-women-color.

22. United Nations Women, "Sluggish Progress on Women in Politics Will Hamper Development," March 10, 2015, http://www.unwomen.org/en/news/stories/2015/3 /press-release-sluggish-progress-on-women-in-politics-will-hamper-development.

23. Catalyst, "List: Women CEOs of the S&P 500," November 19, 2020, http://www .catalyst.org/knowledge/women-ceos-sp-500.

Chapter 3

1. Mary Beard, "The Public Voice of Women," *London Review of Books*, March 20, 2014, https://www.lrb.co.uk/v36/n06/mary-beard/the-public-voice-of-women#fn-03.

2. Find the full letters in John Adams and Abigail Adams, *The Letters of John and Abigail Adams*, ed. Frank Shuffelton (Penguin, 2003). This exchange is widely cited, as in Lily Rothman's "A Cultural History of Mansplaining," *The Atlantic*, November. 1, 2012, https://www.theatlantic.com/sexes/archive/2012/11/a-cultural-history-of-mansplaining /264380.

3. Pamela Barnes Craig, "American Women: Resources from the Law Library," Library of Congress, March 19, 2019, https://memory.loc.gov/ammem/awhhtml /awlaw3/d1.html.

4. Cecilia L. Ridgeway, *Framed by Gender: How Gender Inequality Persists in the Modern World* (Oxford University Press, 2011).

5. Cecilia L. Ridgeway, "Framed by Gender: Cecilia Ridgeway, Stanford Professor," video, YouTube, April 18, 2011, https://www.youtube.com/watch?v=BxkJ4_5qqPc.

6. The American Physical Society tracks comparative rates of women earning PhDs in science, technology, engineering, and math at "Doctoral Degrees Earned by Women, by Major," 2018, https://www.aps.org/programs/education/statistics/fraction-phd.cfm.

7. American Physical Society, "Doctoral Degrees Earned by Women."

8. Jodie T. Allen, "Reluctant Suffragettes: When Women Questioned Their Right to Vote," Pew Research Center, March 18, 2009, http://www.pewresearch.org/2009/03/18/reluctant-suffragettes-when-women-questioned-their-right-to-vote.

9. Allen, "Reluctant Suffragettes."

10. Allen, "Reluctant Suffragettes."

11. Soraya Chemaly, panelist, "We Belong Here: Pushing Back against Online Harassment," keynote panel discussion with moderator Sarah Jeong and panelists Soraya Chemaly, Michelle Ferrier, Amanda Hess, and Laurie Penny, Online News Association 2015 Conference and Awards Banquet (ONA15), September 24–26, 2015.

12. Christopher F. Karpowitz and Tali Mendelberg, *The Silent Sex: Gender, Deliberation and Institutions* (Princeton University Press, 2014), 5.

13. Summarized in Susan C. Herring and Sharon Stoerger, "Gender and (A)nonymity in Computer-Mediated Communication," in *Handbook of Language, Gender, and Sexuality*, 2nd ed., ed. Susan Ehrlich, Miriam Meyerhoff, and Janet Holmes (Wiley-Blackwell, 2014), 567–586.

14. Deborah Fallows, "How Women and Men Use the Internet," Pew Research Center, December 28, 2005, http://www.pewinternet.org/2005/12/28/how-women-and-men-use-the-internet/.

15. David Graddol and Will Swann, *Gender Voices* (Wiley-Blackwell, 1991).

16. For a thorough review of all the scholarly literature on gender and computer-mediated communication, see Herring and Stoerger "Gender and (A)nonymity in Computer-Mediated Communication."

17. S. C. Herring, D. A. Johnson, and T. DiBenedetto, "Participation in Electronic Discourse in a 'Feminist' Field," in *Language and Gender: A Reader*, ed. J. Coates (Blackwell, 1998), http://ella.slis.indiana.edu/~herring/participation.1998.pdf.

18. Cynthia L. Selfe and Paul R. Meyer, "Testing Claims for On-Line Conferences," *Written Communication*, 8, no. 2 (April 1, 1991): 163–192.

19. Herring and Stoerger provide a detailed review of the literature of this period in "Gender and (A)nonymity," 4.

20. Lynn Cherny, "Gender Differences in Text-Based Virtual Reality," in *Cultural Performances: Proceedings of the Third Berkeley Women and Language Conference*, ed. Mary Bucholtz, Anita C. Liang, Laurel A. Sutton, and Caitlin Hines (Berkeley Women and Language Group, University of California, 1994).

21. Karpowitz and Mendelberg, *The Silent Sex*, 7.

22. Paul Djupe, Scott Mcclurg, and Anand Edward Sokhey, "The Political Consequences of Gender in Social Networks," *British Journal of Political Science* 48, no. 3 (June 22, 2016): 1–22.

23. Susan Q. Stranahan, "Susan Estrich on Gender, Missing Voices, and That Nasty Email War," *Columbia Journalism Review*, February 25, 2005, http://archives.cjr.org /the_water_cooler/susan_estrich_on_gender_missin.php.

24. Catherine Orenstein, "About Katie," The OpEd Project, https://www.theoped project.org/about-katie.

25. Catherine Orenstein, interview with the author, June 6, 2017.

26. Katherine Baldiga Coffman, "Evidence on Self-Stereotyping and the Contribution of Ideas," *Quarterly Journal of Economics* 129, no. 4 (November 2014): 1625–1660, https://doi.org/10.1093/qje.qju023.

27. Mary Beard, "The Public Voice of Women," *London Review of Books*, 36, no. 6, https://www.lrb.co.uk/the-paper/v36/n06/mary-beard/the-public-voice-of-women.

28. Benjamin R. Warner et al., "Limbaugh's Social Media Nightmare: Facebook and Twitter as Spaces for Political Action," *Journal of Radio & Audio Media* 19, no. 2 (July 2012): 257–275, https://doi.org/10.1080/19376529.2012.722479.

29. Rosanna Xia, "Most Computer Science Majors in the U.S. Are Men. Not So at Harvey Mudd," *Los Angeles Times*, January 4, 2017, https://www.latimes.com/local /lanow/la-me-ln-harvey-mudd-tech-women-adv-snap-story.htm.

30. Sheryl Sandberg and Nell Scovell, *Lean In: Women, Work, and the Will to Lead* (Alfred A. Knopf, 2013), 147.

31. Jodi Kantor, "Harvard Business School Case Study: Gender Equity," *New York Times*, September 7, 2013, https://www.nytimes.com/2013/09/08/education/harvard -case-study-gender-equity.html.

Chapter 4

1. Michelle Ferrier, panelist, "We Belong Here: Pushing Back against Online Harassment." keynote panel discussion with moderator Sarah Jeong and panelists Soraya

Chemaly, Michelle Ferrier, Amanda Hess, and Laurie Penny, Online News Association 2015 Conference and Awards Banquet (ONA15), Los Angeles, September 24–26, 2015.

2. Committee to Protect Journalists (CPJ), "CPJ Urges U.S. Probe in Hate Mail Case," letter to the U.S. Department of Justice, July 3, 2008, https://cpj.org/2008/07/cpj -urges-us-probe-in-hate-mail-case.php.

3. TrollBusters, "About Us: TrollBusters: Offering Pest Control for Journalists," https://yoursosteam.wordpress.com/about.

4. Michelle Ferrier and Nisha Garud-Patkar, "TrollBusters: Fighting Online Harassment of Women Journalists," in *Mediating Misogyny: Gender, Technology and Harassment*, ed. Jacqueline Ryan Vickery and Tracy Everbach (Palgrave MacMillan, 2018), 311–332.

5. Ferrier, "We Belong Here."

6. Danielle Keats Citron, *Hate Crimes in Cyberspace* (Harvard University Press, 2014), 22.

7. Citron, *Hate Crimes in Cyberspace*.

8. Joseph M. Reagle Jr., *Reading the Comments: Likers, Haters, and Manipulators at the Bottom of the Web* (MIT Press, 2015).

9. Whitney Phillips, *This Is Why We Can't Have Nice Things: Mapping the Relationship between Online Trolling and Mainstream Culture* (MIT Press, 2015).

10. Amanda Lenhart et al., "Online Harassment, Digital Abuse, and Cyberstalking in America" Data and Society Research Institute, November 21, 2016, https://www .datasociety.net/pubs/oh/Online_Harassment_2016.pdf.

11. Andrew Losowsky, "Newsgeist 2015 Ignite Talk by Andrew Losowsky," video, YouTube, November 29, 2015, https://www.youtube.com/watch?v=3a0c2U1T4gs.

12. Karla Mantilla, *Gendertrolling: How Misogyny Went Viral* (Praeger, 2015), 4.

13. Phillips, *This Is Why We Can't Have Nice Things*.

14. Laurie Penny, panelist, "We Belong Here: Pushing Back against Online Harassment," keynote panel discussion with moderator Sarah Jeong and panelists Soraya Chemaly, Michelle Ferrier, Amanda Hess, and Laurie Penny, Online News Association 2015 Conference and Awards Banquet (ONA15), Los Angeles, September 25, 2015, https://livestream.com/accounts/5804560/ona15/videos/100236201.

15. Soraya Chemaly, panelist, "We Belong Here: Pushing Back against Online Harassment," keynote panel discussion with moderator Sarah Jeong and panelists

Soraya Chemaly, Michelle Ferrier, Amanda Hess, and Laurie Penny, Online News Association Conference and Awards Banquet (ONA15), Los Angeles, September 25, 2015, https://livestream.com/accounts/5804560/ona15/videos/100236201.

16. Sarah Kliff, "Writer Lindy West Interviewing Her Cruelest Troll Is an Amazing 20 Minutes of Radio," Vox, February 3, 2015, https://www.vox.com/2015/2/3/7970625/trolls-lindy-west.

17. Stephanie Madden, Melissa Janoske, Rowena Briones Winkler, and Amanda Nell Edgar, "Mediated Misogynoir: Intersecting Race and Gender in Online Harassment," in *Mediating Misogyny: Gender, Technology, and Harassment*, ed. Jacqueline Ryan Vickery and Tracy Everbach (Palgrave Macmillan, 2018).

18. Pew Research Center, "Online Harassment," October 23, 2014, http://www.pewinternet.org/2014/10/23/12113/.

19. Pew Research Center, "Online Harassment."

20. Citron, *Hate Crimes in Cyberspace*.

21. Amanda Lenhart, Michele Ybarra, Kathryn Zickuhr and Myeshia Price-Feeney.] "Online Harassment, Digital Abuse and Cyberstalking in America," November 21, 2016. https://datasociety.net/library/online-harassment-digital-abuse-cyberstalking.

22. Ferrier and Garud-Patkar, "TrollBusters," 323. They include much more data about specific countries for those interested.

23. https://www.symantec.com/en/au/about/newsroom/press-releases/2016/symantec_0906_01.

24. Melissa Dempsey, "Norton Study Shows Online Harassment Nears Epidemic Proportions for Young Australian Women," news release, March 8, 2016, https://www.symantec.com/en/au/about/newsroom/press-releases/2016/symantec_0309_01.

25. https://www.symantec.com.

26. Marie Tessier, "High-Tech Stalking Devices Extend Abusers' Reach," Women's eNews, October 1, 2006, http://womensenews.org/2006/10/hi-tech-stalking-devices-extend-abusers-reach/.

27. Domestic Abuse Intervention Programs, "Understanding the Power and Control Wheel," https://www.theduluthmodel.org/wheels.

28. Soraya Chemaly, "Online Abuse 101," Women's Media Center, http://wmcspeechproject.com/online-abuse-101.

29. Sarah Jeong, *The Internet of Garbage* (Forbes, 2015).

30. Marie Tessier, Kristin Rohlwing, and Humera Lodhi, "Engaging Women: Reflecting the Reality of Your Audience," Reynolds Journalism Institute, Missouri School of Journalism, University of Missouri, March 8, 2016, https://www.rjionline .org/stories/engaging-women-reflecting-the-reality-of-your-audience.

31. Katie Rogers, "Vanessa Williams Receives 'Unexpected' Apology at Miss America," *New York Times*, September 14, 2015, https://www.nytimes.com/2015/09/15 /arts/television/vanessa-williams-returns-to-miss-america-and-receives-an-apology .html.

32. Charlotte Laws, "I've Been Called the 'Erin Brockovich' of Revenge Porn, and for the First Time Ever, Here Is My Entire Uncensored Story of Death Threats, Anonymous, and the FBI," xo Jane, November 21, 2013, http://www.xojane.com /it-happened-to-me/charlotte-laws-hunter-moore-erin-brockovich-revenge-porn.

33. Anita Sarkeesian, "Talking Publicly about Harassment Generates More Harassment," *Feminist Frequency* (blog), July 2015, http://femfreq.tumblr.com/post /132152537305/talking-publicly-about-harassment-generates-more.

34. Jim Edwards, "Video Gamers Are Having a Bizarre Debate over Whether Sending Death Threats to Women Is a Serious Issue," *Business Insider*, October 13, 2014, http://uk.businessinsider.com/gamergate-death-threats-2014-10.

35. Taylor Wofford, "Is GamerGate about Media Ethics or Harassing Women? Harassment, the Data Shows," *Newsweek*, October 25, 2014, http://europe.newsweek .com/gamergate-about-media-ethics-or-harassing-women-harassment-data-show -279736?rm=eu.

36. Jim Edwards, "FBI 'Gamergate' File Says Prosecutors Declined to Charge Men Who Sent Death Threats—Even When They Confessed on Video," Yahoo! Finance, February 16, 2017, https://sg.finance.yahoo.com/news/fbi-gamergate-file-says -prosecutors-101252385.html.

37. Edwards, "FBI 'Gamergate' File."

38. Emma A. James and Nicole A. Vincent, "Random Rape Threat Generator," Rapeglish.com. https://rapethreatgenerator.com.

39. M. C. Black et al., "The National Intimate Partner and Sexual Violence Survey: 2010 Summary Report," Centers for Disease Control and Prevention, National Center for Injury Prevention and Control, http://www.cdc.gov/ViolencePrevention /pdf/NISVS_Report2010-a.pdf.

40. Amanda Taub, "*The Guardian* Study's Hidden Lesson: Trolls Reinforce White Male Dominance in Journalism," Vox, April 13, 2017, https://www.vox.com/2016/4 /13/11414942/guardian-study-harassment.

41. Becky Gardiner et al., "The Dark Side of *Guardian* Comments," *The Guardian*, April 12, 2016, https://www.theguardian.com/technology/2016/apr/12/the-dark-side -of-guardian-comments.

42. Gardiner et al., "The Dark Side."

43. Soraya Chemaly, interview with the author, May 16, 2017.

44. Lindy West, "What Happened When I Confronted My Cruelest Troll," February 2, 2015, *The Guardian,* https://www.theguardian.com/society/2015/feb/02/what -happened-confronted-cruellest-troll-lindy-west#.

45. Phillips, *This Is Why We Can't Have Nice Things*, 15–26.

46. Phillips, *This Is Why We Can't Have Nice Things*, 73.

47. Phillips, *This Is Why We Can't Have Nice Things,* 73–74.

48. Women, Action & Media, "Examples of Gender-Based Hate on Facebook," May 25, 2017, http://www.womenactionmedia.org/examples-of-gender-based-hate -speech-on-facebook.

49. Chemaly, "We Belong Here."

Chapter 5

1. Hanne Jalborg, interview with the author, February 28, 2018.

2. Ben Preston (@RTBenPreston), "In the Newsroom of *Expressen*, a Mighty Swedish Tabloid," Twitter, September 25, 2017, https://twitter.com/RTBenPreston/status /912287281024782336.

3. Renée Kaplan, interview with the author, May 21, 2018.

4. Nina Goswami, interview with the author, September 28, 2020.

5. Olga Stern, interview with the author, May 1, 2018.

6. Laura Zelenko, interview with the author, May 24, 2018.

7. Nina Goswami et al., "The Impact Report 2020: How Our Teams Rose to the 50:50 Challenge," *BBC*, March 2020, https://www.bbc.co.uk/5050/impact2020.

8. Mark Mellman, "Mark Mellman: The Young and the Newsless," *The Hill*, February 4, 2016, https://thehill.com/opinion/mark-mellman/230946-mark-mellman-the -young-and-the-newsless.

9. Laura Hazard Owen, "'If the *Financial Times* Were a Person, It Would Be a Man': Here's How the Paper Is Trying to Change That," *NiemanLab*, April 3, 2018, http:// www.niemanlab.org/2018/04/if-the-financial-times-were-a-person-it-would-be-a -man-heres-how-the-paper-is-trying-to-change-that/.

10. Media Insight Project, "The Personal News Cycle: A Focus on African American and Hispanic News Consumers," American Press Institute and the Associated Press-NORC Center for Public Affairs Research, University of Chicago, September 16, 2014, https://www.americanpressinstitute.org/publications/reports/survey-research/african-american-hispanic-news-consumers.

11. Rick Edmonds, "Newspapers Get $1 in New Digital Ad Revenue for Every $25 in Print Ad Revenue Lost," *Poynter*, September 10, 2012, https://www.poynter.org/news/newspapers-get-1-new-digital-ad-revenue-every-25-print-ad-revenue-lost.

12. Jeremy Peters, "*New York Times* to Impose Fees for Web Readers on March 28," *New York Times*, March 18, 2011, https://www.nytimes.com/2011/03/18/business/media/18times.html.

13. Gerry Smith, "*N.Y. Times* Scales Back Free Articles to Get More Subscribers," *Bloomberg*, December 1, 2017, https://www.bloomberg.com/news/articles/2017-12-01/n-y-times-scales-back-free-articles-to-get-readers-to-subscribe.

14. Owen, "'If the *Financial Times* Were a Person, It Would Be a Man.'"

15. Media Insight Project, "The Personal News Cycle: How Americans Choose to Get Their News," American Press Institute and the Associated Press-NORC Center for Public Affairs Research, University of Chicago, March 17, 2014, http://americanpressinstitute.org/publications/reports/survey-research/personal-news-cycle.

16. Pew Research Center, "Active Science News Consumers Are More Likely to Be Men, College Grads," September 18, 2017, http://www.journalism.org/2017/09/20/science-news-and-information-today/pj_2017-09-20_science-and-news_1-05.

17. Media Insight Project, "How Millennials Get News: Inside the Habits of the First Digital Generation," American Press Institute and the Association Press-NORC Center for Public Affairs Research, University of Chicago, March 16, 2015. https://www.americanpressinstitute.org/publications/reports/survey-research/millennials-news.

18. Nic Newman et al., "Reuters Institute Digital News Report 2020," Reuters Institute for the Study of Journalism, June 2020, https://reutersinstitute.politics.ox.ac.uk/sites/default/files/2020-06/DNR_2020_FINAL.pdf.

19. Sarah Macharia et al., "Who Makes the News? Global Media Monitoring Project 2015," World Association for Christian Communication, November 2015, 8–11, http://cdn.agilitycms.com/who-makes-the-news/Imported/reports_2015/global/gmmp_global_report_en.pdf.

20. Macharia et al., "Who Makes the News?," 9.

21. Macharia et al., "Who Makes the News?," 8–11.

22. Macharia et al., "Who Makes the News?," 10.

23. Macharia et al., "Who Makes the News?," 10.

24. Cristal Williams Chancellor, Diahann Hill, and Katti Gray, "The Status of Women in the U.S. Media 2017," Women's Media Center, 2017, 9, http://www .womensmediacenter.com/reports/the-status-of-women-in-u.s.-media-2017.

25. Goswami et al., "The Impact Report 2020—50:50."

Chapter 6

1. Davey Alba, "Finally, You'll Be Able to Track Your Period in iOS," *Wired*, September 9, 2015, https://www.wired.com/2015/09/finally-youll-able-track-period-ios.

2. Michelle Quinn, "Quinn: Hey Apple Health, Did You Forget about Women?," *The Mercury News*, December 19, 2014, https://www.mercurynews.com/2014/12/19 /quinn-hey-apple-health-did-you-forget-about-women.

3. Sophie Kleeman, "Why Some Left-Handed People Are Having Big Problems with the iPhone," Mic, September 28, 2015, https://www.mic.com/articles/125883 /iphone-6s-6s-plus-ios-9-causing-problems-for-left-handed-users.

4. Center on Media and Human Development, "Teens, Health, and Technology: A National Survey," http://cmhd.northwestern.edu/wp-content/uploads/2015/05 /1886_1_SOC_ConfReport_TeensHealthTech_051115.pdf.

5. Reenita Das, "Femtech: The Digital Revolution in Women's Health," Frost & Sullivan, podcast, October 18, 2019, https://ww2.frost.com/podcasts/femtech-the -digital-revolution-in-womens-health.

6. Ciphercloud, "A Round-Up of Data Breaches in March 2020," Security Boulevard, April 6, 2020, https://securityboulevard.com/2020/04/a-round-up-of-data-breaches -in-march-2020.

7. Genevieve Bell, "We Need Mass Surveillance to Fight COVID-19—But It Doesn't Have to Be Creepy," *MIT Technology Review*, April 12, 2020, https://www .technologyreview.com/2020/04/12/999186/covid-19-contact-tracing-surveillance -data-privacy-anonymity.

8. Frank Konkel, "Report: 2020 Is the Year Data Gets Weaponized," Nextgov, October 30, 2019, http://nextgov.com/cybersecurity/2019/10/report-2020-year-data-gets -weaponized/160984.

9. Natasha Lomas, "Voter Manipulation on Social Media Now a Global Problem, Report Finds," Techcrunch, September 26, 2019, https://techcrunch.com/2019/09 /26/voter-manipulation-on-social-media-now-a-global-problem-report-finds.

10. Lucina Di Meco, "Gendered Disinformation, Fake News, and Women in Politics," Council on Foreign Relations, December 6, 2019, https://www.cfr.org/blog/gendered-disinformation-fake-news-and women-politics.

11. Safiya Umoja Noble, *Algorithms of Oppression: How Search Engines Reinforce Racism* (NYU Press, 2018).

12. Jazmine Ulloa, "How Memes, Text Chains, and Online Conspiracies Have Fueled Coronavirus Protesters and Discord," *Boston Globe*, May 6, 2020, https://www.bostonglobe.com/2020/05/06/nation/how-memes-text-chains-online-conspiracies-haves-fueled-coronavirus-protesters-discord.

13. Queenie Wong, "Twitter under More Pressure to Ban White Supremacists," CNet, November 19, 2019, https://www.cnet.com/news/twitter-under-more-pressure-to-ban-white-supremacists.

14. Emma Grey Ellis, "Greta Thunberg's Online Attackers Reveal a Grim Pattern," *Wired*, March 4, 2020, https://www.wired.com/story/greta-thunberg-online-harassment.

15. David Roe, "Six Security Issues That Will Dominate IoT in 2019," CMS Wire, January 14, 2019, https://www.cmswire.com/internet-of-things/6-security-issues-that-will-dominate-iot-in-2019.

16. Kevin Roose, "The Only Safe Election Is a Low-Tech Election," *New York Times*, February 4, 2020, https://www.nytimes.com/2020/02/04/technology/election-tech.html.

17. Julia Belluz, "Juul Allegedly Shipped 1 Million Contaminated Vaping Products," Vox, October 30, 2019, https://www.vox.com/2019/10/30/20939978/juul-vaping-pods-lawsuit.

18. Daisuke Wakabayashi, "Self-Driving Uber Car Kills Pedestrian in Arizona, Where Robots Roam," *New York Times*, March 19, 2018, https://www.nytimes.com/2018/03/19/technology/uber-driverless-fatality.html.

19. Lydia Ramsey Pflanzer, "The Rise and Fall of Theranos, the Blood-Testing Startup That Went from Silicon Valley Darling to Facing Fraud Charges," *Business Insider*, April 11, 2019, https://www.businessinsider.com/the-history-of-silicon-valley-unicorn-theranos-and-ceo-elizabeth-holmes-2018-5.

20. Catherine Buni and Soraya Chemaly, "The Risk Makers: Viral Hate, Election Interference, and Hacked Accounts. Inside the Tech Industry's Decades-Long Failure to Reckon with Risk," Type Investigations, September 21, 2020, https://www.typeinvestigations.org/investigation/2020/09/21/the-risk-makers.

21. Kat Holmes, *Mismatch: How Inclusion Shapes Design* (MIT Press, 2018).

22. Pinterest's early successes among women were also a problem for a company. In later years, the company worked to attract men and change their perception that the site is only for women.

23. Christopher J. Mendez et al., "Open Source Barriers to Entry, Revisited: A Socio-technical Perspective," in *ICSE '18: Proceedings of the 40th International Conference on Software Engineering* (ACM Press, 2018), https://doi.org/10.1145/3180155.3180241.

24. Y-Vonne Hutchinson, "Biased by Design," *MIT Technology Review*, August 23, 2016, https://www.technologyreview.com/s/602154/biased-by-design.

25. Sasha Costanza-Cook, *Design Justice: Community-Led Practices to Build the Worlds We Need* (MIT Press, 2020).

26. Design Justice Network, "Design Justice Network Principles," summer 2018, https://designjustice.org/read-the-principles.

27. Eric Ries, *The Lean Startup: How Today's Entrepreneurs Use Continuous Innovation to Create Radically Successful Businesses* (Crown, 2011), and http://theleanstartup.com.

28. Eric Ries, "The Lean Startup Methodology," The Lean Startup, http://theleanstartup.com/principles.

29. Ries, "The Lean Startup Methodology."

30. Strategyzer, "The Business Model Canvas." https://www.strategyzer.com/canvas/business-model-canvas.

31. Alexander Osterwalder and Yves Pigneur, *Business Model Generation: A Handbook for Visionaries, Game Changers and Challengers* (John Wiley, 2010).

32. Alexandra Stevenson, "Facebook Admits It Was Used to Incite Violence in Myanmar," *New York Times*, November 6, 2018, https://www.nytimes.com/2018/11/06/technology/myanmar-facebook.html.

33. Daniel Victor, "Microsoft Created a Twitter Bot to Learn from Users: It Quickly Became a Racist Jerk," *New York Times*, March 25, 2016, https://www.nytimes.com/2016/03/25/technology/microsoft-created-a-twitter-bot-to-learn-from-users-it-quickly-became-a-racist-jerk.html.

34. Elaine Glusac, "As Airbnb Grows, So Do Claims of Discrimination," *New York Times*, June 26, 2016, https://www.nytimes.com/2016/06/26/travel/airbnb-discrimination-lawsuit.html.

35. Benjamin Edelman, Michael Luca, and Daniel Svirsky, "Racial Discrimination in the Sharing Economy: Results from a Field Experiment," *American Economic Journal: Applied Economics* 9, no. 2 (April 2017): 1–22.

36. Abba Bhatari, "Airbnb Hires Eric Holder to Help Company Fight Discrimination," *Washington Post*, July 20, 2016, https://www.washingtonpost.com/news/business/wp/2016/07/20/eric-holder-joins-airbnb-to-help-company-fight-discrimination.

37. Hutchinson, "Biased by Design."

Chapter 7

1. Janet Shibley Hyde et al., "The Future of Sex and Gender in Psychology: Five Challenges to the Gender Binary," *American Psychologist* 74, no. 2 (February 2019): 171–193, http://dx.doi.org/10.1037/amp0000307.

2. design-people, "We Are Product & Experience Designers," home page, https://www.design-people.com.

3. Klaus Schroeder, in "Hack for Her Summit," video, YouTube, January 26, 2016, https://www.youtube.com/watch?v=UNOCAEK5fm8.

4. Gendered Innovations in Science, Health & Medicine, Engineering, and Environment, "Inclusive Crash Test Dummies: Rethinking Standards and Reference Models," Stanford University, http://genderedinnovations.stanford.edu/case-studies/crash.html.

5. Gendered Innovations in Science, Health & Medicine, Engineering, and Environment, "Stem Cells: Analyzing Sex," Stanford University, http://genderedinnovations.stanford.edu/case-studies/stem_cells.html.

6. Gendered Innovations in Science, Health & Medicine, Engineering, and Environment, "Osteoporosis Research in Men: Rethinking Standards and Reference Models," Stanford University, http://genderedinnovations.stanford.edu/case-studies/osteoporosis.html.

7. Gendered Innovations in Science, Health & Medicine, Engineering, and Environment, "Housing and Neighborhood Design: Analyzing Gender," Stanford University, http://genderedinnovations.stanford.edu/case-studies/urban.html.

8. Caroline Criado Perez, *Invisible Women: Data Bias in a World Designed for Men* (Abrams Press, 2019), 156.

9. Christopher J. Mendez et al., "Open Source Barriers to Entry, Revisited: A Sociotechnical Perspective," in *ICSE '18: Proceedings of the 40th International Conference on Software Engineering* (ACM Press, 2018), 1004–1015, https//doi.org/10/1145/3180155.3180241.

10. Marie Tessier, Kristin Rohlwing, and Humera Lodhi, unpublished data from the Engaging Women project conducted in 2016 at the Reynolds Journalism Institute, Missouri School of Journalism, University of Missouri.

11. Marie Tessier, Kristin Rohlwing, and Humera Lodhi, "Engaging Women: Reflecting the Reality of Your Audience," Reynolds Journalism Institute, Missouri School of Journalism, University of Missouri, March 8, 2016, https://www.rjionline.org/stories/engaging-women-reflecting-the-reality-of-your-audience.

12. Meredith D. Clark, interview with the author, September 24, 2020.

13. Responsible Research & Innovation Tools, "Welcome to the RRI Toolkit: Towards an Open Science and Innovation System That Tackles the Societal Challenges of Our World," https://www.rri-tools.eu.

14. Marianne Graves Petersen et al., *Guidebook to a Female Interaction Strategy* (design-people, 2012).

15. The GenderMag Project, home page, https://gendermag.org/index.html.

16. Margaret Burnett, "Finding Inclusiveness Software Issues with GenderMag: A Field Investigation," presentation of research results at Computer Human Interaction conference, May 31, 2016. https://www.youtube.com/watch?v=6HYvp5GrPjU.

17. Anita Sarma, "Squashing Inclusivity Bugs in Open Source Software," Opensource.com, August 3, 2018, https://opensource.com/article/18/8/inclusivity-bugs-open-source-software.

18. Sarma, "Squashing Inclusivity Bugs."

19. Margaret Burnett et al., "Finding Gender-Inclusiveness Software Issues with GenderMag: A Field Investigation," in *CHI '16: Proceedings of the 2016 CHI Conference on Human Factors in Computing Systems*, 2586–2598 (ACM Press, 2016), https://doi.org/10.1145/2858036.2858274.

20. Margaret Burnett, interview with the author, January 17, 2020.

21. Gendered Innovations in Science, Health & Medicine, Engineering, and Environment, "Engineering Checklist," Stanford University, http://genderedinnovations.stanford.edu/methods/engineering_checklist.html.

22. Martina Schraudner, "Gender and Innovation: Frauhofer's Discover Gender Research Findings," in *The Innovation Potential of Diversity: Practical Examples for the Innovation Management*, ed. Anne Spritzley, Peter Ohlausen, and Dieter Sprath (Fraunhofer Verlag, 2010).

23. Gendered Innovations in Science, Health & Medicine, Engineering, and Environment, "Gender," in "Terms, Stanford University, http://genderedinnovations.stanford.edu/terms/gender.html.

24. Gendered Innovations, "Gender."

25. RRI Tools, "RRI Tools: A Practical Guide to Responsible Research and Innovation. Key Lessons from RRI Tools," https://www.rri-tools.eu.

26. RRI Tools.

27. RRI Tools.

28. RRI Tools, "Policy Agendas," in "Entering into RRI," https://www.rri-tools.eu.

29. Sasha Costanza-Chock, *Design Justice: Community-Led Practices to Build the Worlds We Need* (MIT Press, 2020).

30. Kat Holmes, *Mismatch: How Inclusion Shapes Design* (MIT Press, 2018), 61.

Conclusion

1. Coral Project, "How Spotlight Uses Ask: 'Discuss Spotlight Part One: Does Boston Deserve Its Racist Reputation?,'" Coral by Vox Media, May 10, 2018, https://coralproject.net/blog/spotlight-ask.

2. Akilah Johnson, Liz Kowalczyk, Todd Wallack, Nicole Dungca, Adrian Walker, Andrew Ryan and Patricia Wen, "Boston. Racism. Image. Reality," *Boston Globe*, December 10, 2017.

3. Davey Alba, Catie Edmondson, and Mike Isaac, "Facebook Expands Definition of Terrorist Organizations to Limit Extremism," *New York Times*, September 17, 2019, https://www.nytimes.com/2019/09/17/technology/facebook-hate-speech-extremism.html.

4. Jennifer Steinhauer, "Gender Gap Closes When Everyone's on the Ballot, Study Shows," *New York Times*, June 24, 2019, https://www.nytimes.com/2019/06/24/us/politics/candidates-women-people-of-color-elections.html.

Bibliography

Alba, Davey. "Finally, You'll Be Able to Track Your Period in iOS." *Wired*, September 9, 2015. https://www.wired.com/2015/09/finally-youll-able-track-period-ios.

Albright, Madeleine. "Madeleine Albright: My Undiplomatic Moment." *New York Times*, February 12, 2016. https://www.nytimes.com/2016/02/13/opinion/madeleine -albright-my-undiplomatic-moment.html.

American National Election Studies. Home page. http://www.electionstudies.org.

The American Physical. "Doctoral Degrees Earned by Women, by Major," 2018, https://www.aps.org/programs/education/statistics/fraction-phd.cfm

American Press Institute. "How African Americans and Hispanics Consume News." September 16, 2014. https://www.americanpressinstitute.org/publications/reports /survey-research/african-american-hispanic-news-consumers.

American Press Institute. "Social and Demographic Differences in News Habits and Attitudes." March 17, 2014. https://www.americanpressinstitute.org/publications /reports/survey-research/social-demographic-differences-news-habits-attitudes/.

Anderson, Ashley A., Dominique Brossard, Dietram A. Scheufele, Michael A. Xenos, and Peter Ladwig. "The 'Nasty Effect': Online Incivility and Risk Perceptions of Emerging Technologies." *Journal of Computer-Mediated Communication* 19, no. 3 (April 1, 2014): 373–387. https://doi.org/10.1111/jcc4.12009.

Andi, Simge, Meera Selva, and Rasmus Kleis Nielsen. "Women and Leadership in the News Media 2020: Evidence from Ten Markets." Reuters Institute for the Study of Journalism, Oxford University, March 8, 2020. https://reutersinstitute.politics.ox .ac.uk/women-and-leadership-news-media-2020-evidence-ten-markets.

Anthony, Susan B., Matilda Joslyn Gage, and Ida Husted Harper. *The History of Woman Suffrage*. 6 vols. Rochester, NY: Anthony, 1881–1922.

"Are Men Not Listening to Women?" *New York Times*, February 29, 2020. https://www.nytimes.com/2020/02/29/opinion/letters/men-women-listening.html.

Atkeson, Lonna Rae, and Ronald B. Rapoport. "The More Things Change the More They Stay the Same: Examining Gender Differences in Political Attitude Expression, 1952–2000." *Public Opinion Quarterly* 67, no. 4 (2003): 495–521. http://www.jstor.org.prxy4.ursus.maine.edu/stable/3521691.

Atkins, Ros. "How We're Bringing Gender Equality to BBC Expert Guests." Huff-Post UK, February 4, 2018. http://www.huffingtonpost.co.uk/entry/bbc-women_uk_5ac1f4e5e4b0a47437ac46cf.

Baek, Young Min, Magdalena Wojcieszak, and Michael X. Delli Carpini. "Online versus Face-to-Face Deliberation: Who? Why? What? With What Effects?" *New Media & Society*, September 19, 2011. https://doi.org/10.1177/1461444811413191.

Bailey, Moya. "New Terms of Resistance: A Response to Zenzele Isoke." *Souls* 15, no. 4 (October 1, 2013): 341–343. https://doi.org/10.1080/10999949.2014.884451.

Banet-Weiser, Sarah, and Kate M. Miltner. "#MasculinitySoFragile: Culture, Structure, and Networked Misogyny." *Feminist Media Studies* 16, no. 1 (January 2, 2016): 171–174. https://doi.org/10.1080/14680777.2016.1120490.

Pamela Barnes Craig, "American Women: Resources from the Law Library," Library of Congress, March 19, 2019, https://memory.loc.gov/ammem/awhhtml/awlaw3/d1.html.

Bartlett, Jamie. "Misogyny on Twitter." *Demos*. February 9, 2017. https://www.demos.co.uk/project/misogyny-on-twitter.

Bates, Laura. "What I Have Learned from Five Years of Everyday Sexism." *The Guardian*, April 17, 2017. https://www.theguardian.com/lifeandstyle/2017/apr/17/what-i-have-learned-from-five-years-of-everyday-sexism?CMP=share_btn_tw.

Beard, Mary. "Internet Fury: Or Having Your Anatomy Dissected Online." *A Don's Life* (blog). *The Times*, April 22, 2017. http://timesonline.typepad.com/dons_life/2013/01/internet-fury.html.

Beard, Mary. "The Public Voice of Women." *London Review of Books*, March 20, 2014. https://www.lrb.co.uk/v36/n06/mary-beard/the-public-voice-of-women.

Beard, Mary. *Women & Power: A Manifesto*. Liveright Publishing, 2017.

Beard, Mary. "Women in Power." *London Review of Books*, March 16, 2017. https://www.lrb.co.uk/v39/n06/mary-beard/women-in-power.

Beaujon, Andrew. "What a Commenter Has to Do to Get Banned from *The New York Times*." Poynter, October 15, 2013. http://www.poynter.org/2013/what-a -commenter-has-to-do-to-get-banned-from-the-new-york-times/225899.

Beck, Kent, et al. "Manifesto for Agile Software Development." 2001. http:// agilemanifesto.org.

Bell, Emily. "Silicon Valley and Journalism: Make Up or Break up?" Video, Reuters Institute for the Study of Journalism, Oxford University, November 21, 2014. http://reutersinstitute.politics.ox.ac.uk/risj-review/emily-bell-silicon-valley-and -journalism-make-or-break. Transcript at Nick Tjaardstra, "Emily Bell's Seminal Speech on the Relationship between Journalism and Technology: It's Time to Make Up or Break Up," WAN-IFRA, November 26, 2014, https://blog.wan-ifra.org/2014 /11/26/emily-bells-seminal-speech-on-the-relationship-between-journalism-and -technology-its-time.

Benesch, Christine. "An Empirical Analysis of the Gender Gap in News Consumption." *Journal of Media Economics* 25, no. 3 (July 1, 2012): 147–167. https://doi.org /10.1080/08997764.2012.700976.

Benton, Joshua. "This Is *The New York Times'* Digital Path Forward." NiemanLab, January 17, 2017. http://www.niemanlab.org/2017/01/this-is-the-new-york-times -digital-path-forward.

Berg, Janne. "Digital Democracy—Studies of Online Political Participation." September 25, 2020. https://www.academia.edu/35491171/Digital_democracy_stud ies_of_online_political_participation.

Bergen, Mark. "Google Overhauls Policies after Uproar over YouTube Videos." Bloomberg, March 21, 2017. https://www.bloomberg.com/news/articles/2017-03-21/google -overhauls-ads-policies-after-uproar-over-youtube-videos.

Bhatari, Abba. "Airbnb Hires Eric Holder to Help Company Fight Discrimination." *Washington Post*, July 20, 2016, https://www.washingtonpost.com/news/business /wp/2016/07/20/eric-holder-joins-airbnb-to-help-company-fight-discrimination.

Bonime-Blanc, Andrea. "Pale, Stale & Male: Does Board Diversity Matter?" *Risk Management*, September 4, 2018. http://www.rmmagazine.com/2018/09/04/pale-stale -male.

Broadwater, Luke, and Catie Edmondson. "A.O.C. Unleashes a Viral Condemnation of Sexism in Congress." *New York Times*, July 23, 2020, https://nyti.ms/2RFBrJQ #permid=108304920.

Brooks, David. "Why Trump Soars." *New York Times*, April 18, 2011, http://www .nytimes.com/2011/04/19/opinion/19brooks.html.

Bryan, Frank M. *Real Democracy: The New England Town Meeting and How It Works.* University of Chicago Press, 2004.

Buni, Catherine, and Soraya Chemaly. "The Risk Makers: Viral Hate, Election Interference, and Hacked Accounts. Inside the Tech Industry's Decades-Long Failure to Reckon with Risk." Type Investigations, September 21, 2020. https://www .typeinvestigations.org/investigation/2020/09/21/the-risk-makers.

Buni, Catherine, and Soraya Chemaly. "The Secret Rules of the Internet." The Verge, April 13, 2016. http://www.theverge.com/2016/4/13/11387934/internet-moderator -history-youtube-facebook-reddit-censorship-free-speech.

Burnett, Margaret. "Finding Gender-Inclusiveness Software Issues with GenderMag: A Field Investigation." Video recorded at the 2016 CHI Conference on Human Factors in Computing Systems in San Jose, California, United States, May 7–12, 2016. https://www.youtube.com/watch?v=6HYvp5GrPjU.

Burnett, Margaret, Anicia Peters, Charles Hill, and Noha Elarief. "Finding Gender-Inclusiveness Software Issues with GenderMag: A Field Investigation." *CHI '16: Proceedings of the 2016 CHI Conference on Human Factors in Computing Systems*, 2586–2598. ACM Press, 2016. https://doi.org/10.1145/2858036.2858274.

Buskirk, Christopher. "Barr Is Right about Everything. Admit You Were Wrong." *New York Times*, April 18, 2019. https://www.nytimes.com/2019/04/18/opinion /barr-media-trump.html.

Campbell, Colin. "Brianna Wu Is Confident a Death Threat Harasser Will Be Caught and Jailed." Polygon, November 4, 2014. http://www.polygon.com/2014/11/4 /7157433/brianna-wu-death-threat-reward.

Captain, Sean. "Disqus Promises to Banish Toxic Reader Comments from Sites Like Breitbart." Fast Company, April 4, 2017. https://www.fastcompany.com/40403181 /diqus-promises-to-banish-toxic-reader-comments-from-sites-like-breitbart.

Catalyst. "Women CEOs of the S&P 500." http://www.catalyst.org/knowledge /women-ceos-sp-500.

Catalyst. "Workplaces That Work for Everyone." Home page. A wide-ranging source of data and research about the status of of women in private business and public leadership. https://www.catalyst.org/research.

Center for American Women and Politics. "Current Numbers." Rutgers University. http://www.cawp.rutgers.edu/current-numbers.

Center for American Women and Politics. "Research and Scholarship." Rutgers University. https://cawp.rutgers.edu/research.

Chavez, Ronald. "Google to Remove Revenge Porn Sites from Search." Mashable, June 19, 2017. http://mashable.com/2015/06/19/google-remove-revenge-porn-sites/.

Chemaly, Soraya. "The Problem with a Technology Revolution Designed Primarily for Men." Quartz, May 7, 2019. https://qz.com/640302/why-is-so-much-of-our-new -technology-designed-primarily-for-men.

Chemaly, Soraya. "10 Simple Words Every Girl Should Learn." *Role Reboot* (blog), May 5, 2014. http://www.rolereboot.org/culture-and-politics/details/2014-05-10 -simple-words-every-girl-learn.

Chemaly, Soraya. "10 Ways Society Can Close the Confidence Gap." Huffington Post, April 23, 2014. http://www.huffingtonpost.com/soraya-chemaly/10-ways -society-can-close-the-confidence-gap_b_5200419.html.

Chemaly, Soraya, and Catherine Buni. "The Unsafety Net: How Social Media Turned against Women." *The Atlantic*, October 9, 2014. https://www.theatlantic .com/technology/archive/2014/10/the-unsafety-net-how-social-media-turned-against -women/381261/.

Cheng, Justin. "The Awkward Truth about Trolls: Any of Us Could Become One." *The Guardian*, February 10, 2017. https://www.theguardian.com/commentisfree /2017/feb/10/truth-trolls-internet-abusive-comments-online.

Cherny, Lynn. "Gender Differences in Text-Based Virtual Reality." In *Cultural Performances: Proceedings of the Third Berkeley Women and Language Conference*, ed. Mary Bucholtz, Anita C. Liang, Laurel A. Sutton, and Caitlin Hines. Berkeley Women and Language Group, University of California, 1994. http://citeseerx.ist.psu.edu /viewdoc/summary?doi=10.1.1.48.9081.

Cristal Williams Chancellor, Katti Gray, Diahann Hill, Faye Wolfe, Tiffany Nguyen. "The Status of Women in the U.S. Media, 2019." Women's Media Center, February 21 2019. https://womensmediacenter.com/reports/the-status-of-women-in-u-s -media-2019.

Chang, S. "Specialization, Homiphily, and Gender in a Social Curation Site: Findings from Pinterest." *CSCW '14: Proceedings of the 17th ACM conference on Computer Supported Cooperative Work & Social Computing*, 674–686. ACM Press, 2014. https:// doi.org/10.1145/2531602.2531660.

Chen, Vivia. "Women and Rejection." *The American Lawyer*, April 7, 2017. http://www .americanlawyer.com/id=1202781816746/Women-and-Rejection.

Chira, Susan. "Opinion: Elizabeth Warren Was Told to Be Quiet. Women Can Relate." *New York Times*, February 8, 2017. https://www.nytimes.com/2017/02/08 /opinion/elizabeth-warren-was-told-to-be-quiet-women-can-relate.html.

Chira, Susan, and Catrin Einhorn. "How Tough Is It to Change a Culture of Harassment? Ask Women at Ford." *New York Times*, December 19, 2017. https://www.nytimes.com/interactive/2017/12/19/us/ford-chicago-sexual-harassment.html.

Citron, Danielle Keats. *Hate Crimes in Cyberspace*. Harvard University Press, 2014.

Clark, Meredith D. "Marginalized Voices and the Comments." Coral by Vox Media, October 2, 2018. https://guides.coralproject.net/survey-marginalized-voices.

Clark, Meredith D. "Marginalized Voices in Comment Spaces." Coral by Vox Media, December 4, 2017. https://coralproject.net/blog/marginalized-voices-in-comment-spaces.

Clifton, Brian, Gilad Lotan, and Emma Pierson. "How to Tell Whether a Twitter User Is Pro-Choice or Pro-Life without Reading Any of Their Tweets." Quartz, January 19, 2017. https://qz.com/520309/how-to-tell-whether-a-twitter-user-is-pro-choice-or-pro-life-without-reading-any-of-their-tweets.

CNN Business. "Insights from 'Red State Christians' Author." Video, December 1, 2019. https://www.cnn.com/videos/business/2019/12/01/insights-from-red-state-christians-author.cnn.

Coffman, Katherine Baldiga. "Evidence on Self-Stereotyping and the Contribution of Ideas." *Quarterly Journal of Economics* 129, no. 4 (November 2014): 1625–1660. https://doi.org/10.1093/qje/qju023.

Collins, Patricia Hill, and Sirma Bilge. *Intersectionality*, 2nd ed. Polity Press, 2020.

Cook, Sarah Gibbard. "Women Lead in Adopting New Technologies." *Women in Higher Education* 21, no. 2 (2012): 24–25. https://doi.org/10.1002/whe.10296.

Cooper, Michael. "Plácido Domingo Leaves Met Opera amid Sexual Harassment Inquiry." *New York Times*, September 24, 2019. https://www.nytimes.com/2019/09/24/arts/music/placido-domingo-met-opera-harassment.html.

Copeland, Libby. "Why Do Women Vote Differently Than Men?" Slate, January 4, 2012. http://www.slate.com/articles/double_x/doublex/2012/01/the_gender_gap_in_politics_why_do_women_vote_differently_than_men_.html.

Coral. "12,000 People Have Something to Say." Vox Media, January 12, 2017. https://coralproject.net/blog/12000-people-have-something-to-say/

Costanza-Chock, Sasha. *Design Justice: Community-Led Practices to Build the Worlds We Need*. MIT Press, 2020.

Crawford, Kate. "Artificial Intelligence's White Guy Problem." *New York Times*, June 26, 2016. https://www.nytimes.com/2016/06/26/opinion/sunday/artificial-intelligences-white-guy-problem.html.

Crenshaw, Kimberlé, Neil Gotanda, Gary Peller, and Kendall Thomas, eds. *Critical Race Theory: The Key Writings That Formed the Movement.* The New Press, 1995.

Crenshaw, Kimberlé Williams, Luke Charles Harris, Daniel Martinez HoSang, and George Lipsitz. *Seeing Race Again: Countering Colorblindness across the Disciplines.* University of California Press, 2019.

Cutler, Anne, and Donia R. Scott. "Speaker Sex and Perceived Apportionment of Talk." *Applied Psycholinguistics* 11 (1990): 253–272. pubman.mpdl.mpg.de/pubman /item/escidoc:68785 . . . /Cutler_1990_Speaker+sex.pdf.

Dam, Rikke Friis, and Teo Yu Siang. "5 Stages in the Design Thinking Process." Interaction Design Foundation, July 13, 2019. https://www.interaction-design.org/literature /article/5-stages-in-the-design-thinking-process.

Das, Reenita. "Femtech: The Digital Revolution in Women's Health," Frost & Sullivan, podcast, October 18, 2019, https://ww2.frost.com/podcasts/femtech-the-digital -revolution-in-womens-health.

Data & Society. "Online Harassment, Digital Abuse." January 18, 2017. https:// datasociety.net/blog/2017/01/18/online-harassment-digital-abuse.

Davis, Julie Hirschfeld. "House Condemns Trump's Attack on Four Congresswomen as Racist." *New York Times*, July 16, 2019. https://www.nytimes.com/2019/07/16/us /politics/trump-tweet-house-vote.html.

Deng, Cathy. "Are Men Talking Too Much? #whotalks Will Show You." Gender-Avenger, August 11, 2017. https://www.genderavenger.com/blog/are-men-talking -too-much.

Design Justice Network. https://designjustice.org.

design-people. "We Are Product & Experience Designers." https://www.design -people.com.

Dewey, Caitlin, and Caitlin Dewey. "Why Women Don't Leave Comments Online." *Washington Post*, January 8, 2015. https://www.washingtonpost.com/news/the -intersect/wp/2015/01/08/why-women-dont-leave-comments-online/?utm_term =.19ab4ae246c0.

Diakopoulos, Nicholas, and Simranjit Singh Sachar. "Changing Names in Online Comments at the *New York Times*." Tenth AAAI International Conference on Web and Social Media, 2016. aaai.org/ocs/index.php/ICWSM/ICWSM16/paper/view /13069.

Digital News Report. "Executive Summary and Key Findings of the 2020 Report." October 1, 2020. http://www.digitalnewsreport.org/survey/2020/overview-key -findings-2020/.

Di Meco, Lucina. "Gendered Disinformation, Fake News, and Women in Politics," Council on Foreign Relations, December 6, 2019, https://www.cfr.org/blog/gendered-disinformation-fake-news and-women-politics.

Dittmar, Kelly. "You Can Try to Silence Women of Color in Congress, But It Won't Work." Vox, June 20, 2017. https://www.vox.com/mischiefs-of-faction/2017/6/20/15840006/women-of-color-congress-silenced-no.

Djupe, Paul, Scott Mcclurg, and Anand Edward Sokhey, "The Political Consequences of Gender in Social Networks," British Journal of Political Science 48, no. 3 (June 22, 2016): 1–22.

Doctor, Ken. "Newsonomics: 10 Numbers on The New York Times' 1 Million Digital-Subscriber Milestone." NiemanLab, December 3, 2017. http://www.niemanlab.org/2015/08/newsonomics-10-numbers-on-the-new-york-times-1-million-digital-subscriber-milestone.

Doctor, Ken. "Newsonomics: The New York Times Is Setting Its Sights on 10 Million Digital Subscribers." NiemanLab, December 5, 2017. http://www.niemanlab.org/2016/12/newsonomics-the-new-york-times-is-setting-its-sights-on-10-million-digital-subscribers.

Doctor, Ken. "Newsonomics: The Thinking (and Dollars) behind The New York Times' New Digital Strategy." NiemanLab, December 5, 2017. http://www.niemanlab.org/2015/10/newsonomics-the-thinking-and-dollars-behind-the-new-york-times-new-digital-strategy.

Dodero, Camille. "Hunter Moore Makes a Living Screwing You." Village Voice, April 4, 2012. http://www.villagevoice.com/news/hunter-moore-makes-a-living-screwing-you-6435187.

Duhigg, Charles. "What Google Learned from Its Quest to Build the Perfect Team." New York Times, February 25, 2016. https://www.nytimes.com/2016/02/28/magazine/what-google-learned-from-its-quest-to-build-the-perfect-team.html.

Duyn, Emily Van, Cynthia Peacock, and Natalie Jomini Stroud. "The Gender Gap in Online News Comment Sections:" Social Science Computer Review (July 26, 2019). https://doi.org/10.1177/0894439319864876.

Dyer, Harry T. "Online Anonymity: The Good, the Bad, and the Ugly." Harry T Dyer (blog), January 4, 2017. https://harrytdyer.com/2017/01/04/online-anonymity-the-good-the-bad-and-the-ugly/.

Edelman, Benjamin, Michael Luca, and Dan Svirsky. "Racial Discrimination in the Sharing Economy: Evidence from a Field Experiment." American Economic Journal: Applied Economics 9, no. 2 (April 2017): 1–22.

Edmonds, Rick. "Newspapers Get $1 in New Digital Ad Revenue for Every $25 in Print Ad Revenue Lost." Poynter, September 10, 2012. https://www.poynter.org /news/newspapers-get-1-new-digital-ad-revenue-every-25-print-ad-revenue-lost.

Edwards, Jim. "FBI's 'Gamergate' File Says Prosecutors Declined to Charge Men Believed to Have Sent Death Threats—Even When They Confessed on Video." Yahoo! Finance, February 16, 2017. https://sg.finance.yahoo.com/news/fbi -gamergate-file-says-prosecutors-101252385.html.

Edwards, Jim. "Video Gamers Are Having a Bizarre Debate over Whether Sending Death Threats to Women Is a Serious Issue," Business Insider, October 13, 2014, http://uk.businessinsider.com/gamergate-death-threats-2014-10.

Elejalde-Ruiz, Alexia. "Is Your Business Male or Female?" Chicago Tribune, May 17, 2019. https://www.chicagotribune.com/business/ct-brand-genders-0903-biz-20150904 -story.html.

Elejalde-Ruiz, Alexia. "To Retain Women, Consulting Firm Targets Gender Communication Differences." Chicago Tribune, September 6, 2016. http://www .chicagotribune.com/business/ct-bcg-women-communication-0906-biz-20160906 -story.html.

Ellis, Emma Grey. "Greta Thunberg's Online Attackers Reveal a Grim Pattern." Wired, March 4, 2020. https://www.wired.com/story/greta-thunberg-online-harassment.

Ellis, Justin. "What Happened after 7 News Sites Got Rid of Reader Comments." NiemanLab, September 16, 2015. http://www.niemanlab.org/2015/09/what -happened-after-7-news-sites-got-rid-of-reader-comments.

Ellison, Jude, and Sady Doyle. "The 'Feminized Society' Myth: How the Gender Perception Gap Makes a Female Minority Feel Like a Majority." In These Times, January 22, 2014. http://inthesetimes.com/article/16157/our_feminized_society.

Eslami, Motahhare, Aimee Rickman, Kristen Vaccaro, Amirhossein Aleyasen, Andy Vuong, Karrie Karahalios, Kevin Hamilton, and Christian Sandvig. "'I Always Assumed That I Wasn't Really That Close to [Her]': Reasoning about Invisible Algorithms in News Feeds." In CHI '15: Proceedings of the 33rd Annual ACM Conference on Human Factors in Computing Systems, 153–162. ACM Press, 2015. https://doi.org/10 .1145/2702123.2702556.

Evans, Garrett. "Mark Mellman: The Young and the Newsless." Text. The Hill, January 27, 2015. https://thehill.com/opinion/mark-mellman/230946-mark-mellman -the-young-and-the-newsless.

Fallows, Deborah. "How Women and Men Use the Internet." Pew Research Center, December 28, 2005. http://www.pewinternet.org/2005/12/28/how-women-and -men-use-the-internet.

Farrow, Dylan. "An Open Letter from Dylan Farrow." *On the Ground* (blog). *New York Times*, February 1, 2014. https://kristof.blogs.nytimes.com/2014/02/01/an-open -letter-from-dylan-farrow.

Felder, Adam. "How Comments Shape Perceptions of Sites' Quality—and Affect Traffic." *The Atlantic*, June 5, 2014. http://www.theatlantic.com/technology /archive/2014/06/internet-comments-and-perceptions-of-quality/371862.

Feldon, David F., James Peugh, Michelle A. Maher, Josipa Roksa, and Colby Tofel-Grehl. "Time-to-Credit Gender Inequities of First-Year PhD Students in the Biological Sciences." *CBE Life Sciences Education* 16, no. 1 (2017). https://doi.org/10.1187 /cbe.16-08-0237.

Feminist Frequency (blog). "Talking Publicly about Harassment Generates More Harassment." May 17, 2017. http://femfreq.tumblr.com/post/132152537305/talking -publicly-about-harassment-generates-more.

Ferrier, Michelle. "TrollBusters: Fighting Online Harassment of Women Journalists." In *Mediating Misogyny: Gender, Technology and Harassment*, ed. Jacqueline Ryan Vickery and Tracy Everbach, 311–332. Palgrave Macmillan, 2018.

Fessler, Leah. "Your Company's Slack Is Probably Sexist." Quartz, November 14, 2017. https://work.qz.com/1128150/your-companys-slack-is-probably-sexist.

Feyer, Thomas, and Susan Mermelstein. "The Editors Respond: We Hear You." *New York Times*, January 31, 2019. https://www.nytimes.com/2019/01/31/opinion /letters/letters-to-editor-new-york-times-women.html.

Feyer, Thomas, and Susan Mermelstein, "Women, Please Speak Out." *New York Times*, February 14, 2020. https://www.nytimes.com/2020/02/14/opinion/letters/letters -editor-nytimes-gender.html.

Flaherty, Colleen. "Study Finds Men Speak Twice as Often as Do Women at Colloquiums." *Inside Higher Ed*, December 19, 2017. https://www.insidehighered.com/news /2017/12/19/study-finds-men-speak-twice-often-do-women-colloquiums.

Flueckiger, Simone. "Practical Advice for Tackling Gender Imbalance in News Media from #WINSummit18." WAN-IFRA. June 12, 2018. wan-ifra.org/2018/12/practical -advice-for-tackling-gender-imbalance-in-news-media-from-winsummit18.

Foxman, Abraham H., and Christopher Wolf. *Viral Hate: Containing Its Spread on the Internet*. St. Martin's Press, 2013.

Fry, Erika. "It's 2012 Already: Why Is Opinion Writing Still Mostly Male?" *Columbia Journalism Review* (May 29, 2012). https://www.cjr.org/behind_the_news/its_2012 _already_why_is_opinio.php.

Fuller, Thomas, and Christopher Flavelle. "A Climate Reckoning in Fire-Stricken California." *New York Times*, September 22, 2020. https://www.nytimes.com/2020/09/10/us/climate-change-california-wildfires.html.

Funke, Daniel. "The Coral Project Talked to More Than 150 Global Newsrooms about Building Better Communities. Here's What It Found." Poynter, August 11, 2017. https://www.poynter.org/tech-tools/2017/the-coral-project-talked-to-more-than-150-global-newsrooms-about-building-better-communities-heres-what-it-found.

Gannon, Megan. "Race Is a Social Construct, Scientists Argue." *Scientific American*, February 5, 2016. https://www.scientificamerican.com/article/race-is-a-social-construct-scientists-argue.

Gardiner, Becky, Mahana Mansfield, Ian Anderson, Josh Holder, Daan Louter, and Monica Ulmanu. "The Dark Side of *Guardian* Comments." *The Guardian*, April 12, 2016. https://www.theguardian.com/technology/2016/apr/12/the-dark-side-of-guardian-comments.

Geiger, A. W., and Lauren Kent. "Number of Women Leaders around the World Has Grown, But They're Still a Small Group." Pew Research Center, July 30, 2015. http://www.pewresearch.org/fact-tank/2015/07/30/about-one-in-ten-of-todays-world-leaders-are-women/.

Gendered Innovations in Science, Health & Medicine, Engineering, and Environment. Home page. Stanford University. http://genderedinnovations.stanford.edu.

Gendered Innovations in Science, Health & Medicine, Engineering, and Environment, "Sex and Gender," Stanford University. http://genderedinnovations.stanford.edu/methods-sex-and-gender-analysis.html.

GenderMag Project, The. https://gendermag.org/index.html.

Ginzberg, Lori D. *Elizabeth Cady Stanton: An American Life*. Hill and Wang, 2010.

Global Media Monitoring Project. *GMMP Global, Regional, and National Reports 1995–2020*. Who Makes the News. http://whomakesthenews.org/gmmp/gmmp-reports.

Glusac, Elaine. "As Airbnb Grows, So Do Claims of Discrimination." *New York Times*, June 26, 2016. https://www.nytimes.com/2016/06/26/travel/airbnb-discrimination-lawsuit.html.

Goel, Vindu. "Facebook Scrambles to Police Content amid Rapid Growth." *New York Times*, May 3, 2017. https://www.nytimes.com/2017/05/03/technology/facebook-moderators-q1-earnings.html.

Goldin, Claudia, Lawrence F. Katz, and Ilyana Kuziemko. "The Homecoming of American College Women: The Reversal of the College Gender Gap." Working Paper 12139, March 2006. National Bureau of Economic Research. http://www.nber.org/papers/w12139.

Golding, J. M., G. S. Bradshaw, E. E. Dunlap, and E. C. Hodell. "The Impact of Mock Jury Gender Composition on Deliberations and Conviction Rates in a Child Sexual Assault Trial." *Child Maltreatment* 12, no. 2 (May 1, 2007): 182–190. https://doi.org/10.1177/1077559506298995.

Goltermann, Lori. "Why Cultivating and Maintaining a Diverse Workforce Is Important." Risk Management, April 11, 2019. http://www.rmmagazine.com/2019/04/11/cultivating-and-maintaining-a-diverse-workforce/.

Gonzalez, Francisco Caro, Maria del Mar Garcia Gordillo, and Ofa Bezunartea Valencia. "Approach to the Reasons for the Low Reading Level of Women's Press." *Studies on the Journalistic Message* 20, no. 2 (2014), https://doi.org/10.5209/rev_ESMP.2014.v20.n2.47045.

Goswami, Nina, Lara Joannides, Angela Henshall, Julia Walker, Ros Atkins, Sarah Holmes, Becky Dale, Alison Benjamin, and Robert Cuffe. "The Impact Report 2020: How Our Teams Rose to the 50:50 Challenge." BBC, March 2020. https://www.bbc.co.uk/5050/impact2020.

Graddol, David, and Will Swann. *Gender Voices*. Wiley-Blackwell, 1991.

Graham, Todd. "Everyday Political Talk in the Internet-Based Public Sphere." *Handbook of Digital Politics*, 247–263. Edward Elgar, 2015. https://www.academia.edu/7369446/Everyday_political_talk_in_the_internet_based_public_sphere.

Graham, Todd, and Scott Wright. "A Tale of Two Stories from 'Below the Line': Comment Fields at the *Guardian*." *International Journal of Press/Politics* 20, no. 3 (July 1, 2015): 317–338. https://doi.org/10.1177/1940161215581926.

Grant, Adam, and Sheryl Sandberg. "Adam Grant and Sheryl Sandberg on Discrimination at Work." *New York Times*, December 6, 2014. https://www.nytimes.com/2014/12/07/opinion/sunday/adam-grant-and-sheryl-sandberg-on-discrimination-at-work.html.

Greenberg, Andy. "Now Anyone Can Deploy Google's Troll-Fighting AI." Wired, February 23, 2017. https://www.wired.com/2017/02/googles-troll-fighting-ai-now-belongs-world.

Grove, Jack. "Female Academics 'Interrupted More in Interviews Than Men.'" *Chronicle of Education*, June 29, 2017. http://thechronicleofeducation.com/2017/06/29/female-academics-interrupted-interviews-men.

Groysberg, Boris, and Deborah Bell. "Dysfunction in the Boardroom." *Harvard Business Review*, June 1, 2013. https://hbr.org/2013/06/dysfunction-in-the-boardroom.

Hafner, Josh. "Here's How Badly Clinton Lost among Women in New Hampshire This Week." *USA Today*, February 10, 2016. https://www.usatoday.com/story/news /politics/onpolitics/2016/02/10/new-hampshire-hillary-clinton-women-voters-bernie -sanders/80198302.

Hancock, Adrienne B., and Benjamin A. Rubin. "Influence of Communication Partner's Gender on Language." *Journal of Language and Social Psychology* 34, no. 1 (January 1, 2015): 46–64. https://doi.org/10.1177/0261927X14533197.

Harmanci, Reyhan. "The Opinion Pages: Mostly a Man's World." SFGate, May 30, 2017. http://www.sfgate.com/entertainment/article/The-opinion-pages-mostly-a-man -s-world-3278707.php.

Harrison, Sara. "Five Years of Tech Diversity Reports—and Little Progress." *Wired*, October 16, 2019. https://www.wired.com/story/five-years-tech-diversity-reports -little-progress.

Hassan, Aisha. "Great Quarter, Guys: Men Dominate 92% of All Corporate Earnings Calls." Quartz, September 13, 2018. https://qz.com/work/1389994/men-dominate -92-of-corporate-conference-calls.

Hawkesworth, Mary. "Congressional Enactments of Race-Gender: Toward a Theory of Raced-Gendered Institutions." *American Political Science Review* 97, no. 4 (2003): 529–550.

Herring, Susan C. "Who's Got the Floor in Computer-Mediated Conversation? Edelsky's Gender Patterns Revisited." *Language@Internet* 7, no. 8 (December 29, 2010). http://www.languageatinternet.org/articles/2010/2857.

Herring, Susan C., and Sharon Stoerger. "Gender and (A)nonymity in Computer-Mediated Communication." In Susan Ehrlich, Miriam Meyerhoff, and Janet Holmes, eds., *Handbook of Language, Gender, and Sexuality*, 2nd ed., 567–586. Wiley-Blackwell, 2014.

Herring, S.C., D.A. Johnson and T. DiBenedetto. "Participation in Electronic Discourse in a 'Feminist' Field. In *Language and Gender: A Reader*, ed. J. Coates. Oxford, 1998.

Hess, Amanda. "Why Women Aren't Welcome on the Internet." Pacific Standard, January 6, 2014. https://psmag.com/why-women-aren-t-welcome-on-the-internet -aa21fdbc8d6.

Hess, Frederick M., and Olivia Meeks. "School Boards circa 2010: Governance in the Accountability Era." National School Board Association, 2010. https://cdn-files.nsba .org/s3fs-public/SBcirca2010_WEB.pdf?Piya0hP.hbJ4QXagUmzbETjNuhDB__kM.

Hicks, Marie. "Why Tech's Gender Problem Is Nothing New." *The Guardian*, October 12, 2018. https://www.theguardian.com/technology/2018/oct/11/tech-gender -problem-amazon-facebook-bias-women.

Hill, Kashmir. "When a Stranger Decides to Destroy Your Life." Gizmodo, July 26, 2018. https://gizmodo.com/when-a-stranger-decides-to-destroy-your-life-1827546385.

Holman, Jordyn. "Silicon Valley Is Using Trade Secrets to Hide Its Race Problem." Bloomberg, February 13, 2019. https://www.bloomberg.com/news/articles/2019-02-13 /silicon-valley-is-using-trade-secrets-to-hide-its-race-problem.

Holmes, Kat. *Mismatch: How Inclusion Shapes Design*. MIT Press, 2018.

Huang, Guanxiong, and Kang Li. "The Effect of Anonymity on Conformity to Group Norms in Online Contexts: A Meta-Analysis." *International Journal of Communication* 10, no. 0 (January 6, 2016): 18. http://ijoc.org/index.php/ijoc/article/view /4037.

Hudson, Laura. "Facebook's Questionable Policy on Violent Content toward Women." Wired, January 24, 2017. https://www.wired.com/2013/01/facebook -violence-women.

Husain, S. Khalid. Comment on "President Obama." Editorial, *New York Times*, January 20, 2009. http://www.nytimes.com/2009/01/21/opinion/21wed1.html #permid=302.

Hutchinson, Y-Vonne. "Bias Manifest." *Include* (blog), August 24, 2016. https:// medium.com/projectinclude/bias-manifest-1b8f62c04af8.

Hutchinson, Y-Vonne. "Biased by Design: Exclusion Hurts Tech Companies More Than They Know." *MIT Technology Review*, August 23, 2016. https://www .technologyreview.com/s/602154/biased-by-design.

Hyde, Janet Shibley, Rebecca S. Bigler, Daphna Joel, Charlotte Chucky Tate, and Sari M. van Anders. "The Future of Sex and Gender in Psychology: Five Challenges to the Gender Binary." *American Psychologist* 74, no. 2 (February 2019): 171–193. https://doi .org/10.1037/amp0000307.

IFEX. "The 50:50 Challenge: Driving Greater Gender Balance at the BBC." April 15, 2018. http://www.ifex.org/united_kingdom/2018/04/15/gender-balance-bbc.

Ingram, Mathew. "While Others Shut Down Comments, the *NYT* Wants to Expand Them." Gigaom, February 25, 2015. https://gigaom.com/2015/02/25/while-others -shut-down-comments-the-nyt-wants-to-expand-them.

International Telecommunications Union. "ICT Facts Figures: The World in 2015." May 2015. https://www.itu.int/en/ITU-D/Statistics/Documents/facts/ICTFacts Figures2015.pdf.

Jackson, Sarah J. "(Re)Imagining Intersectional Democracy from Black Feminism to Hashtag Activism." *Women's Studies in Communication* 39, no. 4 (October 2016): 375–379. https://doi.org/10.1080/07491409.2016.1226654.

Jacobi, Tonja, and Dylan Schweers. "Female Supreme Court Justices Are Interrupted More by Male Justices and Advocates." *Harvard Business Review*, April 11, 2017. https://hbr.org/2017/04/female-supreme-court-justices-are-interrupted-more-by-male-justices-and-advocates.

Jacobi, Tonja, and Dylan Schweers. "How Men Continue to Interrupt Even the Most Powerful Women." Aeon Ideas, May 28, 2017. https://aeon.co/ideas/how-men-continue-to-interrupt-even-the-most-powerful-women.

Jacobi, Tonja, and Dylan Schweers. "Justice, Interrupted: The Effect of Gender, Ideology and Seniority at Supreme Court Oral Arguments." *Virginia Law Review* 103 (2017): 1379. https://papers.ssrn.com/abstract=2933016.

Jacobson, Adam. "From Westeros to Government and Business, Women Have Less Voice." *National Law Review*, June 4, 2019. https://www.natlawreview.com/article/westeros-to-government-and-business-women-have-less-voice.

James, Emma A., and Nicole A. Vincent. "Random Rape Threat Generator." Rapeglish.com. https://rapethreatgenerator.com.

Jensen, Kim D., and Lucy Zhang. "Women in the Economy II: How Implementing a Women's Economic Empowerment Agenda Can Shape the Global Economy." *Citi GPS: Global Perspectives & Solutions*, November 2017. https://ir.citi.com/rxehymXSt WqV7Y6S58ExJLPdJPjqZicwdoxqT%2Fc0qDsBMFxbL%2FzcJiG%2FgKE%2BRxwHca d8oQrgD1w%3D.

Jeong, Sarah. *The Internet of Garbage*. Forbes, 2015.

Johnson, Cathryn. "Gender, Legitimate Authority, and Leader-Subordinate Conversation." *American Sociological Review* 59, no. 1 (February 1994): 122–135. doi: 10.2307/2096136.

"Journalism That Stands Apart: The 2020 Report." *New York Times*, January 17, 2017. http://www.nytimes.com/projects/2020-report.

Kalogeropoulos, Antonis, and Rasmus Kleis Nielsen. "Social Inequalities in News Consumption." Reuters Institute for the Study of Journalism, Oxford University, October 2018. https://reutersinstitute.politics.ox.ac.uk/sites/default/files/2018-10/Kalogeropoulos%20Social%20Inequality%20in%20News%20FINAL.pdf.

Kantor, Jodi. "Harvard Business School Case Study: Gender Equity." *New York Times*, September 7, 2013. https://www.nytimes.com/2013/09/08/education/harvard-case-study-gender-equity.html.

Karpowitz, Christopher F., and Tali Mendelberg. *The Silent Sex: Gender, Deliberation & Institutions*. Princeton University Press, 2014.

King-Slutzky, Johannah. "After Philomela: A History of Women Whose Tongues Have Been Ripped Out." The Hairpin, March 10, 2014. https://www.thehairpin.com /2014/03/after-philomela-a-history-of-women-whose-tongues-have-been-ripped-out.

Kiss, Jemima. "Twitter Planning 'Regular and Consistent Action' to Curb Harassment and Abuse." *The Guardian*, February 9, 2016. https://www.theguardian.com /technology/2016/feb/09/twitter-online-abuse-harassment-nick-pickles.

Kitchener, Caroline. "Why Do So Few Women Write Letters to the Editor?" *The Atlantic*, May 5, 2018. https://www.theatlantic.com/entertainment/archive/2018/05/why-do-so -few-women-write-letters-to-the-editor/559736.

Klein, Ethel. *Gender Politics*. Harvard University Press, 1984.

Klein, L. F., and D'Ignazio, Catherine. *Data Feminism*. MIT Press, 2020.

Kliff, Sarah. "Writer Lindy West Interviewing Her Cruelest Troll Is an Amazing 20 Minutes of Radio." Vox, February 3, 2015. https://www.vox.com/2015/2/3/7970625 /trolls-lindy-west.

LaFrance, Adrienne. "Should We Feed the Trolls?" *The Atlantic*, April 18, 2016. https:// www.theatlantic.com/technology/archive/2016/04/hungry-hungry-trolls/478548.

LaFrance, Adrienne. "Trolls Are Winning the Internet, Technologists Say." *The Atlantic*, March 29, 2017. https://www.theatlantic.com/technology/archive/2017/03/guys-its -time-for-some-troll-theory/521046.

Lam, Monica S. "Keeping the Internet Open with an Open-Source Virtual Assistant." At "MobiCom 2018 - Keynote Talk by Dr. Monica Lam, Stanford University." Video, YouTube, November 8, 2018. https://www.youtube.com/watch?v=R -BHyvli6c0.

Langefeld, Martin. "*Texas Tribune* Is Ramping Up." NiemanLab, July 20, 2009. http://www.niemanlab.org/2009/07/texas-tribun.

Laws, Charlotte. *Rebel in High Heels: True Story about the Fearless Mom Who Battled— and Defeated—the Kingpin of Revenge Porn and the Dangerous Forces of Conformity.* Stroud House Publishing, 2015.

Leibovich, Mark. "For A.O.C., 'Existential Crises' as Her District Becomes the Coronavirus Epicenter." *New York Times*, May 4, 2020. https://www.nytimes.com/2020 /05/04/us/politics/coronavirus-alexandria-ocasio-cortez.html.

Lichterman, Joseph. "*New York Times* Editor: 'We Have to Treat Comments as Content.'" NiemanLab, October 2, 2015. http://www.niemanlab.org/2015/10/new-york -times-editor-we-have-to-treat-comments-as-content.

Lillis, Mike. "Ocasio-Cortez Accosted by GOP Lawmaker over Remarks: 'That Kind of Confrontation Hasn't Ever Happened to Me.'" *The Hill*, July 21, 2020. https://thehill .com/homenews/house/508259-ocaasio-cortez-accosted-by-gop-lawmaker-over -remarks-that-kind-of.

Lipman, Joanne. "Tech Overlords Google and Facebook Have Used Monopoly to Rob Journalism of Its Revenue." *USA Today*, June 11, 2019. https://www.usatoday .com/story/opinion/2019/06/11/google-facebook-antitrust-monopoly-advertising -journalism-revenue-streams-column/1414562001/.

Liptak, Adam. "Chief Justice Samples Eminem in Online Threats Case." *New York Times*, December 1, 2014. https://www.nytimes.com/2014/12/02/us/chief-justice -samples-eminem-in-online-threats-case.html.

Liptak, Adam. "Why Gorsuch May Not Be So Genteel on the Bench." *New York Times*, April 17, 2017. https://www.nytimes.com/2017/04/17/us/politics/why-gorsuch-may -not-be-so-genteel-on-the-bench.html.

Lomas, Natasha. "Voter Manipulation on Social Media Now a Global Problem, Report Finds." Techcrunch, September 26, 2019. https://techcrunch.com/2019/09 /26/voter-manipulation-on-social-media-now-a-global-problem-report-finds.

Macharia, Sarah, et al., "Who Makes the News? Global Media Monitoring Project 2015." World Association for Christian Communication, November 2015. http://cdn.agilitycms .com/who-makes-the-news/Imported/reports_2015/global/gmmp_global_report_en.pdf.

Magistretti, Bérénice. "Frost & Sullivan: Femtech Could Become a $50 Billion Market by 2025." VentureBeat, March 8, 2018. https://venturebeat.com/2018/03/08 /frost-sullivan-femtech-could-become-a-50-billion-market-by-2025.

Magistretti, Bérénice. "The Rise of Femtech: Women, Technology, and Trump." VentureBeat, February 5, 2017. https://venturebeat.com/2017/02/05/the-rise-of-femtech -women-technology-and-trump.

Manne, Kate. *Down Girl: The Logic of Misogyny*. Oxford University Press, 2017.

Manne, Kate. *Entitled: How Male Privilege Hurts Women*. Crown, 2020.

Manne, Kate. "The Logic of Misogyny." *Boston Review*, July 11, 2016. http:// bostonreview.net/forum/kate-manne-logic-misogyny.

Mantilla, Karla. *Gendertrolling: How Misogyny Went Viral*. Praeger, 2015.

Marche, Stephen. "Swallowing the Red Pill: A Journey to the Heart of Modern Misogyny." *The Guardian*, April 14, 2016. https://www.theguardian.com/technology /2016/apr/14/the-red-pill-reddit-modern-misogyny-manosphere-men.

Martin, Fiona. "Getting My Two Cents Worth In: Access, Interaction, Participation and Social Inclusion in Online News Commenting." *#ISOJ* 6, no.1 (April 15, 2015).

https://isojjournal.wordpress.com/2015/04/15/getting-my-two-cents-worth-in
-access-interaction-participation-and-social-inclusion-in-online-news-commenting.

Martin, Fiona. "Women Are Silenced Online, Just as in Real Life. It Will Take More Than Twitter to Change That." *The Guardian*, April 23, 2015. https://www
.theguardian.com/commentisfree/2015/apr/23/women-are-silenced-online-just-as
-in-real-life-it-will-take-more-than-twitter-to-change-that.

Martin, Fiona, and Timothy Dwyer. *Sharing News Online: Commendary Cultures and Social Media News Ecologies*. Palgrave Macmillan, 2019.

Marwick, Alice. "A New Study Suggests Online Harassment Is Pressuring Women and Minorities to Self-Censor." Quartz, November 24, 2016. https://qz.com/844319/a
-new-study-suggests-online-harassment-is-pressuring-women-and-minorities-to-self
-censor.

Matias, J. Nathan. "The Real Name Fallacy." Coral by Vox Media, January 3, 2017. https://coralproject.net/blog/the-real-name-fallacy.

Matias, J. Nathan, T. Simko, and M. Reddan. "Reducing the Silencing Role of Harassment in Online Feminism Discussions." *Citizens and Technology Lab* (blog), June 2020. https://citizensandtech.org/2020/06/reducing_harassment-impacts-in
-feminism online.

McCright, Aaron M. "The Effects of Gender on Climate Change Knowledge and Concern in the American Public." *Population and Environment* 32, no. 1 (2010): 66–87. https://www.jstor.org/stable/40984168.

McDonald, Soraya Nadia. "'Gamergate': Feminist Video Game Critic Anita Sarkeesian Cancels Utah Lecture after Threat." *Washington Post*, October 15, 2014. https://
www.washingtonpost.com/news/morning-mix/wp/2014/10/15/gamergate-feminist
-video-game-critic-anita-sarkeesian-cancels-utah-lecture-after-threat-citing-police
-inability-to-prevent-concealed-weapons-at-event.

Media Insight Project. "How Millennials Get News: Inside the Habits of America's First Digital Generation." American Press Institute and AP-NORC Center, March 16, 2015. http://mediainsight.org:80/Pages/how-millennials-get-news-inside-the-habits
-of-americas-first-digital-generation.aspx.

Media Insight Project, "The Personal News Cycle: A Focus on African American and Hispanic News Consumers." American Press Institute and AP-NORC Center for Public Affairs Research, September 16, 2014. http://www.mediainsight.org/Pages
/focus-on-african-american-and-hispanic-news-consumers.aspx.

Medina, Jennifer. "Campus Killings Set Off Anguished Conversation about the Treatment of Women." *New York Times*, May 26, 2014. https://www.nytimes.com
/2014/05/27/us/campus-killings-set-off-anguished-conversation-about the-treatment
-of-women.html.

Megarry, Jessica. "Online Incivility or Sexual Harassment? Conceptualising Women's Experiences in the Digital Age." *Women's Studies International Forum* 47 (November 1, 2014): 46–55. https://doi.org/10.1016/j.wsif.2014.07.012.

Megarry, Jessica. "Under the Watchful Eyes of Men: Theorising the Implications of Male Surveillance Practices for Feminist Activism on Social Media." *Feminist Media Studies* 18, no. 6 (2017): 1070–1085. https://www.academia.edu/34970007/Under _the_watchful_eyes_of_men_theorising_the_implications_of_male_surveillance _practices_for_feminist_activism_on_social_media.

Mellman, Mark. "Mark Mellman: The Young and the Newsless." *The Hill*, February 4, 2016. https://thehill.com/opinion/mark-mellman/230946-mark-mellman-the -young-and-the-newsless.

Mendelberg, Tali. "Tali Mendelberg Responds to Kate Manne." *Boston Review*, July 11, 2016. http://bostonreview.net/forum/logic-misogyny/tali-mendelberg-tali -mendelberg-responds-kate-manne.

Mendelberg, Tali, and Christopher F. Karpowitz. "Are Women the Silent Sex?" *Boston Review*, April 11, 2016. http://bostonreview.net/books-ideas/tali-mendelberg -christopher-f-karpowitz-are-women-silent-sex.

Mendez, Christopher J., Hema Susmita Padala, Zoe Steine-Hanson, Claudia Hilderbrand, Amber Horvath, Charles G. Hill, Logan Simpson, Nupoor Patil, Anita Sarma, and Margaret M. Burnett. "Open Source Barriers to Entry, Revisited: A Sociotechnical Perspective." In *ICSE '18: Proceedings of the 40th International Conference on Software Engineering*, 1004–1015. ACM Press, 2018. https://doi.org/10.1145/3180155 .3180241.

Metaxa-Kakavouli, Danaë, Kelly Wang, James A. Landay, and Jeff Hancock. "Gender-Inclusive Design: Sense of Belonging and Bias in Web Interfaces." In *CHI '18: Proceedings of the 2018 CHI Conference on Human Factors in Computing Systems*, paper 614, pp. 1–6. ACM Press, 2018. https://doi.org/10.1145/3173574.3174188.

Meyer, Robinson. "90% of Wikipedia's Editors Are Male: Here's What They're Doing about It." *The Atlantic*, October 25, 2013. http://www.theatlantic.com/technology /archive/2013/10/90-of-wikipedias-editors-are-male-heres-what-theyre-doing-about -it/280882.

Miner, Adam S., Arnold Milstein, Stephen Schueller, Roshini Hegde, Christina Mangurian, and Eleni Linos. "Smartphone-Based Conversational Agents and Responses to Questions about Mental Health, Interpersonal Violence, and Physical Health." *JAMA Internal Medicine* 176, no. 5 (May 1, 2016): 619–625. https://doi.org/10.1001 /jamainternmed.2016.0400.

Mislove, Alan, Sune Lehmann, Yong-Yeol Ahn, Jukka-Pekka Onnela, and J. Niels Rosenquist. "Understanding the Demographics of Twitter Users." Association for the Advancement of Artificial Intelligence, 2012. http://www.ccs.neu.edu/home /amislove/publications/Twitter-ICWSM.pdf.

Molla, Rani. "How Facebook Compares to Other Tech Companies in Diversity." Recode, April 11, 2018. https://www.recode.net/2018/4/11/17225574/facebook -tech-diversity-women.

Molla, Rani, and Renee Lightner. "Diversity in Tech." *Wall Street Journal*, April 10, 2016. http://graphics.wsj.com/diversity-in-tech-companies.

Montalvo, Felicia. "Debugging Bias: Busting the Myth of Neutral Technology." Bitch Media, May 17, 2017. https://www.bitchmedia.org/article/debugging-bias -busting-myth-neutral-technology.

Morrison, Patt. "Privilege Makes Them Do It: What a Study of Internet Trolls Reveals." *Los Angeles Times*, July 1, 2015. http://www.latimes.com/opinion/op-ed/la -oe-morrison-phillips-20150701-column.html.

Moses, Lucia. "Inside the *NY Times'* Audience Development Strategy." Digiday, January 14, 2015. https://digiday.com/media/inside-ny-times-audience-development -strategy.

Muddiman, Ashley, and Natalie Jomini Stroud. "10 Things We Learned by Analyzing 9 Million Comments from *The New York Times*." Center for Media Engagement, June 2016. https://engagingnewsproject.org/research/10-things-we-learned-by -analyzing-9-million-comments-from-the-new-york-times.

Mullin, Benjamin. "*The New York Times* Will Use an Algorithm to Moderate Many of Its Comments." Poynter, November 20, 2015. https://www.poynter.org/2015 /the-new-york-times-will-use-an-algorithm-to-moderate-many-of-its-comments /386014/.

Mundy, Liza. "Why Is Silicon Valley So Awful to Women?" *The Atlantic*, April 2017. https://www.theatlantic.com/magazine/archive/2017/04/why-is-silicon-valley-so -awful-to-women/517788.

Murphy, Bill, Jr. "Google and Facebook Now Make More from Ads Than Every Newspaper, Magazine, and Radio Network in the World Combined." *Inc*, June 28, 2017. https://www.inc.com/bill-murphy-jr/google-and-facebook-now-make-more-from-ads -than-every-newspaper-magazine-and-rad.html.

Murphy, Mary Jo. "The Monster Sorority of Women Voters." *New York Times*, October 1, 2016. https://www.nytimes.com/2016/10/02/opinion/sunday/the-monster -sorority-of-women-voters.html.

National Park Service. "1913 Woman Suffrage Procession." https://www.nps.gov /articles/woman-suffrage-procession1913.htm.

Neason, Alexandria. "You're Probably Not Quoting Enough Women. Let Us Help You." *Columbia Journalism Review*, June 7, 2018. https://www.cjr.org/analysis/women-sources.php.

Newman, Nic. "Overview and Key Findings of the 2017 Report" Digital News Report, Reuters Institute for the Study of Journalism, Oxford University, March 22, 2018. http://www.digitalnewsreport.org/survey/2017/overview-key-findings-2017.

Newman, Nic, Richard Fletcher, Anne Schulz, Simge Andi, and Rasmus Kleis Nielsen. "Reuters Institute Digital News Report 2020." Reuters Institute for the Study of Journalism, June 2020. https://reutersinstitute.politics.ox.ac.uk/sites/default/files/2020-06/DNR_2020_FINAL.pdf.

News Leaders Association. "Diversity Survey, 1997–2018." https://members.newsleaders.org/newsroom_diversitysurveyNielsen. "African-American Women: Our Science, Her Magic." September 21, 2017. https://www.nielsen.com/us/en/insights/report/2017/african-american-women-our-science-her-magic.

Nielsen. "Asian American Women Influence Mainstream Shopping and Beauty Trends." May 18, 2017. http://www.nielsen.com/us/en/insights/news/2017/asian-american-women-influence-mainstream-shopping-and-beauty-trends.

Nielsen. "Latinas Are Avid Tech Users, Voracious Video Consumers and Social Trendsetters." September 12, 2017. http://www.nielsen.com/us/en/insights/news/2017/latinas-are-avid-tech-users-voracious-video-consumers-and-social-trendsetters.

Nielsen. "Reaching Black Women across Media Platforms." December 11, 2017. http://www.nielsen.com/us/en/insights/news/2017/reaching-black-women-across-media-platforms.

Nielsen. "U.S. Women Control the Purse Strings." April 2, 2013. http://www.nielsen.com/us/en/insights/news/2013/u-s--women-control-the-purse-strings.

Nielsen, Rasmus Kleis, Meera Selva, and Simge Andi. "Race and Leadership in the News Media 2020: Evidence from Five Markets." Reuters Institute for the Study of Journalism, Oxford University, July 16, 2020. https://reutersinstitute.politics.ox.ac.uk/race-and-leadership-news-media-2020-evidence-five-markets.

Niemeier, Hannah. "Are Millennial Women Reading Newspapers?" *Entity*, September 21, 2016. https://www.entitymag.com/millennials-reading-newspapers/.

Noble, Safiya Umoja. *Algorithms of Oppression: How Search Engines Reinforce Racism.* NYU Press, 2018.

NORC. "How Americans Navigate the Modern Information Environment." University of Chicago, June 15, 2017. http://www.norc.org/Research/Projects/Pages/how-americans-navigate-the-modern-information-environment.aspx.

OpEd Project, The. "The Byline Survey Report, 2012: Who Narrates the World?" *The Byline Blog* (blog), May 29, 2012. https://theopedproject.wordpress.com/2012/05/28/the-byline-survey-2011.

OpEd Project, The. "Who Narrates the World?" June 14, 2017. http://www.theopedproject.org/index.php?option=com_content&view=article&id=817&Itemid=149.

OpEd Project, The. "Why The OpEd Project? An Early Interview with Katie Orenstein Shortly after Our Founding." Accessed May 29, 2017. http://theopedproject.org/index.php?option=com_content&view=article&id=418.

Oppenheim, Maya. "Labour MP Speaks Out on Rape, Receives '600 Threats in One Night.'" *The Independent*, May 31, 2016. http://www.independent.co.uk/news/people/labour-mp-jess-phillips-receives-600-rape-threats-in-one-night-a7058041.html.

Orenstein, Katie. "Time Shifts." Facebook, April 29, 2016. https://www.facebook.com/katie.orenstein/posts/10153629896603358.

Orth, Maureen. "10 Undeniable Facts about the Woody Allen Sexual-Abuse Allegation." *Vanity Fair*, March 6, 2020. https://www.vanityfair.com/news/2014/02/woody-allen-sex-abuse-10-facts.

Osterwalder, Alexander, and Yves Pigneur. *Business Model Generation: A Handbook for Visionaries, Game Changers, and Challengers*. John Wiley, 2010.

Overholser, Geneva, and Kathleen Hall Jamieson. *The Press*. Oxford University Press, 2005.

Owen, Laura Hazard. "'If the *Financial Times* Were a Person, It Would Be a Man': Here's How the Paper Is Trying to Change That." NiemanLab, April 3, 2018. http://www.niemanlab.org/2018/04/if-the-financial-times-were-a-person-it-would-be-a-man-heres-how-the-paper-is-trying-to-change-that.

Pareles, Jon. "Prince: An Artist Who Defined Genre, Is Dead." *New York Times*, April 21, 2016. https://www.nytimes.com/2016/04/22/arts/music/prince-dead.html#permid=18285560.

Park, Deokgun, Simranjit Sachar, Nicholas Diakopoulos, and Niklas Elmqvist. "Supporting Comment Moderators in Identifying High Quality Online News Comments." *CHI '16: Proceedings of the 2016 CHI Conference on Human Factors in Computing Systems*, 1116. ACM Press, 2016. https://doi.org/10.1145/2858036.2858389.

Peacock, Cynthia, and Peter Leavitt. "Improving Civil Discourse: Online Venues Present an Opportunity for People to Engage in Civic Discourse." Center for Media Engagement, University of Texas at Austin, August 2014. https://mediaengagement.org/research/online-discourse.

Pearson, Jordan. "Under the Internet's Bridge with Troll Scholar Whitney Phillips." Motherboard, February 10, 2017. https://motherboard.vice.com/en_us/article/under-the-internets-bridge-with-troll-scholar-whitney-phillips.

Penny, Laurie. *Cybersexism: Sex, Gender and Power on the Internet.* Bloomsbury Publishing, 2013.

Perez, Caroline Criado. *Invisible Women: Data Bias in a World Designed for Men.* Abrams Press, 2019.

Perrin, Andrew J. "'Since This Is the Editorial Section I Intend to Express My Opinion': Inequality and Expressivity in Letters to the Editor." *Communication Review* 19, no. 1 (January 2, 2016): 55–76. https://doi.org/10.1080/10714421.2016.1128188.

Pew Research Center. "Active Science News Consumers Are More Likely to Be Men, College Grads." September 18, 2017. http://www.journalism.org/2017/09/20/science-news-and-information-today/pj_2017-09-20_science-and-news_1-05.

Pew Research Center, "Demographics and Political Views of News Audiences," in "Trends in News Consumption, 1991–2012: In Changing News Landscape, Even Television Is Vulnerable," September 2012.

Pew Research Center. "Internet/Broadband Fact Sheet." January 12, 2017. http://www.pewinternet.org/fact-sheet/internet-broadband.

Pew Research Center. "Online Harassment." October 23, 2014. http://www.pewinternet.org/2014/10/23/12113.

Pew Research Center. "Perceptions of Online Environments." In "Online Harassment." October 22, 2014. http://www.pewinternet.org/2014/10/22/online-harassment/pi_2014-10-22__online-harassment-04.

Pew Research Center. "Reluctant Suffragettes: When Women Questioned Their Right to Vote." March 18, 2009. http://www.pewresearch.org/2009/03/18/reluctant-suffragettes-when-women-questioned-their-right-to-vote.

Pew Research Center. "Section 4: Demographics and Political Views of News Audiences." September 27, 2012. http://www.people-press.org/2012/09/27/section-4-demographics-and-political-views-of-news-audiences.

Pew Research Center. "Trends and Facts on Newspapers: State of the News Media." September 28, 2020. https://www.journalism.org/fact-sheet/newspapers.

Pew Research Center, "Where Men and Women Differ in Following the News." February 6, 2008. http://www.pewresearch.org/2008/02/06/where-men-and-women-differ-in-following-the-news.

Pflanzer, Lydia Ramsey. "The Rise and Fall of Theranos, the Blood-Testing Startup That Went from Silicon Valley Darling to Facing Fraud Charges." *Business Insider,*

April 11, 2019. https://www.businessinsider.com/the-history-of-silicon-valley -unicorn-theranos-and-ceo-elizabeth-holmes-2018-5.

Phillips, Whitney. *This Is Why We Can't Have Nice Things: Mapping the Relationship between Online Trolling and Mainstream Culture*. MIT Press, 2015.

Pierson, Emma. "Fifty Shades of Bias: How Male and Female Movie Critics See Things Differently." Quartz, January 19, 2017. https://qz.com/356249/fifty-shades -of-bias-how-male-and-female-movie-critics-see-things-differently.

Pierson, Emma. "How Men Dominate Online Commenting." Quartz, January 19, 2017. https://qz.com/259149/how-men-dominate-online-commenting.

Pierson, Emma. "How to Get More Women to Join the Debate." *On the Ground* (blog). *New York Times*, January 6, 2015. http://kristof.blogs.nytimes.com/2015/01 /06/how-to-get-more-women-to-join-the-debate.

Pierson, Emma. "How to Get More Women to Join the Debate, Part II." *On the Ground* (blog). *New York Times*, March 9, 2015. http://kristof.blogs.nytimes.com /2015/03/09/how-to-get-more-women-to-join-the-debate-part-ii.

Pierson, Emma. "Is Sexist Rhetoric a Total Frat Move?" *On the Ground* (blog). *New York Times*, May 9, 2016. http://kristof.blogs.nytimes.com/2016/05/09/is-sexist -rhetoric-a-total-frat-move.

Pierson, Emma. "Of Mansplaining and Mastectomies." *On the Ground* (blog). *New York Times*, February 8, 2016. http://kristof.blogs.nytimes.com/2016/02/08/of -mansplaining-and-mastectomies.

Pierson, Emma. "Outnumbered But Well-Spoken: Female Commenters in the *New York Times*." In *CSCW '15: Proceedings of the 18th ACM Conference on Computer Supported Cooperative Work & Social Computing*. ACM, 2015. https://dl.acm.org/doi/10 .1145/2675133.2675134.

Pierson, Emma. "Twitter Data Show That a Few Powerful Users Can Control the Conversation." Quartz, May 5, 2015. https://qz.com/396107/twitter-data-show-that-a-few -powerful-users-can-control-the-conversation.

Pierson, Emma, and Shengwu Li. "A Better Way to Gauge How Common Sexual Assault Is on College Campuses." *Washington Post*. January 19, 2017. https://www .washingtonpost.com/news/grade-point/wp/2015/10/15/a-better-way-to-gauge-how -common-sexual-assault-is-on-college-campuses.

Powell, John A. "The 'Racing' of American Society: Race Functioning as a Verb before Signifying as a Noun." *Law & Inequality* 15, no. 1 (1997): 99–125.

Probolus, Kimberly. "A Woman's Plea: Let's Raise Our Voices." *New York Times*, January 31, 2019. https://www.nytimes.com/2019/01/31/opinion/letters/letters to -editor-new-york-times-women.html.

Quinn, Michelle. "Quinn: Hey Apple Health, Did You Forget about Women?" *The Mercury News*, December 19, 2014. https://www.mercurynews.com/2014/12/19/quinn-hey -apple-health-did-you-forget-about-women.

Quinn, Zoe. *Crash Override: How Gamergate (Nearly) Destroyed My Life, and How We Can Win the Fight against Online Hate*. Public Affairs, 2017.

Rainie, Lee, Janna Anderson, and Jonathan Albright. "The Future of Free Speech, Trolls, Anonymity and Fake News Online." Pew Research Center, March 29, 2017. https://www.pewresearch.org/internet/2017/03/29/the-future-of-free-speech-trolls -anonymity-and-fake-news-online/.

"Random Rape Threat Generator." Accessed April 22, 2017. http://rapethreat generator.com.

Rappeport, Alan. "Gloria Steinem and Madeleine Albright Rebuke Young Women Backing Bernie Sanders." *New York Times*, February 8, 2016. https://www.nytimes .com/2016/02/08/us/politics/gloria-steinem-madeleine-albright-hillary-clinton -bernie-sanders.html.

Reagle, Joseph M., Jr. *Reading the Comments: Likers, Haters, and Manipulators at the Bottom of the Web*. MIT Press, 2015.

Responsible Research & Innovation (RRI). The European Union Programme for Research and Innovation 2014-2020. rri-tools.eu.

Reuters. "Amazon Ditched AI Recruiting Tool That Favored Men for Technical Jobs." *The Guardian*, October 10, 2018. https://www.theguardian.com/technology /2018/oct/10/amazon-hiring-ai-gender-bias-recruiting-engine.

Ridgeway, Cecilia. "Framed by Gender: Cecilia Ridgeway, Stanford Professor." Video, YouTube, April 18, 2011. https://www.youtube.com/watch?v=BxkJ4_5qqPc.

Ridgeway, Cecilia. *Framed by Gender: How Gender Inequality Persists in the Modern World*. Oxford University Press, 2011.

Ries, Eric. *The Lean Startup: How Today's Entrepreneurs Use Continuous Innovation to Create Radically Successful Businesses*. Crown, 2011, and http://theleanstartup.com.

Robb, Alice. "Women Get Interrupted More—Even by Other Women." *New Republic*, May 14, 2014. https://newrepublic.com/article/117757/gender-language -differences-women-get-interrupted-more.

Robinson, Roxana, et al. "A Plea from 33 Writers: Words Matter. Stop Using 'Quid Pro Quo.'" *New York Times*, November 8, 2019. https://www.nytimes.com/2019/11 /08/opinion/letters/quid-pro-quo.html.

Roe, David. "Six Security Issues That Will Dominate IoT in 2019." CMS Wire, January 14, 2019. https://www.cmswire.com/internet-of-things/6-security-issues-that-will -dominate-iot-in-2019.

Rogers, Katie. "Kamala Harris Is (Again) Interrupted While Pressing a Senate Witness." *New York Times*, June 13, 2017. https://www.nytimes.com/2017/06/13/us/politics/kamala-harris-interrupted-jeff-sessions.html.

Rogers, Katie. "Vanessa Williams Receives 'Unexpected' Apology at Miss America." *New York Times*, September 14, 2015. https://www.nytimes.com/2015/09/15/arts/television/vanessa-williams-returns-to-miss-america-and-receives-an-apology.html.

Rogers, Katie, and Nicholas Fandos. "Trump Tells Congresswomen to 'Go Back' to the Countries They Came From." *New York Times*, July 14, 2019. https://www.nytimes.com/2019/07/14/us/politics/trump-twitter-squad-congress.html.

Rolston, Dorian. "Online Story Comments Affect News Perception." *Columbia Journalism Review*, December 14, 2012. http://www.cjr.org/behind_the_news/comments_color_news_perception.php.

Roose, Kevin. "The Only Safe Election Is a Low-Tech Election." *New York Times*, February 4, 2020. https://www.nytimes.com/2020/02/04/technology/election-tech.html.

Rothman, Lily. "A Cultural History of Mansplaining." *The Atlantic*, November 1, 2012. https://www.theatlantic.com/sexes/archive/2012/11/a-cultural-history-of-mansplaining/264380.

Roush, Chris. "Bloomberg to Expand Women's Voices Project." Talking Biz News, April 17, 2018. http://talkingbiznews.com/1/bloomberg-to-expand-womens-voices-project.

Sachar, Simranjit Singh, and Nicholas Diakopoulos. "Changing Names in Online News Comments at the *New York Times*." In *Proceedings of the Tenth International AAAI Conference on Web and Social Media*, 339–347. AAAI Press, 2016. aaai.org/ocs/index.php/ICWSM16/paper/view/13069.

Sandberg, Sheryl, and Adam Grant. "Sheryl Sandberg and Adam Grant on Why Women Stay Quiet at Work." *New York Times*, January 12, 2015. https://www.nytimes.com/2015/01/11/opinion/sunday/speaking-while-female.html.

Sandberg, Sheryl, and Nell Scovell. *Lean In: Women, Work, and the Will to Lead*. Alfred A. Knopf, 2013.

Sarkeesian, Anita. "Talking Publicly about Harassment Generates More Harassment." *Feminist Frequency* (blog), July 2015. http://femfreq.tumblr.com/post/132152537305/talking-publicly-about-harassment-generates-more.

Sarma, Anita. "Squashing Inclusivity Bugs in Open Source Software." Opensource.com, August 3, 2018. https://opensource.com/article/18/8/inclusivity-bugs-open-source-software.

Sayre, Michael J., and Kate Silverstein. "The Female Economy." *Harvard Business Review*, September 1, 2009. https://hbr.org/2009/09/the-female-economy.

Schiebinger, Londa. "Gendered Innovations in Science, Medicine and Engineering." YouTube, May 30, 2018. youtube.com/watch?v=BvnxyORw7To.

Schiebinger, Londa. "Scientific Research Must Take Gender into Account." *Nature News* 507, no. 7490 (March 6, 2014): 9. https://doi.org/10.1038/507009a.

Schmidt, Christine. "'If You Don't Have Gender Equality in Your Newsroom, It's like Running on One Leg. And in the Current Climate, the Male Leg Is Limping.'" NiemanLab, June 21, 2018. http://www.niemanlab.org/2018/06/if-you-dont-have-gender-equality-in-your-newsroom-its-like-running-on-one-leg-and-in-the-current-climate-the-male-leg-is-limping.

Schmidt, Christine. "With Video and Audio, The Skimm Pushes Further into the Daily Routines of Its 6 Million Readers." NiemanLab, November 13, 2017. http://www.niemanlab.org/2017/11/with-video-and-audio-the-skimm-pushes-further-into-the-daily-routines-of-its-6-million-readers.

Schroeder, Klaus, Stine Mosegaard Vilhelmsen, Christina Sogaard Jensen, Mette Jacobsen, Rune Norager, and Marianne Graves Petersen. *Guidebook to a Female Interaction Strategy*. design-people, 2012. design-people.dk

Schwartz, John, and Lisa Friedman. "The 'Straightforward' Link between Climate and California's Fires." *New York Times*, September 14, 2020. https://www.nytimes.com/2020/09/09/climate/nyt-climate-newsletter-california-wildfires.html.

Schwencke, Ken. "How Cloudflare Helps Serve Up Hate on the Web." ProPublica, May 4, 2017. https://www.propublica.org/article/how-cloudflare-helps-serve-up-hate-on-the-web.

"Seeking Gender Parity in Your Letters." *New York Times*, February 29, 2020. https://www.nytimes.com/2020/02/29/opinion/letters/new-york-times-letters-gender.html.

Seelye, Katharine Q. "Molly Ivins, Columnist, Dies at 62." *New York Times*, February 1, 2007. http://www.nytimes.com/2007/02/01/washington/01ivins.html.

Selfe, Cynthia L., and Paul R. Meyer. "Testing Claims for On-Line Conferences." *Written Communication* 8, no. 2 (April 1, 1991): 163–192. https://doi.org/10.1177/0741088391008002002.

Shigeoka, Scott. "The Power of Human Moderation." Coral by Vox Media, January 11, 2019. https://coralproject.net/blog/the-power-of-human-moderation.

Sidner, Sara, and Mallory Simon. "He Tweeted Hate at Her. She Sued. Then She Met Him." CNN, September 16, 2020. https://www.cnn.com/2019/09/21/us/white-supremacist-apology-to-student-soh/index.html.

Smith, Aaron. "Record Share of Americans Now Own Smartphones, Have Home Broadband," Pew Research Center, January 12, 2017. http://www.pewresearch.org/fact-tank/2017/01/12/evolution-of-technology.

Smith, Gerry. "*N.Y. Times* Scales Back Free Articles to Get More Subscribers." Bloomberg, December 1, 2017. https://www.bloomberg.com/news/articles/2017-12-01/n-y-times-scales-back-free-articles-to-get-readers-to-subscribe.

Smith, S. E. "Hashtags Can Create Radical Change—But at What Cost to Their Creators?" Daily Dot, June 2, 2014. http://www.dailydot.com/via/yes-all-women-creator-silenced/.

Snyder, Kieran, and John H. McWhorter. "How to Get Ahead as a Woman in Tech: Interrupt Men." Slate, July 23, 2014. http://www.slate.com/blogs/lexicon_valley/2014/07/23/study_men_interrupt_women_more_in_tech_workplaces_but_high_ranking_women.html.

Solnit, Rebecca. "Men Explain Things to Me." Guernica, August 20, 2012. https://www.guernicamag.com/rebecca-solnit-men-explain-things-to-me/.

Southern Poverty Law Center. "Woman Hatred, Fueled by Presidential Campaign, on the Rise." February 15, 2017. https://www.splcenter.org/fighting-hate/intelligence-report/2017/woman-hatred-fueled-presidential-campaign-rise.

Steinhauer, Jennifer. "Gender Gap Closes When Everyone's on the Ballot, Study Shows." *New York Times*, June 24, 2019, https://www.nytimes.com/2019/06/24/us/politics/candidates-women-people-of-color-elections.html.

Stephens, Bret. "The Smearing of Woody Allen." *New York Times*, February 9, 2018. https://www.nytimes.com/2018/02/09/opinion/smearing-of-woody-allen.html.

Stevenson, Alexandra. "Facebook Admits It Was Used to Incite Violence in Myanmar." *New York Times*, November 6, 2018. https://www.nytimes.com/2018/11/06/technology/myanmar-facebook.html.

Stranahan, Susan Q. "Susan Estrich on Gender, Missing Voices, and That Nasty Email War." *Columbia Journalism Review*, February 25, 2005. http://archives.cjr.org/the_water_cooler/susan_estrich_on_gender_missin.php.

Strandberg, Kim, and Janne Berg. "Online Newspapers' Readers' Comments: Democratic Conversation Platforms or Virtual Soapboxes?" *Comunicação e Sociedade* 23 (2013): 132–152. https://doi.org/10.17231/comsoc.23(2013).1618.

Strategyzer AG. "The Business Model Canvas." Accessed April 23, 2019. https://www.strategyzer.com/canvas/business-model-canvas.

Streitfeld, David. "Inside eBay's Cockroach Cult: The Ghastly Story of a Stalking Scandal." *New York Times*, September 26, 2020. https://www.nytimes.com/2020/09/26/technology/ebay-cockroaches-stalking-scandal.html.

Stroud, Natalie Jomini, Emily Van Duyn, and Cynthia Peacock. "Survey of Commenters and Comment Readers." Center for Media Engagement University of

Texas at Austin, March 2016. https://mediaengagement.org/research/survey-of
-commenters-and-comment-readers.

Stuart, Keith. "Brianna Wu and the Human Cost of Gamergate: 'Every Woman
I Know in the Industry Is Scared.'" *The Guardian*, October 17, 2014. https://www
.theguardian.com/technology/2014/oct/17/brianna-wu-gamergate-human-cost.

Swanson, Ian. "Ocasio-Cortez Accosted by GOP Lawmaker over Remarks: 'That Kind
of Confrontation Hasn't Ever Happened to Me.'" *The Hill*, July 21, 2020. https://thehill
.com/homenews/house/508259-ocaasio-cortez-accosted-by-gop-lawmaker-over
-remarks-that-kind-of.

Tannen, Deborah. "Who Does the Talking Here?" *Washington Post*, July 15, 2007.
http://www.washingtonpost.com/wp-dyn/content/article/2007/07/13/AR200
7071301815.html.

Taub, Amanda. "*The Guardian* Study's Hidden Lesson: Trolls Reinforce White Male
Dominance in Journalism." Vox, April 13, 2016. https://www.vox.com/2016/4/13
/11414942/guardian-study-harassment.

Taylor, Astra. *The People's Platform: Taking Back Power and Culture in the Digital Age.*
Metropolitan Books, 2014.

Technology Safety. Home page. Accessed May 23, 2017. https://www.techsafety
.org/.

Tenore, Mallary Jean. "Why Women Don't Contribute to Opinion Pages as Often
as Men & What We Can Do about It." Poynter, February 25, 2011. https://www
.poynter.org/reporting-editing/2011/why-women-dont-contribute-to-opinion-pages
-as-often-as-men-what-we-can-do-about-it.

Tessier, Marie. "Hi-Tech Stalking Devices Extend Abusers' Reach." Women's eNews.
October 1, 2006. http://womensnews.org/2006/10/hi-tech-stalking-devices-extend
-abusers-reach.

Tessier, Marie. "Raising Women's Voices." Coral Project by Vox Media. https://blog
.coralproject.net/raising-womens-voices.

Tessier, Marie. "Seeking More Women's Voices in the Digital Public Square." *New
York Times*, May 10, 2019. https://www.nytimes.com/2019/05/10/opinion/letters
/women-voices.html.

Tessier, Marie. "Speaking While Female, and at a Disadvantage." *New York Times*,
October 27, 2016. https://www.nytimes.com/2016/10/27/upshot/speaking-while
-female-and-at-a-disadvantage.html#permid=20297956.

Tessier, Marie. "What Women Want in a Community." Coral by Vox Media, January 25, 2017. https://blog.coralproject.net/what-women-want-in-community.

Tessier, Marie, Kristin Rohlwing, and Humera Lodhi. "Engaging Women: Reflecting the Reality of Your Audience." Reynolds Journalism Institute, Missouri School of Journalism, University of Missouri, March 8, 2016. https://www.rjionline.org/stories /engaging-women-reflecting-the-reality-of-your-audience.

Thorson, Esther. "Mobilizing Citizen Participation." In Geneva Overholser and Kathleen Hall Jamieson, eds., *The Institutions of American Democracy: The Press*, 203–220. Oxford University Press, 2006.

Tiffany, Kaitlyn. "Who Are Period-Tracking Apps Really Built For?" Vox, November 13, 2018. https://www.vox.com/the-goods/2018/11/13/18079458/menstrual-tracking -surveillance-glow-clue-apple-health.

Tiku, Nitasha. "Twitter CEO: 'We Suck at Dealing with Abuse.'" The Verge, February 4, 2015. https://www.theverge.com/2015/2/4/7982099/twitter-ceo-sent-memo -taking-personal-responsibility-for-the.

TrollBusters. "AboutUs: TrollBusters: Offering Pest Control for Journalists." http:// www.troll-busters.com.

Ulloa, Jazmine. "How Memes, Text Chains, and Online Conspiracies Have Fueled Coronavirus Protesters and Discord." *Boston Globe*, May 6, 2020. https://www .bostonglobe.com/2020/05/06/nation/how-memes-text-chains-online-conspiracies -haves-fueled-coronavirus-protesters-discord.

United Nations Women. "Sluggish Progress on Women in Politics Will Hamper Development." March 10, 2015. http://www.unwomen.org/en/news/stories/2015/3 /press-release-sluggish-progress-on-women-in-politics-will-hamper-development.

United Nations Women. "Urgent Action Needed to Combat Online Violence against Women and Girls, Says New UN Report." Press release, September 24, 2015. http://www.unwomen.org/en/news/stories/2015/9/cyber-violence-report-press-re lease.

Van Duyn, Emily, Cynthia Peacock, and Natalie Jomini Stroud. "The Gender Gap in Online News Comment Sections." *Social Science Computer Review* (July 26, 2019). DOI: 10.1177/0894439319864876.

Vernasco, Lucy. "Seven Studies That Prove Mansplaining Exists." Bitch Media, July 14, 2014. https://www.bitchmedia.org/post/seven-studies-proving-mansplaining -exists.

Vickery, Jacqueline Ryan, and Tracy Everbach, eds. *Mediating Misogyny: Gender, Technology and Harassment*. Palgrave MacMillan, 2018.

Victor, Daniel. "Microsoft Created a Twitter Bot to Learn from Users: It Quickly Became a Racist Jerk." *New York Times*, March 24, 2016. https://www.nytimes.com

/2016/03/25/technology/microsoft-created-a-twitter-bot-to-learn-from-users-it-quickly
-became-a-racist-jerk.html.

Vyas, Darshali A., Leo G. Eisenstein, and David S. Jones. "Hidden in Plain Sight: Reconsidering the Use of Race Correction in Clinical Algorithms." *New England Journal of Medicine*, August 27, 2020. https://www.nejm.org/doi/full/10.1056 /NEJMms2004740.

Wachter-Boettcher, Sara. *Technically Wrong: Sexist Apps, Biased Algorithms, and Other Threats of Toxic Tech.* Norton, 2017.

Wang, Shan. "The Gender Gap Persists at Many Top News Outlets in the U.S., and It's Reflected in How Stories Are Reported." NiemanLab, March 22, 2017. http://www .niemanlab.org/2017/03/the-gender-gap-persists-at-many-top-news-outlets-in-the-u-s -and-its-reflected-in-how-stories-are-reported.

Wang, Shan. "*The New York Times* Is Trying to Narrow the Distance between Reporters and Analytics Data." NiemanLab, July 25, 2016. http://www.niemanlab.org /2016/07/the-new-york-times-is-trying-to-narrow-the-distance-between-reporters-and -analytics-data/.

Warner, Benjamin R., Sarah Turner McGowen, and Joshua Hawthorne. "Limbaugh's Social Media Nightmare: Facebook and Twitter as Spaces for Political Action." *Journal of Radio & Audio Media* 19, no. 2 (July 2012): 257–275. https://doi.org/10.1080 /19376529.2012.722479.

Warner, Fara. "Nike's Women's Movement." Fast Company, July 31, 2002. https:// www.fastcompany.com/45135/nikes-womens-movement.

Warren, Rossalyn. *Targeted and Trolled: The Reality of Being a Woman Online.* Transworld Digital, 2015.

Weckerle, Andrea. *Civility in the Digital Age: How Companies and People Can Triumph over Haters, Trolls, Bullies and Other Jerks.* Que Publishing, 2013.

Weiss, Debra Cassens. "Interruptions of Female Justices Has Increased with Their Representation on SCOTUS, Study Finds." *ABA Journal*, April 6, 2017. http://www .abajournal.com/news/article/interruptions_of_female_justices_has_increased_with _their_representation_on.

West, Lindy. *Shrill: Notes from a Loud Woman.* Hachette Books, 2016.

West, Lindy. "What Happened When I Confronted My Cruellest Troll." *The Guardian*, February 2, 2015. https://www.theguardian.com/society/2015/feb/02/what -happened-confronted-cruellest-troll-lindy-west.

Williams, Jamillah Bowman. "Why Companies Shouldn't Be Allowed to Treat Their Diversity Numbers as Trade Secrets." *Harvard Business Review*, February 15,

2019. https://hbr.org/2019/02/why-companies-shouldnt-be-allowed-to-treat-their-diversity-numbers-as-trade-secrets.

Williams, Joan C. "Hacking Tech's Diversity Problem." *Harvard Business Review*, October 1, 2014. https://hbr.org/2014/10/hacking-techs-diversity-problem.

Williams, Mary Elizabeth. "Pinterest's Gender Trouble." Salon, May 2, 2012. https://www.salon.com/2012/05/02/pinterests_gender_trouble/.

Wofford, Taylor. "Is GamerGate about Media Ethics or Harassing Women? Harassment, the Data Shows." *Newsweek*, October 25, 2014. http://europe.newsweek.com/gamergate-about-media-ethics-or-harassing-women-harassment-data-show-279736.

Women, Action & Media. "Examples of Gender-Based Hate Speech on Facebook." May 25, 2017. http://www.womenactionmedia.org/examples-of-gender-based-hate-speech-on-facebook.

Women, Action & Media. "Reporting, Reviewing, and Responding to Harassment on Twitter: Infographic." April 22, 2017. http://womenactionmedia.org/twitter-report/twitter-abuse-infographic.

Women, Action & Media. "Twitter's Abuse Problem: Now with Actual Solutions and Science." April 22, 2017. http://womenactionmedia.org/twitter-report.

Women in the World in Association with *The New York Times*. "Why Men Are Prone to Interrupting Women." March 19, 2015. http://nytlive.nytimes.com/womenintheworld/2015/03/19/google-chief-blasted-for-repeatedly-interrupting-female-government-official.

Women's Media Center. "The Gender Gap in Coverage of Reproductive Issues." 2016. http://wmc.3cdn.net/3d96e35840d10fafd1_7wm6v3gy2.pdf.

Women's Media Center. "The Status of Women in U.S. Media 2017." April 13, 2017. http://www.womensmediacenter.com/pages/the-status-of-women-in-u.s.-media-2017.

Women's Media Center. "The Status of Women of Color in the U.S. News Media 2018." March 23, 2018. http://www.womensmediacenter.com/reports/the-status-of-women-of-color-in-the-u-s-media-2018-full-report.

Women's Media Center. "WMC Speech Project: Online Abuse 101." April 25, 2017. http://wmcspeechproject.com/online-abuse-101.

Women's Media Center. "WMC Speech Project: What the Random Rape Threat Generator Tells Us about Online Misogyny." January 18, 2017. http://wmcspeechproject.com/2017/01/18/what-the-random-rape-threat-generator-tells-us-about-online-misogyny.

Wong, Queenie. "Twitter under More Pressure to Ban White Supremacists." CNet, November 19, 2019. https://www.cnet.com/news/twitter-under-more-pressure-to-ban-white-supremacists.

Woolley, Anita Williams, Christopher F. Chabris, Alex Pentland, Nada Hashmi, and Thomas W. Malone. "Evidence for a Collective Intelligence Factor in the Performance of Human Groups." *Science* 330, no. 6004 (October 29, 2010): 686–688. https://doi.org/10.1126/science.1193147.

World Editors Forum. "Online Comment Moderation: Emerging Best Practices." WAN-IFRA, October 4, 2013. http://www.wan-ifra.org/reports/2013/10/04/online-comment-moderation-emerging-best-practices.

Wortham, Jenna. "What Do Women Want in a Laptop?" Bits Blog, 1242338021. //bits.blogs.nytimes.com/2009/05/14/what-do-women-want-in-a-laptop/.

Wu, Nicholas. "'I Am Someone's Daughter Too.' Read Rep. Ocasio-Cortez's Full Speech Responding to Rep. Ted Yoho." *USA Today*, July 24, 2020. https://www.usatoday.com/story/news/politics/2020/07/24/aoc-response-ted-yoho-read-text-rep-ocasio-cortezs-speech/5500633002.

Xia, Rosanna. "Most Computer Science Majors in the U.S. Are Men. Not So at Harvey Mudd." *Los Angeles Times*, January 4, 2017. https://www.latimes.com/local/lanow/la-me-ln-harvey-mudd-tech-women-adv-snap-story.html.

Index